IS DIPLOMACY DEAD?

Leslie Fielding

read History at Cambridge, where he is an Honorary Fellow of Emmanuel College, and Persian at the School of Oriental and African Studies, London. He joined the then Foreign Service in 1956, working initially in Tehran and (briefly) Singapore, before being put in charge of the British Embassy in Phnom Penh, Cambodia, in his early 30s. His subsequent diplomatic career took him to Paris, in the political section; Brussels, as a Director in the European Commission; Tokyo, as EU Ambassador; and back to Brussels, as Director-General for External Relations. He has been a Visiting Fellow at St Antony's College, Oxford, and Vice-Chancellor of the University of Sussex. His autobiography, Kindly Call Me God, was published in 2009 and his Before the Killing Fields: Witness to Cambodia and the Viet-Nam War, in 2008. Subsequently, he has published two works of fiction: a screenplay, Twilight over the Temples: The Close of Cambodia's Belle Epoque; and a novel, The Mistress of the Bees, both in 2011. Previously, he had contributed to two travel anthologies: Travellers' Tales, in 1999 and More Travellers' Tales, in 2005. He is married to the medievalist, Sally Harvey; they have two children, and live in Shropshire. Sir Leslie was knighted in 1988. He is a Reader Emeritus in Hereford Diocese.

IS DIPLOMACY DEAD?

by

Sir Leslie Fielding OE.

Boermans Books

Second edition (revised and enlarged), 2014

ISBN 978-0-9562167-5-5

A full CIP record for this book is available from the British Library.
A full CIP record is available from the Library of Congress
Library of Congress Catalog Card Number: available
Published March 2012 by Boermans Books (Second edition, 2013)
Printed in Gentium Book Basic 12
Printed and bound in Great Britain by York Publishing Services.

THE SECOND EDITION

The first edition of this book was launched at the Oxford Literary Festival, in 2012, under the title "Mentioned in Despatches, Phnom Penh, Paris, Tokyo, Brussels. Is Diplomacy Dead?" This second edition has been revised, enlarged and re-titled simply "Is Diplomacy Dead?

IS DIPLOMACY DEAD?

Sir Leslie Fielding's latest book is for both modern diplomatic historians and the informed general public.

The central part focuses on four major international issues of the 1960s-1980s—the Cambodian tragedy, the French 'veto', the challenge of Japan and the freeing up of world trade. The author reveals state confidences and explains the traditional techniques of diplomatic reporting—and how diplomats were monitored.

But times have changed. Things have moved on. In recent years, our Diplomatic Service has suffered. So the author puts the rhetorical question: "Is Diplomacy Dead?"

In an authoritative Foreword, Sir Christopher Meyer (former Ambassador in Washington, author of 'DC Confidential' and 'Getting Our Way') writes: "The short answer to the question posed by Leslie Fielding is "no". The long answer is set out by the author, elegantly and rigorously .... Weak leadership at the top of the Foreign Office. A Downing Street deaf to what it did not want to hear ...."

Sir Leslie concludes that the tide is beginning to turn and the Diplomatic Service under the Coalition and William Hague is now once more able to fulfil its potential—ever more essential, as power centres shift and potential conflicts over climate change and fuel supplies loom. It is far too soon to start preparing the coffin for British diplomacy.

Amusingly, the Confidential FO Personnel ("INDIV") Reports on Sir Leslie, procured under the Freedom of Information Act, and published for the first time, describe the young Fielding as "brusque", "irritating", "inclined to corpulence", "startlingly flamboyant in dress", "needing to be sat on, periodically", and requiring to "find himself the right wife"! If only on the last count, things did eventually get a little better!

READERS' COMMENTS

An excellent book. Obviously an historic and thoughtful piece of work.
Lord Howe of Aberavon

"Is Diplomacy Dead?" is moving and most interesting.
Matthew Parris

As I expected, it is lively and entertaining.
Lord Hurd of Westwell

Greatly enjoyed it ..... The despatches read really well.
Lord Hannay of Chiswick

Much enjoyed reading it. I went straight to Chapter 8—the reports say as much about the reporting officers as they do about the author.
Lord Wilson of Dinton

A most interesting and significant book.
Rt Rev Lord Carey of Clifton

I was interested to read these reflections on the FCO and on the nature of diplomacy. I am encouraged by the current Foreign Secretary's vision for strengthening the FCO.
Richard Ottaway MP, (Chair, Foreign Affairs Committee, House of Commons)

Leslie Fielding's 1965 despatch analysing Prince Norodom Sihanouk is an outstanding and accurate appreciation of a leader far too few foreign observers understood. Its perceptive detail and insights into the Prince's personality are the more remarkable given the time it was written, when Norodom Sihanouk's failings were little recognised.'

Milton Osborne, (author of 'Sihanouk: Prince of Light, Prince of Darkness')

The book is a good read, throughout, for ex-Eurocrats—written with the wry humour we have come to expect from the author. He provides a textbook lesson in the techniques of diplomacy, by publishing some of his restricted newsletters round the world, to Heads of EU Delegations, when he was in charge of External Relations.

Robert Elphick, (Editor, Journal of AIACE-UK)

A brilliant and instructive narrative .... I admire the professionalism, seriousness and dedication to service, displayed in these despatches.

Sir James Adams

I read 'Is Diplomacy Dead?' with huge interest—full of wisdom.

Sir Sherard Cowper-Coles

I was fascinated by the Paris and Planning Staff despatches about France and de Gaulle. I don't think I've ever read a more perceptive account of the General and his achievements.

John Shakespeare

Never has diplomacy been more necessary than today, as this fine book demonstrates so eloquently.

Sir Christopher Meyer

CONTENTS

FOREWORD

By

Sir Christopher Meyer

The short answer to the question posed by Leslie Fielding is "no". The long answer is set out by the author, elegantly and rigorously, in this important book.

It is extraordinary that the case has to be made at all for the modern relevance of diplomacy. A great part of the problem is the lazy stereo-typing that still clings to the diplomatic profession, much of it fuelled by the media. The popular image of the diplomat has moved little from the Terry-Thomas lampoon in the 1959 film, Carlton-Browne of the FO—a bumbling, upper-class twit, enjoying an aristocratic lifestyle at the taxpayer's expense. It is a caricature recently refreshed and revived by the highly successful advertising campaigns for Ferrero Rocher chocolates and (in the US) for Grey Poupon mustard, both of which link their products to the gracious living of an imagined diplomatic life-style.

It is but a short step from this caricature to a belief that diplomacy is an anachronism with as much relevance to the contemporary world as hereditary peers in an unreformed House of Lords. This is not a uniquely British phenomenon—I have heard French and German diplomats bitterly complain about the decline of their respective foreign ministries—but it is one which has hit the Foreign and Commonwealth Office especially hard. It has struggled since the 1970s to change its image, especially by emphasising the economic and commercial content of a diplomat's work. The modest success attending these efforts has been recently underlined by the Coalition government's decision to re-invent the wheel and make commerce a top priority for British diplomacy. With a distressing loss of self-confidence, the FCO has put itself through various hoops designed by outside consultants to appear relevant and modern. "Change" has been a mantra, frequently without a clear idea of where this permanent revolution is meant to lead—even though "change management" has been entrusted to a senior official. The net result of all this upheaval has been to damage, not enhance, the FCO's effectiveness. Political correctness has run riot, as morale has plunged. Personnel management has been supplanted by the latest fads of the "human resources" industry, whose main effect seems to have been to drive prematurely from the Service some of its most capable senior members.

Leslie Fielding quotes William Hague's speech of September 2011, a blueprint, if not exactly for the renaissance of former glories, at least for the restoration of what should be the core attributes and purpose of a Foreign Office: a clear sense of the national interest, the primacy of policy-making and negotiation, and profound understanding of foreign countries, with the language skills to make this possible. Those whom the gods wish to destroy, they first make mad. It was suicidal lunacy to have shut down the FCO Language School and Library and to dispose of the latter's invaluable archive of historic documents. Rescuing British subjects in distress abroad, however laudable, is no substitute, even if it gives you the fleeting satisfaction of a good headline or two (which it usually does not, since the Briton abroad is an incurable whinger).

Much else has done damage to British diplomacy. Weak leadership at the top of the Foreign Office. A Downing Street deaf to what it did not want to hear. The Treasury's repeated assaults on the FCO budget, such that the Department for International Development, with its grotesquely inflated budget, was able under New Labour to

2

run an alternative foreign policy (the global ambition of overseas aid is perhaps the last remaining twitch of the British imperial instinct). An obsession with process at the expense of substance. There is now general acceptance that the box-ticking, target-setting culture of the last ten years or more has been damaging to the public service as a whole. It has been particularly harmful to the Foreign Office in attempting to measure quantitatively activities, such as the exercise of influence in foreign capitals, which are unquantifiable.

All these things are reversible; and it seems that William Hague wants to reverse them. For the sake of our country we must wish him luck. But something else has to change too. It is to be found in the realms of technology and ideology. It is a commonplace that the world in which diplomacy operates has changed radically in the last half-century. This often leads to the further argument that diplomacy is therefore dead. Who needs an embassy when there is instant electronic communication and heads of government and others can converse with each other through high-definition video links? This is a strange argument. Communication can be as fast as you like; but the last time I looked it was always two-way. To a nimble ambassador instant communication is a blessing. It means that he or she can get their views onto ministers' desks in virtual real-time, so influencing (provided someone is taking notice) policy decisions as they are being made. As for direct video contacts between capitals, they are of limited use unless underpinned by a deep understanding of context, which can come only from Our Man or Woman on the spot. If the truth be told, I spent a fair amount of time as ambassador clearing up misunderstandings after the Great Men had spoken to each other.

But, above all, it is ideology that makes this volume so timely. We are witnessing the death throes of several conventional wisdoms about international relations. They are all based on the naïve belief that there is such a thing as progress in world affairs. Typical was the argument made by the American political scientist, Francis Fukuyama, after the demise of the Soviet Union, that history had ended with the triumph of liberal capitalism. In fact, as the last two decades have shown, history has returned with a vengeance, not least in the Balkans where all manner of deadly irredentism re-emerged as the frozen glaciers of the Cold War melted away.

In a triumph of hope over reason, people like Tony Blair talk today about global values trumping "narrow" national interest. Others, usually based in EU institutions in Brussels, have invented a thing called the "post-modern state", a construct derived from a view of European integration and the impact of globalisation. Yet others speak of the rise of multilateral diplomacy, which will put paid to the traditional bilateralism of international relations.

The common thread running through all these received wisdoms is that the day of the nation-state is over.

This has always been a fallacy; but it has taken hard economic times to reveal it to be so. Globalisation is repeatedly invoked, without ever being properly defined. It is perfectly true that frontiers are now much more porous than they used to be. People, money, culture, electronic communications, cross national boundaries as never before. But, paradoxically, this has led neither to a harmonisation of polities nor to any diminution of nationalism. To the contrary, it is almost as if national sentiments, and protectionism, have grown to compensate for the pressures of globalisation. Five minutes in Beijing, Moscow, Delhi or Washington—to name but four—will make that plain as a pikestaff.

It is also true that the world is confronted by problems, such as climate change, which are beyond the power of any single nation to solve. If there is any place where "global values" should prevail, it is surely here. But at conference after conference—Copenhagen, Cancun, Durban—climate change has been the plaything of warring national interests. Multilateralism is an emperor with very few clothes. The harsh truth is that what matters at these grand diplomatic gatherings is less what the delegates say to each other, more the instructions they receive from their respective capitals. That is where the lobbying has to be done to get governments to change their positions and it can only be done by diplomats with deep understanding of the local power structure.

The gap between ideology and reality is nowhere greater than in the EU, home of the "post-modern state". The Eurozone crisis has revealed the EU for what it has always been at base—an area for the advance and, where possible, reconciliation of national interests. In times of prosperity, this could be camouflaged by the rhetoric of European unity. But, nothing more concentrates the minds of elected politicians, nor reminds them of their political morality, than an economic crisis which tests the patience, even endurance, of their national electorates. No wonder "ever closer union" seems to have given way to *"sauve qui peut"*.

As always in times of economic hardship, the world becomes a less predictable and more dangerous place. Uncertainty hangs over the globe. The Four Horses of the Apocalypse are stamping their feet in the stables. Never has diplomacy been more necessary than today, as this fine book demonstrates so eloquently.

1. INTRODUCTION

I joined the then Foreign Service (later re-designated Diplomatic Service, when the Foreign Office and the Commonwealth Relations Office merged to form today's Foreign and Commonwealth Office) in 1956, having been placed second equal in the Open Competition for entry, and gained a First in Part II of the Historical Tripos at Cambridge.

I was not in all respects a happy bunny as an undergraduate. Emmanuel was a relaxed and friendly College. But two years military service had unsettled me. I did not know who I was or what I really wanted to do in life. In the grip of other interests and preoccupations in my first two years—socialising, pursuing psychical research in haunted houses, dabbling in Christian theology and testing my vocation to the Anglican priesthood—I attended no university lectures after my first term, and did only the necessary minimum reading for the weekly essay for my supervisor. I was lucky to scrape an Upper Second in Part I of the Tripos. I began to look for a way out from academe (despite still toying with the idea of writing a doctoral thesis on medieval Christian heresies). Money was tight—P. Fielding Ltd, the small family business, teetering on the brink of bankruptcy; my religious vocation in crisis, and shelved for the time being. So I decided to go abroad, as far away as possible from Europe—and from Christianity! Rudyard Kipling's words, in 'Mandalay', summed it all up:

> "Ship me somewheres east of Suez, where the
> best is like the worst,
> Where there aren't no Ten Commandments, an'
> a man can raise a thirst."

But, how? Then I saw the Open Competition advertised in the national press and cast my hat into the FO ring, despite having only 'dead language' competence in French and German, and knowing nothing of abroad beyond Paris, Florence and Rome. Also, despite absolutely no personal background of the kind normative in the Diplomatic before the Second World War: I was not only a neophyte but also an 'arriviste', coming from a 'trade' background and a London day school.

Slightly against my wishes, I was corralled by the FO into following an intensive two year Persian language course, first at SOAS in London and then up-country in Iran. After which, I served in the Tehran Embassy for a couple of years as the Ambassador's Private Secretary. Also, as general dogsbody in the Chancery (i.e. the Political Section—where I wrote inter alia a commended study of Tehran taxi drivers: a powerful and volatile body). In 1960, I was transferred back to the Foreign Office in London, to comparable dogsbody duties on the NATO and WEU desk in the Western, later Western Organisations Department. After a year, I took the concomitant job of Foreign Office Resident Clerk. In the spring of 1964, I was promoted to First Secretary and posted to the Office of the Political Advisor to the Commander in Chief, Far East in Singapore. After barely a month, as an expendable bachelor I was shunted up to Phnom Penh, to serve for an indefinite period as Chargé d'Affaires in Cambodia (the Embassy had been attacked by a mob; the wives and children and all non-essential staff pulled out; the Ambassador in the process of being withdrawn). I stayed there until the autumn of 1966, when conditions had normalised and a new Ambassador could be accredited in my place.

It was an interesting time to be serving East of Suez. In Indo-China, Harold Wilson had been right to resist repeated US pressure in the early 1960s to commit British troops to the unnecessary, unjust and unwinnable war in Viet-Nam; and to concentrate instead, as Prime Minister Sir Anthony Eden had done at the time of the French defeat and withdrawal in the mid-1950s, on the search for a realistic settlement through negotiation. The so-called Geneva Conference on Indo-China, established on Eden's personal initiative in 1964, and co-chaired by the UK and the USSR, was kept in being for this purpose. It was used to limited good effect over Laos, in the early 1960s; but failed to gain a purchase on Cambodia. The tragedy lay in British inability to convince President Johnson to go for a neutralised Cambodia, before it was too late. If Kennedy had lived, and Macmillan not fallen sick, it might have been different. *Hinc illae lacrimae!*

I felt sorry for the Cambodian Head of State, Prince Norodom Sihanouk. On leaving the post, I reported officially that he was "likely to control the destiny of the Kingdom for as far ahead as one can see" (which was not far). But privately I advised James Cable (Head of South East Asia Department in London) that "he seems likely to decline and eventually be ushered off the Cambodian scene"[1]. In the event, Sihanouk was deposed by a microcephalic general four years later, in 1970. I still feel horror over the Pol Pot episode which followed from 1975 to 1979, in which up to a quarter of the population was murdered or worked to death. (I recently wrote a semi-fictional, semi-autobiographical screenplay about the whole business— 'Twilight over the Temples: The Close of Cambodia's Belle Epoque').

It was in this period, as an unusually young Head of Mission (in my early '30s), that I wrote the twelve despatches to the Foreign Secretary reprinted in Chapter 4 of this book. For two of them, I received a personal word of thanks from the Foreign Secretary of the day (R. A. Butler, on 'Cambodian Neutrality: Its Nature and Prospects'; and Patrick Gordon Walker, on 'The Americans as Sihanouk Sees Them'). My farewell despatch pleased the Prime Minister (Harold Wilson). Apparently, I had performed adequately in the eyes of my superiors—even if some in the Service were a little incredulous, and a few were (as usual) frankly irritated.

At this point, it would normally have been time for me for me to return to Iran, probably as Commercial Secretary,

---

[1] Before the Killing Fields, p.206

and to keep my Persian well-honed against the day when I might be needed there as Ambassador (which, in the event, never happened). Instead, I was posted to the Embassy in Paris (because I was supposed by then to speak the language fluently, and get on well with the French). While in Paris, I drafted for my Ambassador's signature the three Paris despatches on French foreign policy in Chapter Five.

These were followed by a paper I wrote on arrival, in 1970, in the Planning Staff of the FCO in London, called 'The French Analogy', produced in response to the demand of the Prime Minister to know "Why can't we be more like the French?" (Edward Heath had complexes on the subject). My sceptical superior, Percy Cradock, took the precaution of asking the Paris Embassy whether I had got it entirely right, in order to forearm himself against any challenge from the Prime Minister. Fortunately, the Number Two in Paris, Michael Palliser, subsequently head of the Diplomatic Service, replied positively.

In Paris, it was once again an interesting time to be on the spot. France had been a close friend and ally, since the '*Entente Cordiale*'. But Charles de Gaulle had vetoed UK accession to the European Community in 1963; was to do so again, in 1967. Anglo-French relations had accordingly to be rebuilt, from the ground up, once the General had gone and the more sympathetic Georges Pompidou taken over. This demanded rather more thought to Paris and things Gallic than we had always thitherto been inclined to give.

I had worked steadily in my first assignments, in the Tehran Embassy and in London; even, at times, quite hard. But in Phnom Penh I had had to work my socks off night and day—doing six people's jobs (previously those of the Ambassador, the Head of Chancery, the Consul and the Commercial, Information and Political Officers). Paris was more relaxing, even if it knew its moments of crisis and drama—not least during the popular uprising (what the French call "the events") of May 1968. I enjoyed being a cog in a great Embassy machine and had the time of my life. It was too good to last.

In 1970, I was sent back to London to become the number two in the prestigious policy planning unit ('Planning Staff') of the FCO. This was a small but influential "Think Tank" and came directly under the Permanent Under-Secretary of State. The appointment was supposed to be a great compliment. But the three years I spent there, while both reflective and creative, were also a little frustrating, both because what I had wanted was a job in the team negotiating British entry into the European Community, and because I did not see entirely eye-to-eye with my respected first boss, Percy Cradock, nor measure up to his expectations. I thought his approach to foreign affairs too academic and theoretical; he in his turn found me no intellectual. Yet I produced my share of the work. This included authorship of possibly the first ever FO reflection on international terrorism, quaintly entitled— 9/11 lay far ahead—'Low Level Political Violence'. (In character, Percy insisted on inserting at the beginning that "A major trap to avoid .... is to exaggerate its importance. The world is, and has always been, a violent place ...." But he did leave unchanged my conclusion: "Low Level Political Violence is not new. But it is on balance likely to be an increasingly frequent and awkward phenomenon throughout the world, over the next decade and beyond").

Whenever I could, I escaped from the Planning Staff. I improved my German. I studied different aspects of economics on a series of three-week courses at the Civil Service College—wanting to build upon the GCE 'A' Level in Economics which I had taken by correspondence while I was still in Paris, and upon the two months I had spent at a French Business School on temporary detachment from the Embassy. In the evenings, I wrote a novel (unpublished because I did not agree with the modifications which my then literary agent requested—it eventually came out in 2011, as 'The Mistress of the Bees') and finalised the MS of a book about the Cambodia crisis (permission to publish initially refused by the FCO; it was cleared only in 2008, appearing as 'Before the Killing Fields: Witness to

Cambodia and the Viet-Nam War'). Also in my spare time as a planner, I ghosted a book for a friend engaged in research into alcohol and drug addiction and was eventually even promoted to Counsellor.

In 1973, it was with initial relief that I moved to the European Commission on secondment from the Diplomatic Service, at the urgent request of Christopher Soames[2] (previously my Ambassador in Paris and now freshly appointed Vice-President in Brussels), and with the encouragement of Denis Greenhill, my Permanent Under-Secretary—an ally of mine who had been instructed by Edward Heath to beat the bushes for suitable birds.

Interestingly, there was no conflict of loyalty. In the Diplomatic Service, the natural priority had been the promotion of British national interests. In Brussels, I was concerned with the interests of Britain in Europe and found it equally natural. But the workload was extremely heavy; the subject matter initially unfamiliar; the working methods strange and at times repugnant; the overall 'culture shock' much greater than I had expected. Language alone was a problem. I had, while in Paris, passed the Civil Service Higher Level French examination *summa cum laude*; and I was apparently judged by Personnel Department to be one of the best speakers in the Service. But that did not make me completely bilingual. To draft and to speak all day in French in Brussels demanded a level of effort greater than that which I had previously had to make during three years in Cambodia and four years in France. The French language demands facial exertions different from those required when one mutters away in English. Consequently, my throat, cheeks and lips began to rebel after eight or nine hours non-stop; and I regularly suffered from initial 'French face-ache', for which the best relief was to swear copiously in German or Dutch— different muscles—when back in Brussels again, after the summer holidays.

---

[2] He wrote to me that "it will be a mixture of fun and frustration, but it has got to work".

Nevertheless, my face fitted and I thrived. After four years serving as the Director responsible for the Community's relations with the United States and the Old Commonwealth and for a range of other matters (including agricultural trade policy, a real headache), I volunteered to go out to Tokyo (after a nine month sabbatical at St. Antony's College, Oxford to read up about the country and acquire some basics of the language), to take over the diplomatic Delegation recently opened there.

I had always been drawn to Japan (having volunteered, without success, to learn Japanese rather than Persian, back in 1956; and subsequently travelled up and down the country, on leave from Phnom Penh). But I also felt that it was time for a proper professional diplomat (little me) to take over one of these curious new overseas Delegations of the European Community, just to show how they should really be run. This may seem condescending and even arrogant. But one of my afore-mentioned multiple responsibilities while Director had been oversight of the growing network of external offices. I had appointed wherever I could some sensible people to run them. But this was a new game for the Commission, and individual performances varied. The man in Tokyo, Wolfgang Ernst, had not proved the brightest jewel in our overseas crown; and was coming up to retirement. I replaced him in 1978.

From Tokyo, I wrote the official 'diplomatic' despatches in Chapter 6—a practice thitherto unfamiliar to the Commission in Brussels. It was certainly a challenging assignment. Trade tension between Japan and the European Community was rising and had to be contained; Japan herself was becoming an economic super-power ('Japan as Number One' was the title of a then fashionable book by Ezra Vogel). Brussels needed to be not only persistent with its well-founded commercial complaints, but also patient and committed to the development of partnership with Tokyo. Japan mattered—and had come fully of age. It was while serving in Tokyo that I transferred formally from the Diplomatic Service, to become a permanent EC Official.

In 1982, at the age of fifty, I was promoted to Grade One and brought back to Brussels to take over from Sir Roy Denman as the Director-General for External Relations (effectively, the Permanent Secretary). The department was a big one—I had four Deputy Director-Generals under me, plus nine Directors and twenty-five Division Chiefs (in Whitehall terminology, four Deputy Secretaries, nine Under Secretaries and twenty-five Assistant Secretaries); plus a network of thirty odd external delegations and offices. It took some co-ordinating. Remembering how cut-off our people abroad could feel, and following a discreet Foreign Office precedent, I used to write a regular monthly newsletter to the individual Heads of external Commission posts, to keep them in the political picture at headquarters. My letters were not shown to Commissioners, nor were they officially recorded. They were written in demotic English, rather than the slightly stilted French then more customary in Brussels, to give them a fully private and personal flavour. A selection is to be found in Chapter 7.

After five years of that, I decided in 1987 that it was time to come home—in the event, to the University of Sussex as its Vice-Chancellor. In some ways, I regretted leaving; it would have been tempting, for example, to have put my hat in the ring to become the next Director-General of the GATT in succession to my friend and accomplice Arthur Dunkel (for which move I was well placed); or to have moved on to Washington, as the EC ambassador (which would have been the normal conclusion of my particular *cursus honorum*). But, for family reasons, the decision to return home was probably right.

The foregoing will, I hope, set the context, not only of the despatches and reports already mentioned, but also of the Staff in Confidence reports, in Chapter 8 below. For me, they make at times embarrassing reading. Some of the compliments are unexpected. But the criticisms are sharp— and accurate. There is no moment, in this series of INDIV reports, at which I can rightly claim to find myself unfairly treated. Yet to see oneself as others see one can be disconcerting.

Thus, on the one hand it is flattering to find that my Persian was considered good enough for me to be taken as an Iranian. I am encouraged that I was thought to be 'quite tough', 'quick in action', 'very valuable in a tight corner' or 'first-class in a crisis'. But I can well imagine why my first Ambassador might have found my exterior 'whimsical', my second Ambassador detected 'excessive pomposity', my third Ambassador considered my dress flamboyant. It was perfectly true that I 'denied myself nothing' and was inclined to corpulence (eventually cured by marriage and children). On the other hand, I disbelieve and deny that I ever had any 'effeminate traits'. And I recall that it was boring to be perpetually told to get married to a suitable girl: love, I thought, was not a career move.

With hindsight, however, I understand what they meant when various bosses in the Foreign Office commented: 'brusque and needing to be sat upon'; or 'probably irritates a few' or showed too much 'bravura'; or stood 'in need of correction because of his tendency to over-value his capacity'. Percy Cradock, for his part, casting around for something positive, may have found me a 'first class diplomat'; but was clear that, even if 'Fielding thinks more than his manner suggests', nevertheless he shows 'some lack of intellectual power and incisiveness'. (By Percy's personal standard, he was probably right). But these shortcomings happily did not prevent me from showing, a few years later in Brussels, 'great aptitude' for political and economic work (David Hannay); and for proving "an extremely effective official" (Crispin Tickell).

All in all, there is no denying that the Foreign Office knew their man. Nor is there any doubt, each in his own way, of the calibre of the men who reported on me, nor the shrewdness and humanity with which they wrote. (My own assessment of each of *them* comes in the next Chapter.)

I, for my part, am proud to have served in the Diplomatic Service in its heyday—and subsequently in the Directorate-General for External Relations ('The Coldstream Guards' of the Commission, being *Nulli Secundus*). Starting again today, I doubt whether I should want to choose any other career. Yet things are not now entirely what they used to be, either in London or Brussels. Perhaps, after all, I saw the best of it? History will tell, but I cannot. But let me move on, to 'Things As They Used to Be' (Chapter 2); then 'Change – And Decay' (Chapter 3).

2. THINGS AS THEY USED TO BE

As a career diplomat and later 'Eurocrat', I was privileged to observe at close hand the workings of foreign policy; and to have a part to play, on some issues. My assignments, almost without exception, were quite fascinating.

To begin with, there was the Middle East, as seen from Tehran; next, the Western alliance, defence and security, in London and Singapore. But the four issues which most stand out in my mind arose in Phnom Penh, Paris, Tokyo and Brussels, as follows:

- in Phnom Penh: how to limit the escalation of the disastrous Viet-Nam War, by using the Anglo-Soviet Geneva Conference on Indochina, to underpin Cambodia's neutral status. Despite every effort, we failed;
- in Paris: how to overcome the Gaullist veto on UK accession to the European Community and restore confidence and cooperation to Anglo-French relations. After President de Gaulle's resignation, we succeeded;
- in Tokyo: for the European Community, how to face up to the challenge of an economically resurgent Japan. We and our European partners largely succeeded;
- in Brussels: how to make use of a united Europe to liberate and expand international trade, speaking with one voice in the GATT/OECD/UN/G7. We largely succeeded; as also with the opening up of the European Single Market, another mainly British inspired initiative. Sadly, foreign policy and defence cooperation lagged behind; the Euro disaster, and the rise of Tory 'Euroscepticism,' came later.

A major part of this book is concerned with diplomatic reporting on these issues: the confidential despatches which I wrote—and the equally confidential personnel reports written on me by my superiors. There was a symbiosis between the two; fully to assess any despatch, the Foreign Office needed to know something about the despatcher. I continued despatch-writing, FO-style, while serving on secondment to the European Commission in the late 1970s and '80s —and FO personnel reports kept track of me in Brussels.

The Diplomatic Service despatches reproduced below are drawn from the National Archives, where they are now open to the public. My confidential personnel file at the Foreign and Commonwealth Office, which I had never seen before, was recently made available to me under the Data Protection Act of 1998. The official despatches which I wrote from Tokyo while serving as a 'Eurocrat' are reproduced with the *nihil obstat* of the European Commission.

These matters are handled differently today. Among other things, there has been a revolution in communications technology, including an absolute digital 'tsunami'. But, in my day, the system was as follows. British Embassies overseas could communicate on urgent matters daily with London by telegrams, usually ciphered, sent across the ether by the Diplomatic Wireless Service. More routine communications took the form of letters sent to London in a weekly or fortnightly 'Diplomatic Bag' carried by a Queen's Messenger. By the same route, but less frequently, Heads of Mission sent formal despatches to the Foreign Secretary. The sender was invariably an Ambassador; but could, in his absence, be his stand-in or substitute—a 'Chargé d'Affaires'. These despatches were sometimes of a routine character: the 'Annual Review' of developments in the foreign country concerned; the annually updated 'Personalities Report' on the local foreign 'movers and shakers'; the report on the State Visit of a foreign Potentate. But they were rarely trivial. On occasion, a despatch could be a stimulating piece of 'blue sky thinking', outside the box. In between, despatches were employed to put down an important marker, by addressing a major issue arising in the country in which the British Embassy was located, to which more measured consideration deserved to be given than was always possible in the mostly tactical cut-and-thrust of day-to-day diplomatic telegrams.

The less ephemeral of such ambassadorial despatches (printed impressively in double columns on grey-green paper) were circulated to potentially interested top brass— ministerial as well as senior official—throughout the Foreign Office and Whitehall, as well as to all other British Heads of Mission overseas and sometimes also to select British Commonwealth and foreign governments. There could on occasion be a touch of exhibitionism in such documents, or evidence of a burning desire to put across home truths or set wrongs to right. The final Valedictory Despatch, written when the Ambassador was on the eve of retirement from the Service, traditionally released the sender from the usual diplomatic constraints. A celebrated example is that of Sir Nicholas Henderson's Valedictory from Paris in 1979 (which leaked to the press and made such an impression on Mrs Thatcher that 'Nicko' was brought back from retirement after the general election and sent to Washington as Ambassador).

In parallel with diplomatic reporting went another practice of the Service, not advertised to the public at large, but entirely familiar to the professionals themselves. This was the system of regular confidential reports on each of us, classified 'INDIV' or 'Staff in Confidence'.

For this purpose, a comprehensive form had to be completed by the reporting officer, usually the subject's immediate boss, and counter-signed (and if appropriate commented upon) by the latter's superior—at a post abroad, invariably the Ambassador himself. The early part of the form comprised two sections, with tick boxes. The first section, 'Basic Proficiency', dealt with knowledge of the work, output, attention to detail, management skills, interest in the welfare of subordinate staff and acceptability as a colleague. The reporting officer had to put his tick—for example as to 'output'—in one of five boxes, from "Gets through a great deal of work" to "Does too little". If the subject of the report was up for promotion, these boxes were more numerous and more detailed. There then followed a section on 'Positive Qualities' such as judgement, quickness of apprehension, or fertility of ideas. Moving on from the tick boxes (which each had space for brief amplifying comment), observations were invited on the officer's health and what his wife was like. The report had to conclude with a pen portrait of the officer (hand-written, not typed—secretaries were not permitted to handle the form), for which up to a page was allocated. Space was allowed for any recommendation for future training and postings and on the general direction which the officer's future career might take. Also, for an assessment of his likely terminal rank in the Service. The countersigning officer was assigned half a page for any final comments or glosses on what had gone before.

These Staff In Confidence reports were handled with great discretion by the Personnel Department in London, almost as if they were secrets of state. The subject of a report was never permitted to see it, although could be informed of any observed major shortcoming which he or she should endeavour to correct. The reports were taken carefully into consideration by a committee of the Powers That Be when promotion or completion of probation in a higher grade had to be decided. The system was scrupulously fair. The Personnel Department themselves took into account the record of the reporting officer as a balanced assessor.

This system was essential in a small Service (around 800 members in 'Branch A', when I was recruited in 1956), scattered around the world (some of us were indeed never to meet each other). The FO was not like a Home Civil Service Ministry, where everyone served together in one building for years on end, and (metaphorically) took the same train or bus home at close of play. True, with the passage of time, almost every individual came to know, and be known by, a wide cohort of peers. 'High-flyers' quite soon established their reputations. It followed that political despatches did not come out of the blue: the man was usually as clear as his message. Nevertheless, tabs had to be kept on people. Some of the criteria for doing so were those of an age now gone. But others have stood the test of time. The general atmosphere was one of trust; but conditional trust, because the monitoring was on-going, and people could—and occasionally did—go off the boil.

The practice did not exist in the same form, or meet the same high standard, in the bureaucracy of the European Commission in Brussels, as I discovered on transfer there in 1973. Personnel Reports had to be shown to, and counter-signed by, their subjects. Perhaps this was as well, given the different nationalities and public service traditions represented in the Commission. In the original European Community of the Six (the Benelux countries, Italy, France and Germany), there was little homogeneity. Even less so, with the accession of Denmark, Ireland and the UK, and the subsequent arrival of the Greeks, Iberians and Scandinavians. (Latterly, of course, also Baltic, East European and Balkan Member States.)

Nevertheless, the disadvantage of non-confidentiality was that Commission Personnel Reports in my day were invariably bland and not uncommonly deficient. Any Director or Head of Division in Brussels to whom a new official was proposed invariably checked—orally and privately—with the individual's previous boss, to find out what he or she was really made of.

Chapters 4-7 of this book reproduce some of the despatches, in both the Diplomatic Service and the European Civil Service, for which I was responsible—against the background of the revelatory (and at times slightly tongue-in-cheek) Staff in Confidence reports in Chapter 8.

But these despatches and reports do give rise to the more fundamental questions posed next, in Chapter 3. When all is said and done, and all the papers filed away, what did it all add up to? In John le Carré's novel *"Tinker, Tailor, Soldier, Spy"*, a colleague of George Smiley says, of the English *élite*: "Trained to Empire; trained to rule the world. All gone. All taken away". Is that true, of our diplomats? And is diplomacy now dead?

3. CHANGE – AND DECAY

The elegant court sword that I carried with my diplomatic uniform was a glittering object of display. With its gilded hilt and golden pommel, it was carried in a shiny black scabbard. But the chased and ciphered blade, so discreetly concealed in lacquered leather, was long and thin and endowed with a wickedly sharp point. Beneath the urbanities and apparently civilised conventions, diplomacy —and the promotion of this nation's interests overseas— could be a fierce affair.

In September 2012, the murder of the US Ambassador to Libya—a country which America was endeavouring to assist—served as a reminder that a diplomatic career can have its hazards. The fact is that the profession, like rugby football, is a contact sport; it is not for the faint-hearted. As The Times once put it: 'A modern diplomat can expect to spend more time in posts wearing dusty boots and flak jackets than sipping cocktails and munching canapés at embassy receptions'.

I admit that I had been under the vague impression, on joining the Diplomatic Service, that I was signing up for a civilised career of elegance and ease, waltzing under the chandeliers with beautiful bare-shouldered Contessas, and consorting with Monarchs, Presidents, Prime Ministers and the like, in the Chancelleries of the Great Powers. But I was soon to be disabused. In my day, as a British diplomat, I have been stoned by religious fanatics in the Middle East;

pushed about by mobs, shot at, and driven to conduct peace talks in an opium bordello in Indo-China; chased, with intent, by riot police in Europe; routinely expected to work through the night, and the jet lag, in faraway places— and once, at a UN Ministerial Conference, to negotiate for seventy-two hours entirely without sleep.

The profession, nevertheless, still suffers from an image problem. Sir Christopher Meyer acknowledges this, in his Foreword to the present volume:

> 'The popular image of the diplomat has moved little from the Terry-Thomas lampoon in the 1959 film, Carlton-Browne of the FO—a bumbling, upper-class twit, enjoying an aristocratic lifestyle at the taxpayer's expense'.

Two or three years ago, the foreign editor of The Times, in what he presumably intended as positive copy, felt able to comment that:

> 'Today the FCO takes pride in adapting to new realities. Gone are the stuffy pinstriped suits and overbearing diplomats. In their place is a new breed of young officials, who look more like friendly bank managers than the snobbish Whitehall élite'.

I am baffled by the clichés. The hitherto strictly confidential 'INDIV' personnel reports on me, recently extracted from the Foreign Office under the Freedom of Information Act, and reproduced in the Chapter 8 below, offered an entirely different picture. My first boss in London had noted what he called my *fin de siècle* appearance. The Inspector from London who came to check up on me, when I was a 31 year old Chargé d'Affaires in Cambodia, wrote that "Mr. Fielding has a pop painting on the wall in the Residence, and a Beatles record on his gramophone. How 'With It' can the younger generation get"? A year later, I was teaching the King's favourite daughter 'The Twist', to the tune of Chubby Checker. Later on, I was judged by my superior in Paris to be 'often startlingly flamboyant in dress' (a reference, probably, to the trendy, 'Flower Power', kipper ties I wore when calling on senior officials at the *Quai d'Orsay*, to their outward horror but no doubt also inward envy).

But, to be serious, the Service has recently had its downs as well as its ups. Despite the headlines, Diplomacy is not today actually Dead. But it has at times seemed to be more absent than present.

It might therefore be tempting to dismiss the major content of this book (Chapters 4-9) as outmoded and past its sell-by date—"a handful of grey despatches, long, long ago, at rest" (to misapply Callimachus, on Heraclitus of Halicarnassus[3]). In any case, some people sometimes say, everyone knows that the FO is not what it was. So, who cares?

Of course, diplomats have always had a bad name, in some quarters. Is not an Ambassador "an honest man sent to lie abroad for the good of his country" (in the deliberately ambiguous quip of the Elizabethan Provost of Eton and sometime overseas Envoy, Sir Henry Wootton)? Didn't the 19th Century Italian diplomatist, Count Cavour, once say: "If we did for ourselves what we do for our country, what rogues we should be". When Karl von Clausewitz said that "war is the continuation of politics by other means", was he not implying that diplomacy is the extension of war, by other means?

But any sane person would argue that, these days, diplomacy, far from being a partner to warfare, must now actually replace it. Foreign affairs are not a Vicarage Tea Party, with cucumber sandwiches; the world has never been a cosy place, a Victorian Sunday School, the Queensberry Rules at work. But we can no longer solve our problems—if indeed we ever always could—simply by

---

[3] "They told me, Heraclitus, they told me you were dead . A handful of grey ashes, long, long ago at rest". Trans. William Johnson Cory

sending a gunboat. It didn't work, in our 'Cod War' with Iceland in the early 1970s, even if it did boot fascist Argentina out of the Falklands. We cannot readily use such means in the Maghreb or Middle East or Central Asia today.

Furthermore, diplomacy is not, as so often assumed, a moral desert. At its best, it can be about charm, not coercion; good manners, not ill; persuasion, not deception. About empathy and respect for other people. About meeting others half way; and being ready to go the extra mile. About building where possible on trust and on common interests, rather than on mendacity and aggrandisement. Of course, compromise and "splitting the difference" is not invariably the right way forward. To be fair, one must sometimes also be firm. There is always, and understandably, the ever-resilient strand of national self-interest. But intertwined with it is often a second, idealistic strand: the sense of justice; the belief that there is some over-arching standard beyond the narrow national interest, by which diplomacy can and should be judged.

A word here about individual freedom of conscience. The modern British diplomat is a civil servant. If he has a sympathy for one British political party rather than another (as he is entitled to, in a free society), he keeps it to himself and loyally serves the elected Government of the day. He is also bound by the Official Secrets Act and needs permission to publish. But he is not obliged to help carry through a major foreign policy with which he profoundly disagrees on moral grounds. He can advise against it. If overruled, he may request to be assigned to other duties. In an extreme scenario, he can resign: in which case the basic requirement is that he should do so discreetly. While still a member of the Diplomatic Service, and always in a situation of crisis, he must not betray the trust vested in him, or in effect blackmail the government of the day, by public disclosure of dissent or by the overnight withdrawal of expertise and manpower. Diplomacy, as conducted by professionals, has never been a "Kiss-and-Tell" calling.

But back to the wider picture. What stands out a mile today, to readers of Ernest Satow, Harold Nicolson and the memoirs of an earlier age, is the extent and complexity of the change which diplomacy has undergone over the past fifty years.

People still matter. Individuals do play, as they always did, an immensely crucial part. Social and interpersonal skills remain as essential as ever. Foreign languages, foreign social customs, foreign political and psychological realities—despite their de-emphasis and denial under the last Labour government (see below)—all continue to have to be understood and respected. But the *shape*, *style* and *content* of diplomacy have changed.

Embassies have proliferated in number, as newly independent countries have established their overseas representation. International and regional organisations have burgeoned. The work of an Embassy has extended from the political and consular to the cultural and (in spades, these days) commercial. New concerns, such as the global environment, post-Cold War peacekeeping and international terrorism, have been added to the diplomatic agenda. *Multilateral* diplomacy, in international organisations such as the EU, the UN, the WTO, NATO etc., has become a mega-phenomenon. Also, 'Summit diplomacy', for instance, in the G20. Both, in my experience, demanding new knowledge and novel professional techniques. Improvements in communication and facility of contact have brought greatly increased ministerial travel and instant and constant consultation between Ministry and Embassy, between home government and foreign government. In Whitehall, there has been a coming together of foreign and domestic policy, necessarily blurring the distinction between bureaucrats and diplomats—Home Civil Servants and Diplomatic Service Officers.

Up to and even beyond the Napoleonic Wars, very few Europeans concerned themselves directly with foreign affairs; it was the preserve of Princes and a small body of

Ministers Potentiary, Envoys Extraordinary and Aristocratic Diplomatists who probably had more in common with their foreign counterparts than with their own ill-informed and impassive co-nationals back home. The English public, as a rule, were notably indifferent. To be sure, young gentlemen of good family, accompanied by their chaplains and tutors, dragomans and domestics, embarked on the Grand Tour. The Duchess of Richmond even gave a ball in Brussels, and was gravely inconvenienced by the unexpected clash with the subsequently arranged battle of Waterloo—but what else could one expect of that jumped-up little Corsican, Signor Buonaparte? Jane Austen's novels, and Parson Woodforde's diaries, record an English social scene which appears largely oblivious of the clash of continental armies and indifferent to the knavish tricks of foreigners.

Today, however, we live in a global political village, as well as in a global economy. In the contemporary West, almost everyone has some view of foreign policy. Far from being a closed preserve, it has become, like our views on education and our notions of the shortcomings of the young, a public park where anyone is free to kick a ball about. In Europe and America, not only learned institutions (like the RIIA and the IISS, with us) but also party-political and private "think-tanks" abound, challenging and second-guessing the professionals in the Foreign Ministries.

The media too. I personally deplore the over-simplified world of the sound-bite and the short attention span of the TV screen; the know-all assurance of the teenage scribblers on the broadsheets and the bar-stool arrogance of interviewers on the 'Today' programme. Nevertheless, these guys and dolls do have their role to play—as, famously, did US television cameramen, press commentators and news agency reporters in Indo-China in the 'Sixties, to my direct experience and awed admiration. The Viet-Nam War seemed to me—stationed, as I was, in the area—misconceived, ill-directed and above all unwinnable. This message was eventually relayed to the

American people back home, too. So media men have their value.

But, if they are necessary, they are not sufficient. Leaving aside the phone-hacking and the muck-raking, the media offer only episodic, not continuous, coverage of people, places and events. They are also highly derivative and dependent on others. I was once cynically amused by a senior and respected American journalist who spent hours being comprehensively briefed by me in a foreign country with which he was totally unfamiliar, and from which US diplomatic representation had been temporarily withdrawn; only for him to offer the opinion, having returned home and published his articles to wide acclaim, that newsmen had made Embassies redundant.

I mentioned sound-bites and simplifications. It goes almost without saying that such trivial chirpiness and dumbing-down cut no mustard when applied to the sheer complexity of many world issues. The global waters are often opaque, even muddy. There is the old diplomatic joke: to every many-sided and entangled international issue, there is always one answer which is simple, lucid and compelling—but which is invariably wrong.

Which brings me to media-fixated 'Sofa Government', as the Butler Report called it. Features of it were the political advisors and appointees and spin-doctors. Fairly recent phenomena, in London, they have long been a part of the Washington scene. That is not necessarily a recommendation; such folk—who are not entirely chosen on merit—can have real limitations. Not the least of these is their liability—the supreme fallacy in foreign policy—to see the world as they want it to be, or as they fondly assume it must be, rather than as it really is.

Let me move from the general to the particular, to look at the UK as such, and then—quite closely—at our own Foreign Office.

Internationally, as is widely acknowledged, the UK continues on the path of its long-drawn-out decline from Empire and global outreach. In the course of this process, and in a world that was changing anyway, we have sometimes been uncertain of our path. (See Lord Hannay's, *Britain's Quest for a Role: A Diplomatic Memoir from Europe to the UN*, 2013).

Domestically also, however, the country has entered a period of change and possible decay and accordingly stands in urgent need of reform.

In particular, our *politics* has seemingly changed for the worse. Thus, membership of the House of Commons has become, for many, a professional career—what 'The Economist' recently described as "a game now played by slick graduates, who work in think tanks or back rooms before climbing the pole to their own (parliamentary) seat". Lord Turnbull, Cabinet Secretary and Head of the Civil Service 2002-2005, in testimony to a House of Lords Committee in August 2009, stated his belief that many MPs had entered parliament too young and that their leaders were not always "people of seniority or wisdom".

Meanwhile, in the absence of the checks and balances of a written Constitution, the Presidential-type patronage of the British Prime Minister has extended massively, on almost an 18th Century scale. In the last Parliament, Tony Blair had the gift of over 90 odd junior ministerial posts, outside the actual Cabinet; and almost 80 well-paid 'Special Political Adviserships' to bestow on apparatchiks (twenty of them in No. 10). Things got only marginally better, under the LibCons—initially, 70 junior ministers and 66 special advisers (eighteen of them in No. 10). But numbers soon rose again (to as many as 83 special advisers, by mid-2012), and will continue to rise, under the plans for 'Extended Ministerial Offices' announced in July, 2013.

In consequence, the old Whitehall ethos, the tradition of the Northcote/Trevelyan reforms of the 19th Century, the duty of "Telling Truth to Power", are all in retreat and may never quite come back, despite the best effort of successive Cabinet Secretaries and Heads of the Civil Service, and notwithstanding the passage of the Constitutional Reform and Governance Act of 2010.

Which is a huge pity. The PM and his Cabinet colleagues deserve not to be surrounded by too many 'Yes Men' and seekers after preferment (all those 'asking faces', as King Charles II described some of his courtiers, after the Restoration). As Lord Howe put it, in a lecture at Buckingham University, in 1997 ("Diplomacy: A Diet of Diversity"): "The Secretary of State does need professional guidance; and he or she is entitled to expect professional candour".

Furthermore, sheer ugly reality has the habit of breaking in. In an article in Prospect in November 2008 entitled, *'Anyone for Realpolitik?*, Sir Rodric Braithwaite, a top flight diplomat and former Ambassador in Moscow, argued that Britain's foreign policy, like its banks, had run out of capital, and become largely irrelevant in world affairs; and that a more realistic approach was called for, in a multipolar world. Sir Jeremy Greenstock—a former Ambassador to the United Nations and ill-fated Special Representative for Iraq, shackled to the arrogant and ignorant Paul Bremer III—began his St. Michael and St. George lecture on 'Freedom, Order and Shifting Sands', delivered in the Locarno Room of the Foreign Office in June 2011, with the affirmation that 'the rocks of the old order are fracturing'. Whether we like it or not, and whatever courtiers may counsel, palpable external dangers do lie ahead of us, in the present century.

Is the world, as we British know it, coming to an end? There has been a spate of books on this subject (see Reading List). In one of the latest, *'Going South'*, 2012, Larry Elliott and Dan Atkinson affirm that the UK is on the way to becoming a Third World economy. In my own view, not. Or, at least, not quite yet. But the authors insist that:

> "The empire on which the sun never set is no more, and the United Kingdom has slipped down almost every international league table: for manufacturing strength, for the size of its economy and for living standards ..... For almost

a century, the United Kingdom has deluded
herself, first into believing that the days of
global dominance will return, then into
thinking that the symptoms of decline can be
relatively easily tackled."

Certainly, we do have to face the fact that the tectonic
plates of global power and security are grinding and
shifting, not very evidently to UK advantage. There is much
to play for; but we are going to need every ounce of
professional insight and expertise, just to get by. The
challenge is not for amateurs, let alone 'shamateurs'. Good
diplomacy has to be part of the response.

Mr. William Hague said, in a well-argued presentation to
the International Institute of Strategic Studies in July 2009:

"Any informed assessment of likely trends in
world affairs, over the next decade, on which
our whole national future heavily depends, is a
sobering one ...... the pattern of events we might
expect leads unmistakably and ·uncomfortably
to a world environment in which it will be more
difficult for this country and its traditional
allies to achieve their foreign policy goals,
unless we improve the way we go about them."

William Hague pointed to "powerful forces of economics
and demography elsewhere in the world;" and gave
reasons why the world looked likely to be a more
dangerous place in the coming decades. On this melancholy
but all too plausible prospect, I was myself lecturing to my
undergraduates, over twenty years ago; so Hague is not
inventing the wheel. But he was absolutely right to give
prominent mention to 'failed states', terrorism, risk of
irreversible climate change and shortages of water.
(Indeed, as we see currently in the Horn of Africa, over-
grazing, poor soil and water conservation and rash
deforestation are bringing destitution and famine to

millions.) Hague also mentioned demography. The hard fact is that we face an on-going exponential increase in the world's population. This has tripled, in my own lifetime. Today, two thirds of all Africans are reported to be below the age of 25. The previous Pope said that there was room for all of us on this planet. I myself am not sure that this will remain true much longer, since half again more of us are predicted, by 2050. The future risks of political instability, mass migration and open warfare cannot yet be quantified but clearly do exist. To all of which have to be added, in the light of the 2010 Reith Lectures by the then President of the Royal Society, the future potential dangers of 'Bio-Error' and 'Bio-Terror'.

William Hague correctly noted the declining relative power of many Western nations, in the face of the huge expansion of economies such as China's and India's and even Brazil's (the so-called "Big Emerging Economies" or B.E.E.s—sometimes also called the B.R.I.C.s, to include modern Russia). Possibly even, as Matthew Parris put it in The Times in November 2011: "The imperium of the West is over, never to return." Certainly, Europe's share of the world economy is projected to decline from 18% to 10% by 2050. Not entirely surprisingly, since China today reportedly exports in less than 6 hours what she did in the whole of 1978. Her share of world trade in 2030 is predicted to be twice that of the US.

I am not of the view that China will inevitably become the new top Super Power, nor put the first man on Mars. She has problems of her own. And remember when the experts were predicting that Japan would be 'Number One'? Nor do I anticipate that India, struggling with a population explosion which will carry her numbers to 1.6 billion over the next 30 years, will necessarily become a world shaker. But both India and China are definitely on the up escalator, where we are not.

On terrorism, we are faced with the rise of a Jihadist/Salafist Muslim fundamentalism, which reaches into the heart of even British society. Not all of this new phenomenon is criminal and fanatical. But we would do well occasionally to try to see ourselves as others see us. In his valedictory despatch from Saudi Arabia, back in 2000, Sir Andrew Green, himself an Arabist, had this to say—truer today than ever:

> "Recent campaigns based on the Western concept of human rights miss the mark and engender hostility .... the bulk of the Saudi population reject many of our concepts on both religious and social grounds. They are aware of the rate of divorce, abortion, fatherless children, drug abuse and crime in Western societies and do not accept that we can give them lessons how to organise a society. But, even more important to them, they see us as a Godless society."

Think about that, the next time you walk through the Muslim areas of Birmingham, Bradford, East London, Leeds, Leicester, or Luton.

Then there are the current stresses and strains in the fabric and functioning of international collaboration itself. Lord Hannay has this to say, in the Envoi to *Britain's Quest for a Role*:

> "My principal concern is that we may be at a point when the main international structures which have been so laboriously built up since the end of the Second World War, and even more so since the end of the Cold War—the UN, the IMF, the World Bank, the WTO, the EU, NATO to name the most prominent—may begin to fray and crack and to lose their relevance."

And again:

> "Either the world will surmount the current crises and continue the painful process of edging towards a more rules-based international community capable of mastering, or at least managing, the main global challenges which face us: or it will drift towards a new world disorder, with pretty unpleasant consequences for all concerned."

The EU is, of course, already is now in serious crisis. This was true even before the Greek financial meltdown and consequent shock waves, within and beyond the Euro-zone. To quote a high level 'Reflection Group' report submitted way back in 2010 to the European Council of Heads of State and Government:

> "The EU stands at a critical point in its history..... We now face a choice ..... follow a path to sustainable economic recovery and a more influential role on the world stage, or prepare for a managed decline into irrelevance"[4].

Europe has, of course, been in difficulties in the past. It can be argued that she has a habit of turning a crisis into an opportunity. Nevertheless, we have serious cause to be worried. Britain may be glad not to have joined the Euro. But we are part and parcel of the EU—whatever the new caucus of 'Eurosceptics' in the Tory Party may argue—for compelling reasons of national self-interest. If Europe founders, there may be nowhere else viable to head for, even if we can find a lifeboat.

Indeed, even the US now has its problems. We have moved from a world in which America thought it had limitless resources and unbounded options, to one where the constraints are clear; from a world in which the US could work in the G7 or G8, to one where Washington has

---

[4] Project Europe 2030, Challenge and Opportunities, May 2010

to work in the context of the G20; a world where new technologies and new powers play a bigger role.

If that is true of America, how much the more is it true of Britain?

The UK is not broken. But parts of it—to practise British understatement—are less functional than they used to be. True, as the FCO website boasts: "We are an influential member of key international organisations such as the United Nations, the European Union, NATO and the Commonwealth, and we have strong links with many parts of the world". Immodestly, the website then continues that: "Britain is emerging as a global hub for ideas and a primary force in the search for answers to global problems". Maybe. But let's not kid ourselves. We face serious domestic problems, financial, economic and social, which cannot easily be solved. Perhaps even a problem of national identity. (I think of David Goodheart's "The British Dream", 2012.) Internationally, not merely are we no longer 'Top Dog' in the 'Great Game', as in the days of Palmerston and Salisbury; it is also that we are no more by a long chalk even a Number Two, capable of playing a world policeman. Some go further and argue that the UK has become too much concerned with international Human Rights and with the political and military behaviour of other States (even sometimes with—whisper it—'régime change' in mind), to the neglect of the protection of British national interests and security; perhaps even that we are incapable of acting significantly at all, other than quite cautiously, and in any case in concert wherever possible with our European partners. Certainly, as Sir Rodric Braithwaite has argued (Financial Times, August 2011), Britain needs finally to work out what sort of country it is— "a floundering former empire still dreaming of a global reach, or a serious medium sized power with a realistic view of its national interest".

The Anglo/US so-called 'Special Relationship', while still operative, is no longer what it was. As Lord Hurd once expressed it: "In the penny-farthing relationship which we now have with the United States, the farthing is gradually getting smaller". There are currently signs that the US is beginning to recalibrate the relationship and seek new partners, in a changing world. Accordingly, we should neither expect too much from it (noteworthy, not so long ago, were Mrs Clinton's detachment over the Falklands; President Obama's attack on '*British* Petroleum'), nor allow ourselves, on the other hand, to be 'satellised' by it, as latterly in policy towards the Middle East and Central Asia. Remember the resolute way in which Prime Minister Harold Wilson flatly refused to cave in to White House pressure to commit British troops to the Vietnam War.

I turn to the nuts and bolts of specifically British diplomacy. After successes in Kosovo and Sierra Leone, Britain over-reached herself in Iraq and sleep-walked into an unwinnable conflict in Afghanistan. Were our diplomats to blame? Not over Iraq. They were not brought into the act—or not fully or early enough. Nor were their equally expert State Department opposite numbers, incidentally, thanks to Bush and Rumsfeld. Yet the professionals on both sides of the Atlantic—the 'Camel Corps' as our own FO Arabists are sometimes called—were perfectly well aware, as Rudyard Kipling once put it, that: "Asia is not going to be civilized after the methods of the West. There is too much Asia and she is too old".

Sadly, the over assertive-nature of presidential-style government—tentatively under Margaret Thatcher and then much more markedly Tony Blair—ended up reducing not only the FCO and the Foreign Secretary, but even the Cabinet as a whole, to a cipher—with the House of Commons more than usually a rubber stamp in a Westminster ink-pad. (Even today, MPs are often "bored and underused", to quote David Rennie, political editor of The Economist). And pretty well everyone now concedes that the romantic amateurism and sofa-style decision-making of Labour's Downing Street have been destructive and at times downright dangerous. As Lord Patten once put it (in "*Cousins and Strangers*", 2006):

"One of the government departments most affected by the accumulation of power in Downing Street has been the Foreign Office ...... It cannot have been helpful in the build-up to the Iraq war and in its aftermath that the Prime Minister was divorced from the informed scepticism that the Foreign Office would have brought to a discussion of the available policy options."

Lord Hurd, went further, and wrote of Iraq (in *British Diplomacy*, 2007) that:

"The post-war plan was based on assumptions in the Pentagon which quickly proved false. They ignored their own ignorance and trusted advisers who others knew were untrustworthy. The British Government subordinated its thinking so completely to the United States that no serious questions were asked about the plan and no attempt made to modify it in the light of British experience in Iraq or the Middle East. No attention was paid to those who predicted correctly that while most Iraqis would rejoice at Saddam Hussein's overthrow, it did not follow that they would welcome foreign military occupation. The recklessness of these assumptions in the Pentagon passes belief. So does the failure of Britain to question them."

So much for Iraq (until the Chilcot Inquiry finally releases its much delayed report, possibly now not until 2014.) The Libyan outlook is still uncertain. What about policy towards Afghanistan? In his memoirs[5], a former US Defence Secretary wrote ruefully that: "We viewed the people and leaders of South Viet-Nam in terms of our own

---

[5] Robert McNamara: *In Retrospect*, 1995

experience". Alas, the lesson has not been fully learned. The world has always had, will always have, a plurality of political systems. Afghanistan was seen too much in Western categories. Yet anyone who speaks the languages, or who has served there, like Lord Hannay, or who has even visited the place and travelled a bit (as I have), will know that it is far from being a country yearning to become a "P.C." Scandinavian democracy, anxiously waiting to be saved by Western military "surge" tactics. Nor is it even *one* country, in the usual Western sense. Conflict in Afghanistan is always multi-dimensional: Sunni and Shia; farmer and nomad; Pashtun and Tajik, Uzbek and Hazara. This is not to say that the Western military assault was unjustified, once the Taleban had offered the provocation of giving safe haven to Bin Laden and Al Qaeda, But, beyond that, the initial Western policy seems to have been too 'local-reality-lite', and too 'crusader-heavy'; and the allies focussed too much, as one Tory MP and Central Asian expert has put it, on what they would like to achieve, and not enough on what they could actually achieve[6]. A distinguished former ambassador and special envoy to Afghanistan[7] has put it less diplomatically:

> "The enterprise has proved to be a model of how not to go about such things, breaking all the rules of grand strategy: getting in without having any idea of how to get out; almost wilful misdiagnosis of the challenges; changing objectives, and no coherent or consistent plan; mission creep on an heroic scale; disunity of political and military command, also on an heroic scale."

Fortunately, this policy is now changing; but not before time. In the process, one prays that professional experts

---

[6] Adam Holloway: *In Blood Stepp'd Too Far? Towards a Realistic Policy for Afghanistan*, 2009
[7] Sir Sherard Cowper-Coles: *Cables from Kabul*, 2009

may have more scope to exercise their skills than they did at the outset. And Syria is the next case in point, and an even more tangled mess: variously at odds with neighbours, and full of longstanding domestic rivalries and fault lines of race and religion. The régime is obviously odious; but any successors may well not prove much better, particularly if they end up being dominated by religious extremists.

On, to the FCO, as such. Ours has always been, and still remains, one of the world's most respected diplomatic services. (I can attest to that, having observed it for fifteen years, from the outside, while serving in the Brussels Commission). The Service has always had a remarkable *esprit de corps*. 'The Office' continues to muster, at and near the top, first class men and women—balanced, well-informed and tough-minded. But it has had not only to cope with the party political problems touched on above, but also to face massive internal change in its administration and traditional working methods. These have been driven by revolutionary (and no doubt inescapable) new communications technology; 'political correctness'; 'managerialism'; and unrelenting and quite excessive budget cuts. The Service has been shaken almost to its foundations.

In the Foreword to my own autobiography[8], Lord Hannay wrote:

> "It is hard to exaggerate the changes that have taken place over the period of some fifty years since Leslie Fielding (and I) first joined the Foreign Office in the 1950s. Then, newly-joined desk officers arrived at the gentlemanly hour of 10 o'clock to work in offices still heated (perhaps warmed gets it better) by open coke fires. Telegrams arrived intermittently by a system of vacuum-driven tubes, then were carried along the corridors by elderly

[8] *Kindly Call Me God*, 2009

messengers on massive trolleys which clattered and banged incessantly. A pervasive smell of boiled cabbage percolated round the Palmerstonian building from the canteen far below. Every paper that entered the Foreign Office was carefully registered by an army of clerks and then, resplendently covered by a separate folder, began to make its way up through the hierarchy, gathering comments— often long, copious and self-indulgent comments—appended in manuscript at each stage. No fax machines, no photocopiers, no e-mails. Now, several communications revolutions later, that pattern of work would be unrecognisable to today's officials, hard-driven by the demand for instant reactions to fast-moving events around the world and the requirements of the 24-hour, seven-days-a-week media scene. Not much of that great diplomat Talleyrand's *douceur de vivre* left now."

Undeniably, across the board, in recent years, spirits have been on the low side. Thus, one ex-High Commissioner (the late Sir Hilary Synnott) wrote to me, just before the last general election, that:

"things aren't what they were. There has been a significant decline in available resources—due to personnel cuts as well as financial stringency. At the same time, activity in 'services' such as consular and immigration work has increased enormously, as have the burdens of accountability and Freedom of Information. This has taken its toll on political analysis and expertise. And morale seems to be pretty poor."

Let us look at some of these changes.

Confidential 'INDIV' Personnel Reports (see Chapter 8) are sadly now no more. There are, I believe, 'assessments' of officers by their supervisors; but they have to be shown to the individual concerned and will, therefore, I suspect— if practice in the European Commission is anything to go by —be liable to pull their punches, for fear of contention, perhaps even appeal to the European Court of Human Rights! Would it be possible, today, I wonder, for my bosses to have written privately, behind my back, of my being "sometimes a bit brash .... needs to be sat upon periodically"; or "already inclined to corpulence"; or to have claimed that "it is time he got married and had children"; and that "if he could find himself the right wife, he would get to the top all the quicker".

The least objectionable changes lie in the social field. British society has itself evolved, and—quite rightly—the Service with it. Women are no longer required to resign on marriage. Diplomatic wives can pursue careers of their own. Ethnic composition goes some way to reflect contemporary British society. Short sleeves are more the order of the day than stiff collars and morning coats. The rights of sexual minorities are respected, even upheld. No doubt rightly, in the modern age, 'Inclusiveness' and 'Equal Opportunities' are the watchwords.

Or I am perhaps being too indulgent and a touch P.C. myself? Under the last government, the 'Politically Correct' approached the point of self-parody. The official website trumpeted the news that "the FCO is emerging as one of the UK's top employers for lesbian, gay and bisexual staff". And one wondered why the 'Human Resources' side of the Office could afford, in the financial climate—let alone see the need for—an 'Anti-Bullying Unit'. A more forthright view than mine was expressed, ten years ago, in a letter to the FT, entitled "Once proud Foreign Office sacrificed to 'Cool'". It was written by John Shakespeare, an experienced ex-ambassador (and also, incidentally, the hero of the mob attack on the British Chancery in Phnom Penh on 11 March

1964—I relieved him there, later that year, and have always admired him immensely). He wrote:

> "Old-timers like me look on in stunned disbelief at the tide of political correctness now engulfing the Foreign and Commonwealth Office: reverse discrimination, "inclusion" courses, and FCO lesbian and gay groups, a "gender advisory group", tax-free foreign allowances for "partners" (of whatever sex), the banning of the use of "junior" and "senior", mentoring programmes, stress audits .... You name it. Our cool new FCO will have it."

Other socially influenced change has definitely not been for the better. Sir Roger Carrick, a former High Commissioner in Canberra, was earlier a much respected Head of the small, highly effective (but subsequently abolished), Personnel Operations Department. In his memoir, *'Diplomatic Anecdotage'*, 2012, he has this to say:

> "Postings of diplomats used to be considered carefully against a detailed brief and personal knowledge. Nowadays, officers themselves bid for jobs on the computer screen. Their own skills and judgment in arguing for their preference will not be even. The results might include—and I suspect they have done so—the early promotion of the particularly bright and skilled in advocacy and lobbying, and the by-passing of less self-promoting yet able and experienced officers."

I deplore this. In my day, and Carrick's, we were simply designated and sent, by those who knew us intimately and had a knack of choosing 'horses for courses'—mostly without argument on our side and never by self-selection.

The impact of the communications revolution has been more fundamental. Printing of despatches is very much a thing of the past. British representatives abroad—where they are not using their mobile telephones and engaging in video conference calls—now use email, and for more important reports, what they call 'E-grams'. Emails apparently go only to named officers, or short distribution lists such as members of a particular department in the FCO. I understand that E-grams have a wider circulation, but usually confined to functional or geographic Directorates—such as Middle East/North Africa or Defence and Security. 'Foreign Office and Whitehall' distribution no longer happens. Valedictory and other formal, carefully considered, despatches of the kind reproduced later in this volume are now no more and (in the case of Valedictories) strictly forbidden.

Altogether, a sad business, even if unavoidable. More haste may have brought less speed—resulted in less reflection and more reflex action. Economy—mainly of people's time—is probably one reason for the change. Ministerial sensitivity to criticism has been another. But security and the risk of embarrassing leaks (see below), are also factors.

Certainly, it has become more difficult for officials to tender dispassionate advice in confidence. There is a fear of indiscretion—or even public release, under the Freedom of Information Act. Some ambassadors, I am told, now think twice before speaking their mind—for example, about a foreign potentate in the news. Interviewed on his 37 years in the Diplomatic Service, the former High Commissioner and Ambassador, Sir Nicholas Fenn, said in February 2010 that:

> "Another destructive element has been the popular enthusiasm for open government. Diplomacy demands discretion. Premature publicity arouses populist pressures which all too often destroy the possibility of progress.

> Confidentiality is indispensable to good governance and also to democracy. Far from being a bastion of our liberties, the Freedom of Information Act was a disaster for democracy. Time was when policy was declared by elected Ministers in Parliament and scrutinised by elected MPs—not aired in advance on the *Today* program. The advice tendered by unelected officials was not a legitimate matter for enquiry. Open that advice to public scrutiny, and you turn first class public servants into second class politicians; we are not good at it. The danger is obvious: officials no longer tender exclusively the advice they believe to be in the public interest; they have to consider the likelihood of leak or publication. And this corrodes democracy. Advice can be exploited for electoral advantage. Intelligence reports can be used to influence public opinion on the eve of a war. A Prime Minister can ask about a candidate for senior office, 'Is he one of us?'"

Even more damaging, however, has been the imposition (manifest throughout Whitehall, but totally inappropriate to the Diplomatic Service) of what I will term 'managerialism'—described graphically by Sir Christopher Meyer at the beginning of this book as "the box-ticking, target-setting culture of the last ten years .... obsession with process at the expense of substance". In "*Getting Our Way*" (see Background Reading), he describes this inapplicable and absurd managerial paradigm, the invention of expensive outside consultants, as leading to a "bureaucratic exercise of elephantine proportions". Sir Ivor Roberts, now President of Trinity College, Oxford, but then our Ambassador in Rome, commented in his Valedictory Despatch in 2006, that:

"Too much of the change management agenda is written in Wall Street management-speak which is already tired and discredited by the time it is introduced. Synergies, vfm, best practice, benchmarking, siloworking, roll-out, stakeholder, empower, push-back and deliver the agenda, fit for purpose are all prime candidates for a game of bullshit bingo, a substitute for clarity and succinctness."

He puts the rhetorical question:

"Can it be that in wading through the plethora of business plans, capability reviews, skills audits, zero-based reviews and other excrescences of the management age, we have indeed forgotten what diplomacy is all about?"

Personally, I agree and am unimpressed by 'managerialism'. For what it may be worth, I write as someone who received serious mid-career training in economics, and attended a French Business School, before being let loose on international trade policy in Brussels; who ran one of the largest departments of the European Commission; and who was, later on, a non-executive director of two multinational enterprises as well as the chief executive of a modern British University.

Probably the most devastating blow of all, however, came from the 'slash and burn' budget cuts imposed by the Treasury on the Diplomatic Service in the Blair/Brown years.

The FCO's relatively modest budget (tiny, in comparison to expenditure on defence and overseas aid) was cut to the bone. The previous government closed forty overseas embassies and other diplomatic posts, on grounds of economy. The Language School (on which more below) was also closed. There was a fire sale of assets. 'The Office' found itself under yet further budgetary pressure, as a result of the decline in the international parity of Sterling (due to the removal by the Treasury, without compensating measures, of the overseas price mechanism under which the FCO used to be able to arrange sensible hedging in currencies). Long years of all that finally led the Foreign Affairs Select Committee of the House of Commons, after the General Election, to sound the alarm: budget cuts had damaged the Department's ability to safeguard UK interest overseas.

The foregoing is self-evidently the more regrettable for the stark fact that, more than ever in our history, we now need good diplomacy.

The point was made succinctly, in the foreign policy debate in the House of Lords on 1 July 2010. Lord Howe called for Britain to "find its rightful place in the vanguard —not the slipstream—of the development which will define the future of our continent"; but made it clear that "we can be effective only if we are successful in persuading others to work with us". To that end, later in the debate, Lord Montgomery expressed the hope that the LibCon Coalition would "turn the Foreign Office back into the policy-making department it once was". On the same day, William Hague was in the FCO, delivering much the same message, in his first policy statement after taking office as Secretary of State.

I shall revert to this, in the Envoy. Meanwhile, it is time to move from the general to the particular.

4. DESPATCHES FROM PHNOM PENH

CAMBODIAN NEUTRALITY : ITS NATURE AND PROSPECTS

Mr. Fielding to Mr. R.A. Butler

SUMMARY

Although Prince Sihanouk claims that Cambodia is neutral, current appearances are to the contrary. (Paragraphs 1-2.)

His policy is premised on Cambodia's innate weakness and vulnerability and on certain long-term political assumptions: China is the future major Power in South-East Asia; the United States will be defeated and ejected from Indo-China; Cambodia's biggest enemy is Viet-Nam, whom only China can restrain. (Paragraphs 3-6.)

Nevertheless Sihanouk genuinely dislikes Communism and does not consider it suited to the Cambodian people. (Paragraph 6.)

Hence his compromise, termed a policy of "neutrality"; Indo-China ought to be neutralised by a Geneva Conference and made a buffer zone. Meanwhile Cambodia is to strike an East/West balance which leans more than somewhat in China's direction. (Paragraphs 7-8.)

The neutrality policy is under strain from within and without. (Paragraphs 9-11.)

Sihanouk is adroit and will continue to walk the tight-rope as long as possible. But he may in the end feel obliged to seek a Communist alignment. (Paragraphs 12-14.)

Confidential   British Embassy
No. 52   Phnom Penh
Sir,   September 16, 1964

On the 23rd of September, Prince Sihanouk is leaving for Peking, where he hopes to conduct important talks affecting Cambodia's future relations with China, North Viet-Nam, the Neo Lao Haksat and the National Liberation Front. Emissaries are passing to and fro, rumours come thick and fast, and speculation is rife as to the probable consequences of this latest Eastward genuflection. Detailed developments over the coming months will be reported faithfully to your department. No doubt there will be many false alarms and nine-day wonders which blossom and fade with the brisk fecundity and decay of tropical vegetation. But our botanical enthusiasm must not be entirely diverted from the underlying roots and soil from which these exotics will have drawn their nourishment. Prince Sihanouk's tactics may be unpredictable but his strategy is always clear and consistent. In this despatch, I have the honour to submit some thoughts on the basic character of Sihanouk's foreign policy and on the more general prospects for the survival of a neutral Cambodia.

2. Sihanouk is fond of proclaiming that his country is strictly neutral. Appearances in Cambodia at present hardly bear out this claim in the literal sense. The Press is heavily censored and devotedly toes the line laid down by the Government. There is no freedom of public debate. Even strictly factual Western reporting (other than the highly tendentious coverage afforded by Agence France Presse) rarely finds its way into print. But everything Chinese, including Hsin-Hua propaganda of all descriptions, is joyously received and acclaimed. Muted voices from the Soviet bloc are heard in the background; the foreground is reserved to Prince Sihanouk and the People's Republic of China, who both profess to speak with one voice. Information and cultural activity by Western

diplomatic missions is heavily circumscribed. The United States Information Service in Cambodia, formerly an ambitious organisation, is now operating almost on a care and maintenance basis; its vacated headquarters stand gutted, painted with "Yankee go home" slogans and alive only to the sound of rats' feet over broken glass. Measures of socialisation are being applied to the economy which threaten the existing trading links with the West; the foreign banks have already been pushed out and the Western oil companies face nationalisation with exiguous compensation. No compensation whatsoever has been paid (although promised) to this Embassy for the extensive damage caused by mob action on the 11th of March. American economic aid has been rejected. The British and Americans are forbidden to have social contacts with Cambodians. Their Governments are subjected to daily public abuse. Economic and military aid has been demanded of, and is to some extent forthcoming from, the Communist nations. Far, therefore, from presenting a picture of neutrality in any genuine sense, Cambodia gives the appearance of occupying a position on the Left of the non-aligned group of nations.

3. Nevertheless this impression, which has been deliberately fostered largely for reasons of foreign policy, should not be taken entirely at its face value.

4. The underlying reality which dictates all Prince Sihanouk's policies is the utter weakness of his country. Cambodia is a viable ethnic and economic unit, with the mass of its people reasonably content with their lot and united in profound affection for and acceptance of Sihanouk as their leader. But these are the Prince's only resources. Otherwise, he is set about by what he considers to be traditional enemies. Thailand, however genuine her subsequent sea-change into a well-scrubbed pro-Western democracy, did in fact seize wide and fertile areas of Cambodia during the war and did not disgorge them until

1947. Laos still maintains on paper (and could well pursue by force of arms, if she fell entirely to the Communists) a claim to the province of Stung Treng. To the east are the Viet-Namese, whom Sihanouk fears the most. The Viet-Namese posed a serious threat to Cambodia in history right up to the days of French colonial intervention. The average Cambodian today, and Sihanouk himself, both dislikes and distrusts them. In the fifteenth century, the Annamites wiped out a nation, the Cham, of similar stock and racial origins to the Cambodians. Sihanouk constantly reverts to their fate when discussing his Eastern frontier. He sees the Viet-Namese as more ruthless, talented and industrious than the Cambodians; as a people irresistibly drawn by their greed and by their own population pressures towards the rich under-populated and under-developed Cambodian rice-lands. Cambodia has no effective armed forces and no friendly neighbours. Amid an Indo-China torn with war and civil and political dissensions, Cambodia's vulnerability is, like Allah, closer to Sihanouk than his own jugular vein.

5. Against this background, Sihanouk has formulated certain long-term assumptions which have dictated most of his recent policies and actions and which emerge clearly from his voluminous but generally frank public utterances. They are as follows. First, the power most seriously to be reckoned with in the future is People's China. In the middle and long term, and perhaps before then, the whole of Indo-China will become a sphere of Chinese influence. Second, the Chinese, even in their present militant mood, are not bound on conquest and annexation; they will be content to exclude Western influence and to assert their own; eventually they will probably become prosperous and go soft like the Russians; if he steps softly, therefore, Cambodia may yet survive the ascendency of China in Asia. Third, Sihanouk considers that the United States is shortly to be subjected to humiliation and defeat in South Viet-Nam, and to lose all direct influence in the area. Fourth, the greatest threat to Cambodia is posed by Viet-Nam.

Viet-Nam will shortly be united under Communist rule; but he fears that Communism will not mitigate, it will merely make more formidable than ever before, the traditional expansionist threat described in paragraph 4 above. Fifth, he feels certain that Cambodia's only hope of national survival is, therefore, to establish a *modus vivendi* with the Viet-Namese Communists and to rely on Big Brother China to prevent Viet-Nam from being beastly.

6. At the same time, there is no doubt that Sihanouk personally dislikes Communism, considers it inappropriate as a political and social creed for the Cambodian people and is firmly bent on preserving for as long as possible the integrity, independence and national character of his country and nation. At home, he has rigorously suppressed his own Khmer Rouge and keeps his Khmer Rose on a tight rein. He proclaims in his speeches, and evidently believes, that the strict regimentation, harsh application to ceaseless labour and general lack of *joie de vivre* which he has witnessed with his own eyes in Communist China, would be profoundly repugnant to the care-free Cambodian national character. Sihanouk also considers that Communism would conflict with the profoundly religious and monarchical traditions of Cambodia. Nor does he profess to any delusion about the friendship which the Communists offer. "The Communists are deceitful to us and we are to them . . . the day that they are not interested in our country, I will no longer be able to deceive them and ask for their aid. They will refuse to give me aid and will whip me or devour the Cambodian people."

7. Sihanouk at present is therefore striking a precarious balance. He has felt it necessary to reject American aid and advice and to present the Americans to his people as enemies and potential aggressors. Fundamentally, he has probably done so because he sees the Americans as unable to protect their allies in South Viet-Nam and because he deems it expedient to strike a posture pleasing to Peking.

But he does not wish the Americans to disappear altogether from the scene. In an interview with *Le Figaro* during his State visit to France in June, he made it clear that, although the Americans were bidden to leave Indo-China, they should remain in Thailand and the Philippines, and anywhere else where they were welcome. Otherwise "neutrality would be impossible because equilibrium would be broken". To help maintain this equilibrium, he is making the most of his longstanding but newly enthusiastic friendship with France and of the modest support of the Soviet bloc and Yugoslavia. He has given strict instructions that no assistance is to be given to the Viet Cong. He has been quick to harness Indonesian diplomatic support to his chariot, but at the same time has refrained from riding down Malaysia. If he is hostile to Great Britain, this is almost entirely because he sees us a wilfully obstructing the convening of a Geneva Conference.

8. It is still the Geneva Conference solution which he seeks: a Conference which would endorse Cambodian neutrality, set a formal seal on his present frontiers, and bind as closely as any written agreement could the Governments of North Viet-Nam and People's China. He would like such a Geneva Conference to be extended to the whole of Indo-China (except North Viet-Nam, which he considers irremediably Communist). "I consider that now is the time to apply a diplomatic and political solution, in making South Viet-Nam, Laos and Cambodia a buffer zone effectively separating the Communists from the West."

9. The question arises as to whether Cambodia's policies of neutrality can long continue in their present form. I regret to report that the prospects, whether short term or long, do not appear very bright. Sihanouk may find that he has now leaned so far in the Chinese direction that he cannot recover his balance.

10. Economically and socially, Cambodia is already beginning to slide down the slippery slope. The inept and half-baked measures of socialisation embarked upon with such gay abandon last autumn have since proved a sorry venture and may be difficult to reverse. If left to themselves they could eventually bring the economy to a point from which it would be able to recover only at the cost of extensive Communist, and no doubt in large measure Chinese, economic alignments. Financial troubles and economic dislocation could in turn quicken the developing Left-wing and fellow-travelling elements in Cambodian urban life.

11. In the context of foreign affairs, Sihanouk cannot persist indefinitely in his attempt to obtain a Geneva solution. He has announced his intention, and could well mean it, of waiting after the American elections until only the turn of the year. As the situation in South Viet-Nam apparently deteriorates and the Viet Cong advance their banners, the need to hop off the fence and do a deal becomes for Sihanouk more and more acute. He cannot hope to earn sympathy and influence in Hanoi if he offers recognition only after victory has been won. Already he may fear that the situation in South Viet-Nam is developing faster than he had anticipated. Meanwhile, feeling seriously exposed on his solitary neutralist perch, he has qualms that his anti-American actions may one day come home to roost. Lacking any real understanding of the Americans or their way of life, and completely without insight into their current intentions and planning, Sihanouk has shown in recent months increasing anxiety that the United States will resort to desperate expedients to save the Saigon regime, and bring vengeance to bear on Cambodia. In his speeches he warns against (and may, himself, even half-believe) various C.I.A. assassination plots and Pentagon plans for invasion.

12. Sihanouk is therefore likely sooner or later to take seriously the possible need for specific alignment with Peking. He has already spoken of the possibility of signing a defence agreement with China to guard against an attack by the Imperialists, and of buying national survival at the price of a complete change of regime involving passage into the Socialist-Communist camp. The logic of his established policies, and the exigencies to which they give rise, may finally combine to make this consequence inevitable. If so, Sihanouk will have the consolation of history. Following the decline and fall of the Empires of Angkor, the Cambodians have spun out a precarious existence as the Satellite of this and that ascendant Power for the past 450 years.

13. There still remain, however, one or two encouraging signs. The Prince has said that he will if necessary become the first Cambodian Commissar; but he has also publicly forecast that thorough-going Communism would end the monarchy and drive him into exile. He will not willingly therefore press too deep into the Chinese embrace. He has also begun to sense a double-cross. Sihanouk is discouraged and to some extent disillusioned by the caution with which the North Viet-Namese have responded to his feelers. Hanoi may prefer not to recognise Cambodia's frontiers in advance of a final victory in the south and perhaps not even then. This could promote an agonising re-appraisal of Cambodian alignments. While Sihanouk would never permit himself openly to oppose China, he might attempt to insulate himself from his immediate Communist neighbours by a policy of self-reliance; and an austerity regime devoted to building up Cambodia's military strength could conceivably command substantial assistance inter alia from the Soviet bloc. Finally, if the developing situation in Indo-China over the coming months should offer even the ghost of a chance of negotiation and neutralisation, Sihanouk, who still has some freedom of manoeuvre, will be quick to exploit it.

14. Prince Sihanouk once said that Cambodia needed for its survival a strong leader and a strong friend. The leadership he supplies himself; it is still largely unchallenged throughout the land. The chosen friend is to be China rather than the United States; if China honours this friendship and accepts its responsibilities, Cambodia will reciprocate. Sihanouk is attached to his own concept of neutrality and will not abandon it freely. But he is even more attached to preserving intact the country and people of Cambodia. Deeply repugnant though this would be, he might prefer to become something like a Satellite of China than to see his people swamped and his country dismembered in a Communist free-for-all in Indo-China. It is in this setting that the events of the next few months will be played through to their conclusion. Cambodian neutrality has reached a turning point. Cambodia is now free to pivot like a weather-cock; the winds of change will determine the direction which she finally faces; in the end, the North-Easter may dash her to pieces.

I have, &c.

Leslie Fielding

(Chargé d'Affaires)

<u>Letter to Mr. Fielding from Head of South-East Asia Department, FO, September 24, 1964</u>

1. Thank you for your interesting and entertaining Despatch No 52 on the nature and prospects of Cambodian neutrality. The eve of Sihanouk's departure for Peking is a timely moment for a fresh survey of this question and we are having the Despatch printed for distribution.

2. One additional argument which supports your thesis and, perhaps, takes it even a little further is Sihanouk's "educational insurance policy"—the presence of his eldest son at school in Peking with (typical Sihanouk) other sons at Moscow and Prague.

3. As you will meanwhile have seen from the record of the Secretary of State's talk with Bundy, our own policy remains unchanged: we would like to support such remnants of Cambodian neutrality as can be preserved and, when our allies will permit it, would still like a Cambodian Conference.

(J. E. Cable)

<u>Response of Foreign Secretary, Mr. R.A. Butler, passed on by his Private Secretary, October 12, 1964</u>

Dear Leslie

The Secretary of State has asked me to say how much he admires your despatch No. 52 about Cambodian neutrality, which enables him to understand Prince Sihanouk a little more.

Yours ever,
Nicko Henderson

THE CHINESE PRESENCE AND PURPOSE IN CAMBODIA

Mr. Fielding to Mr. Gordon Walker

SUMMARY

Cambodia is associated by geography and history with China. (Paragraph 2.)

There is an important Chinese community in Cambodia. (Paragraphs 3-4.) But it is not exploited for purposes of subversion. (Paragraph 5.)

Communist China's presence is chiefly asserted through the economic and military aid programmes, and by careful cultivation of Prince Sihanouk. (Paragraphs 6-8.)

The ultimate aim of the Chinese Communists is probably to make Cambodia not a Satellite, but a subservient State. (Paragraphs 9-10.)

In the short term however they are making a good thing out of Cambodian "neutrality". (Paragraph 11.)

For the present, the Chinese are in one sense a restraining influence over Sihanouk. (Paragraph 13.) But the future prospect is sombre. (Paragraphs 14-15.)

Secret   British Embassy
No. 57   Phnom Penh
Sir,   November 17, 1964

Communist China has cast a long shadow into Cambodia since the early years of her existence. In a speech to the Philippine Congress in February 1956, Prince Sihanouk said that "as long as the feelings of the Government of

Communist China .... are not belied by some signs of change, I cannot, as the present leader of .... a small people of only 5 million inhabitants, under any circumstances rebuff the friendship of the leader of a people of 600 million". There were in the event no subsequent "signs of change" in China's steady policy of friendship towards Cambodia. As a result, Sihanouk's foreign policy acquired an increasingly pro-Chinese bias. In my despatch No. 52 of the 16th of September, I reported that Sihanouk was likely sooner or later to take seriously the possible need for specific alignment with Peking. The present despatch is concerned with the other side of the coin: if Sihanouk is prepared to sell, will he find a buyer? I have the honour to submit an account of the Chinese presence in Cambodia, and to offer a tentative assessment of the underlying Chinese purpose here.

2. A measure of Chinese interest in Cambodia is dictated by the facts of geography and history. Geographically, Cambodia (although there is no common frontier) is a close neighbour of China's. For Yunnan province, she is the second doorstep down into the South-East Asian street. Historically, Indo-China has been the traditional boundary between the ancient Indian and Chinese civilisations. The first known written record of the existence of Cambodia under the name of Funan is to be found in the early Chinese chronicles. Embassies were sent to China from Funan in the European Dark Ages. The Chinese diplomat, Chou Ta-kuan, visited Angkor in 1283 on a mission to negotiate Chinese suzerainty over Cambodia. Another diplomatic mission was sent in the 15th century, following Chinese annexation of Annam. Chinese cultural influence, the glory and power of the imperial courts, has asserted itself in varying degree in Cambodia for most of the Christian era. The modern Cambodians significantly interpret China's historical role as that of a sort of Indo-China policeman, a powerful but respected neighbour,

anxious that peace should prevail along the imperial boundaries.

3. From the proximity of China, the tide of history has swept into Cambodia a considerable human jetsam. The existence of a small Chinese minority of tradesmen was reported by Chou Ta-kuan. Today, out of an approximate population in Cambodia of 6 million it has been estimated that between 5 and 6 per cent are Chinese. Almost all this small but influential racial minority is centred in the towns. In the capital city of Phnom Penh, where less than half the inhabitants are Cambodian, perhaps a quarter are of definite Chinese descent. As financiers, entrepreneurs, traders, shopkeepers and skilled workers, the Chinese have traditionally controlled much of the nation's commerce and have thereby acquired relative affluence. Despite growing resentment in recent years of their high economic status, the Chinese minority as a whole is respected and admired by the Cambodians. Thing Chinese are auspicious and prestige-laden. More Cambodians wear jewellery inscribed with lucky Chinese characters than can read Chinese. The ambitious and go-ahead eagerly seek Chinese partners in marriage.

4. Inter-marriage has not significantly diminished the homogeneity and national consciousness of the expatriate Chinese. As so often elsewhere in Asia, they are broadly in sympathy with Peking and heavily infiltrated by pro-Communist elements. There is an equally large and urban-centred Viet-Namese minority, who are also economically influential and are also Communist infiltrated. It follows, therefore, that at least 10 per cent of the population of Cambodia, including half that of Phnom Penh, is an element in Cambodian society susceptible to influence from Peking and potentially a medium for subversive activities.

5. There is, however, no evidence to suggest that Peking is at present pursuing a policy directly designed to subvert the Cambodian State, fruitful though the field would be. In 1956, Mao Tse-tung and Chou En-lai congratulated Sihanouk on his far-sighted decision to be neutral, offered economic assistance to Cambodia (the first offer to a non-Communist country ever made by People's China) and let it be understood that if ever the Prince had trouble with the Viet Minh, he need only appeal to Peking to have it stopped. In a joint statement made by the Prime Ministers of Cambodia and China in Peking in August 1958, Chou En-lai specifically advised the Chinese residing in Cambodia to refrain from all political activity in their host country. Since then, the Chinese Government have made no apparent effort to intervene on behalf of proscribed Cambodian Communists, or to prevent the deliberate attack on the economic ascendency of the expatriate Chinese launched by Prince Sihanouk in his various measures of reform. There is a large and active Chinese diplomatic mission in Phnom Penh: although we must assume that it has established a widespread network of informers and agents of influence, the mission seems mainly to concentrate, with considerable success, on information and propaganda activities of a kind calculated not to give offence to the Cambodian Government.

6. Facts and figures about the Chinese programme of economic aid to Cambodia are not readily available, but we know that its impact is being increasingly felt, both in economic and political terms. A Sino-Cambodian trade and payments agreement of June 1956 provided for the annual exchange of goods between the two countries, and it may be significant that China appears prepared to accept the sort of Cambodian export which is not normally marketable outside the country. In June of that year, £8 million worth of equipment, merchandise and constructional material was promised as an outright gift. Subsequent aid in 1960 may have been worth £10 million.

Factories for the manufacture of plywood, textiles, paper and cement have been constructed, equipped and set to work by the Chinese Government. Further textile, paper and glass factories are promised, together with more equipment for factories already in existence. A floating population of up to 300 experts has helped to carry these projects through. Some of these experts are currently drawing up plans for the construction of a large airport, ostensibly civil, but with what seems to me obvious military significance, at Battambang towards the frontier with Thailand. These projects have sometimes proved uneconomic "white elephants"; but the Cambodians do not seem to mind (albinos have always held a special place of honour in the elephant stables of the Khmer god-kings). To the Cambodians, what is important is that all of this aid is apparently being given without strings; impressive industrial installations have been handed over free of charge to the Cambodian Government for operation by the Cambodians themselves. The United States aid programme which Sihanouk abruptly terminated in November 1963 was generous (to the tune of some $370 million since 1951), constructive and prudently administered. But somehow the Americans never got the full credit and it is now the Chinese who lead the field.

7. China also runs a military aid programme. A number of vehicles and automatic weapons have already been provided. Light weapons have been promised for 22,000 men (over two-thirds of the entire Cambodian Army), plus a workshop for their maintenance and repair. The navy has been ignored as unimportant. For the air force, the Cambodians have been told to turn to the French or the Russians. No tanks or heavy artillery have been provided for the Cambodian Army—the Cambodian terrain is not greatly suited to tank action, nor the Cambodian soldier to the effective use of complex modern equipment. The Chinese have concentrated instead on what for the Cambodians are the essentials. Although the French,

Russians and Czechs are all providing considerable quantities of arms to Cambodia, and the former still maintain a military training mission, the Chinese will probably succeed in establishing a special position with the Cambodian land forces in the course of the next year or two.

8. It is, however, on the diplomatic front where China has been most demonstrably active in supporting Cambodia, and establishing influence over Prince Sihanouk personally. Sihanouk's son and possible heir, Prince Naradipo, has been joyfully received for education in Peking. In May 1963, a Treaty of Friendship was signed between the two countries. Over the past year, the Chinese have been outspoken in their support for the political project closest to Sihanouk's heart: that of a Geneva Conference to endorse Cambodian neutrality and territorial integrity. They have taken Sihanouk's side throughout the series of frontier incidents in which with monotonous regularity Viet-Namese regular forces have attacked Cambodian villages and peasants allegedly harbouring the Viet Cong. They have issued a series of statements, the texts of which are set out in the enclosure to this despatch, affirming the "total support" of the Chinese people in the event of a Western attack on Cambodia. Above all, they have assiduously paid open court to the egotism and conceit of the Prince; the latter was profoundly flattered by the lavishness of his reception in Peking in October and by the personal attention accorded to him by the highest personalities of the Chinese State.

9. So much for the Chinese "presence". What of the Chinese "purpose"? If I correctly understand his despatch from Peking No. 30 of the 8th of April, 1964, about China and South-East Asia, Mr. Garvey suggested that China's present objective was not to subjugate South-East Asia in the sense of conquering it militarily, so much as to exclude Western

influence and to establish control through local governments which need not be Communist in complexion.

10. In my view, this is exactly what the Chinese are up to in Cambodia. No doubt they reason to themselves as follows. China at present has only a limited military capacity for intervention in this country; subversion is for the time being ruled out as imprudent. But time itself is on China's side. Events must, therefore, be permitted to follow their dialectically inevitable course. There must be no forcing from Prince Sihanouk; too much is at stake in Indo-China for the Phnom Penh tail to be allowed to wag the Peking dog. But on the other hand, the eventual objective must be to convert Cambodia, not into a formal "Satellite", but into one of a string of Asian States subservient to the People's Republic.

11. So far, Chinese patience and pragmatism appear to have reaped ample rewards. The American position in Cambodia has been at least for the time being destroyed. China has been permitted freely to extend her foothold. Prince Sihanouk has given increasing diplomatic support to Peking on the world stage. The People's Republic of China received de jure recognition from Cambodia in July 1958; at the Colombo Conference in December 1962, Sihanouk refused to lend himself to schemes of conciliation between India and China which were unwelcome to the latter; in July 1963, Cambodia refused to sign the Nuclear Test Ban Treaty, which Sihanouk denounced as a bargain of dupes and a demagogic act; in 1964, Cambodia has given full diplomatic support to China over the Gulf of Tonkin incidents, has effusively welcomed the explosion of the first Chinese nuclear device, and has undertaken to lead the van at New York in calling for the admission of Peking to the United Nations.

12. What are the consequences for the West of China's Cambodia policy? As seen from here, China's patience

offers us some immediate and fleeting consolation. But beyond that, Chinese thoroughness seems all too likely to leave nought for our comfort.

13. Our consolation lies in the fact that, at the present critical juncture, China is, by a curious paradox, exercising a certain restraint on Prince Sihanouk's actions. Impatient of obtaining the guarantee of his neutrality which he thinks a Geneva Conference would offer, Sihanouk has come round more and more to the view that he must without delay recognise North Viet-Nam and the National Liberation Front and accept the consequences. Such consequences would almost certainly be adverse to the West. The Saigon regime might find it necessary to cut Cambodia's life-line of trade and supply up the Mekong river. This would quickly reduce Cambodia to a chaos in which Prince Sihanouk would be compelled to retaliate by even more desperate action. Military facilities would probably be granted to the Viet Cong insurrectionaries, South Viet-Nam would no doubt want to launch military reprisals and the whole affair could escalate into a regional crisis from which the Chinese would be unable to stand aloof. The dangers of this appear to be better understood in Peking than anywhere else. The Chinese have skilfully avoided formally committing themselves to military intervention in Cambodia. They have declined to sign a defence treaty with Sihanouk; the statements in the Annex would probably bind China only in the event of an out-and-out invasion by the forces of "imperialism". During his last visit to Peking in October, Sihanouk was on the brink of precipitate recognition of the Viet-Namese Communists. He is said to have been dissuaded from this course by Chou En-lai, who pointed out that Cambodia's greatest present asset was her neutrality. Like virginity, it was not to be lightly discarded. In so far therefore as the British Government may still envisage a Geneva conference as a possible operative cure for Cambodia's troublesome condition, they appear to be able to call on the services of a

Chinese anaesthetist to keep Sihanouk quiet while the table is got ready.

14. On the other hand, in the absence of an agreed international settlement, the longer-term Chinese influence in Cambodia seems likely to prove distinctly unhelpful. In his despatch referred to above, Mr. Garvey confessed to little doubt that the pace of Chinese activities abroad would increase as time went on and the Chinese separatist Neo-Comintern got established. In Cambodia, this could mean an extension of the Chinese presence, a growth of extreme Left-wing and anti-Western influence the gradual imposition of State control on Communist lines in all sectors of the economy and of society, and the eventual penetration and control by China of the Cambodian Army. The greater the difficulties which Cambodia would be having with land-hungry neighbours, the more firmly rooted would Chinese hegemony become. The probable effect of all this on the stability of Laos, on the morale of South Viet-Nam and on Thailand's confidence in her Western alignment is not for this post to assess. But these three countries all have common frontiers with Cambodia and, as seen from here, none would stand to gain if Cambodia became in fact, if not in name, a Chinese fellow traveller.

15. When Britain was attempting, some 12 months ago, to prepare the way towards a Geneva conference on Cambodia, there was some difference of view between Her Majesty's Missions in this area as to whether Sihanouk would permit, or China would wish, the conversion of Cambodia into a Chinese satellite. It all depends, of course, on what one means by the word "Satellite". The position as seen from this post today might be summarised as follows. Sihanouk will not turn Cambodia over to thorough-going Communism unless this is the only way to prevent her dismemberment. The Chinese for their part do not wish physically to take the country over, and are prepared for

the present to support the continuance of Cambodian "neutrality". Nevertheless the course of Chinese activity inside Cambodia and of Cambodia's present relations with her immediate neighbours seems likely to lead to an increasingly intimate alignment of Peking and Phnom Penh, to the general detriment of the West and the particular discomfort of Bangkok and Saigon.

I have &c.

Leslie Fielding

(Chargé d'Affaires)

Letter to Mr. Fielding in Phnom Penh from Head of South-East Asia Department, Foreign Office, December 15, 1964

We were glad to have your useful and stimulating despatch, No. 57 of November 17, about the Chinese presence and purpose in Cambodia. It is being printed; and a copy is now doing the rounds of the Office.

2. I am not sure that I entirely agree with you about the effectiveness of Chinese aid. Once the glamour has worn off, I would have thought it possible that the worthlessness of white elephants, such as uneconomic cement plants, would become apparent—even to a people who have a soft spot for albinos. I find myself much more in agreement with your suggestion in paragraph 7 that the Chinese will succeed in establishing a special position with the Cambodian land forces because they have concentrated on supplying essential equipment and have eschewed the white elephants of complex weapons which the Cambodians may never be able to handle. This gives weight to your forecast in paragraph 14 that the Chinese might eventually gain control of the Cambodian army. Nevertheless Sihanouk—in common with other potentates, not all of them oriental—has a liking for toys; and perhaps

if the Chinese do not provide nice, impressive and complicated equipment—even tanks—he will go elsewhere for them.

3. The general line of argument in the despatch seems to me to be right. I, too, would expect Cambodia to become more and more of a nuisance in international affairs while avoiding, as far as possible, outright Communism and I agree that China will probably try to avoid physically taking over the country. Our hope is, of course, Prince Sihanouk's spirit of independence. His present fawning on China is the product of circumstances which may well be short lived. If eventually some kind of neutralist solution for South East Asia is accepted, we might be able to pursue policies which would help to redress the balance of attractiveness between ourselves and the Chinese in the eyes of Sihanouk. He is always likely to remain a thorn in the Western flesh, but it is possible that we shall be able once again to establish some sort of working relationship with him. What happens when he disappears from the scene is impossible to predict, but here again perhaps the French heritage would provide a nucleus from which could grow a neutralism which might not essentially be anti-Western.

(J.E. Cable)

THE AMERICANS AS SIHANOUK SEES THEM

Mr. Fielding to Mr. Gordon Walker

SUMMARY

The American position in Cambodia has been largely destroyed by Prince Sihanouk. Why has he done this? (Paragraph 2.)

Prince Sihanouk's grievances are the following. He resents the apparent failure of United States policies in South Viet-Nam (paragraph 3). He believes that the Americans look down upon him (paragraph 4), are backing the Thais and the Viet-Namese against Cambodia (paragraph 5) and are conspiring to overthrow him (paragraphs 6-7).

Sihanouk also dislikes the Americans as people (paragraph 8). American personal diplomacy has had its failures (paragraph 9).

The present outlook for Cambodian-American relations is discouraging (paragraph 10).

There is a great deal of nonsense and injustice in Sihanouk's attitude to the Americans (paragraph 12).

The chances of a rapprochement are slight but nevertheless exist (paragraphs 13-14).

Confidential and Guard   British Embassy
No. 59   Phnom Penh
Sir,   November 25, 1964

In this despatch I have the honour to describe American activities and policy in Cambodia, not necessarily as they are, but as they are seen by Prince Sihanouk, the Cambodian Head of State. An assessment of the relations of the United States with Cambodia since the latter gained independence in 1954 is the task of the historian, not the diplomat. The British diplomat is particularly unqualified to adopt a balanced viewpoint in this country because his personal sympathies will inevitably lie with his American colleagues, just as his professional approach will reflect a cardinal feature of the policy of Her Majesty's Government in South-East Asia—that of the closest cooperation and support for the Government of the United States. But the fact remains that Prince Sihanouk sees the Americans through strangely tinted spectacles; it is the duty of this Mission to report, with appropriate reserve, the prospect of the United States so afforded.

2. In my despatch No. 57 of November 17, on the Chinese presence and purpose in Cambodia, I reported that the American position in this country had been, at least for the time being destroyed. The United States economic and military aid programme, worth $370 million over the years, was abruptly terminated by Sihanouk in November 1963. The American Embassy was attacked and partly sacked (as was our own) in March 1964. In September, Mr. Randolph Kidder, the American Ambassador-designate, whose appointment had already received the *agrément* of the Royal Cambodian Government, was refused the right to present his credentials, and was suffered ignominiously to depart. In November, threats to dismiss the United States Embassy from Phnom Penh, and thereby completely to sever diplomatic relations with Washington, reached their apogee in an ultimatum issued by the Head of State. As I write, Sihanouk has suspended this threat and accepted an American suggestion for talks on neutral ground; but this development is itself a measure of the chronic state of American-Cambodian relations. The Americans were well received in Cambodia 10 years ago; their prestige stood high as a result of the victories of the United States in the Second World War and by virtue of American championship of the under-developed and smaller nations. What, from Sihanouk's point of view, are the causes of this profound fall from grace?

3. The most fundamental reproach which Sihanouk has for the United States is probably that of failure. As I wrote in my despatch No. 52 of September 16, he thinks that the United States is shortly to be subjected to humiliation and defeat in South Viet-Nam and to lose all direct influence in the area. Sihanouk has at present no confidence in the ability of the Americans to protect their friends in Indo-China. He considers that they have directed Communist lightning a good deal too close to Cambodia for comfort. He calculates that the Americans, having made (in his view) a mess of Indo-China, will wash their hands of it and sail away to safety across the Pacific, leaving the locals to fend for themselves. In the interests of preserving Phnom Penh from the likely fate of Saigon, he now prefers to keep the Americans at arm's length and to embrace the friendship of the ascendant power of China. He will not begin to change his posture until American policy in South Viet-Nam, and perhaps also in Laos, shows unmistakable signs of success.

4. Sihanouk apparently believes that what really determines the policy of the United States Government towards him is the size and the neutral status of his country. Cambodia has a population of only 6 million. Sihanouk once said that if she had 100 million, like Indonesia, the United States would soon change their tune. He feels great pride as the descendant of a long line of kings and is conscious of the past glories of the Khmer Empire; he is therefore the more resentful of the fact that Cambodia is not what it was. Sihanouk knows his country is small and backward; but, like a cripple with his deformity, he hates people to notice it. On a recent visit to Phnom Penh, the Director of South-East Asian Affairs in the State Department told me that Cambodia was not in his view the key to anything. Unhappily, Sihanouk also is aware or this view, which he describes as one of "scorn and contempt" for his country. His sense of frustration and annoyance is compounded by the attitude of a certain section of the American press, to which he is morbidly sensitive, and

which has consistently ridiculed him and belittled his achievements. In recent years, the State Department has made it plain that the United States accepts and supports the neutrality of Cambodia. But these assurances have somehow never carried conviction to the deaf ears of Prince Sihanouk.

5. But the princely grudge against the Americans unfortunately seems to extend much further back than the present and the recent past. In April and again in September of 1954, Sihanouk appealed to the United States for military help against the Communist Viet Minh operating on Cambodian soil. Sihanouk claims that his doubts about the value of American support began when, as a result of this appeal, it became clear to him that they would not commit ground troops against the Communists in Cambodia, just as they had refused to commit them at Dien Bien Phu. Cambodia's policy of neutrality was accordingly proclaimed in October 1954 (during an official visit to Phnom Penh by Pandit Nehru) and confirmed at the Bandung Conference in April 1955 (following Sihanouk's conversations with Chou En-lai). Sihanouk dislikes the Thais and hates and fears the Viet-Namese; for him it is an article of faith that these people are bent on completing the destruction of Cambodia which they began centuries ago. Communism is for him only one problem among many. Accordingly, in 1956 Sihanouk began to protest against SEATO manoeuvres. Just as the Russians these day sometimes profess to fear that it is the Germans who run NATO, so Sihanouk maintained that it was the Thais who were setting the SEATO pace. The acid test came when the South Viet-Namese occupied parts of Stung Treng (now Ratanakiri) Province in 1958. On that occasion, the State Department is said to have warned Cambodia not to use American weapons to oust the intruder, on the grounds that these weapons had been given to Cambodia for use only against the Communists. It was probably at this point that Sihanouk concluded that American aid gave him

effective protection neither from the Communists on the one hand, nor his Western-aligned neighbours on the other.

6. Sihanouk professes to find confirmation for his distrust of Washington in what he conceives to be the clandestine and subversive activity directed against him by the United States in concert with Thailand and South Viet-Nam. He seems to fear that the United States may even one day wish to occupy his country for some wider strategic purpose connected with the hot war in Indo-China. For Sihanouk, there are three American Governments, each with its own policy towards him; those of the President and the State Department, of the Central Intelligence Agency and of the Pentagon. Sihanouk publicly professes, and inwardly may more than half believe, that the latter two organisations are implacably opposed to him and bent on securing his downfall.

7. In his speeches, Sihanouk repeatedly unfolds a long list of alleged conspiracies. In 1958 there was the Dap Chhuon affair, in which the Governor of Siem Reap Province was said to have plotted an uprising with the approval of Thailand and South Viet-Nam. He was caught, with two Viet-Namese agents, in possession of espionage material of alleged American origin. A diplomat on the staff of the American Embassy in Phnom Penh who may have had some contact with Dap Chhuon left the country precipitately. In 1959 the Americans were blamed for the flight to Viet-Nam in January of Sam Sary, a former confidant of the Prince, under charges of treason, and for the parcel bomb which nearly killed the Queen Mother in August. Above all, the Americans are held to aid and abet the activities of Sihanouk's mortal rival, Son Ngoc Thanh, in exile in South Viet-Nam, where he heads the anti-Sihanouk Khmer Serei ("Free Khmer") movement. The Khmer Serei direct subversive radio broadcasts into Cambodia from mobile stations in South Viet-Nam and

Thailand. Sihanouk maintains that this is done with equipment supplied by the United States. These events have greatly hardened Sihanouk in his distrust and fear of the Americans. He now sees their complicity in everything, and finds it frankly incredible that they could not put an end to the activities of his enemies if they so chose. The dismissal of United States aid last November was due in part to this atmosphere of mystery and myth. Sihanouk held the Americans responsible for the deposition of President Diem in South Viet-Nam, and apparently felt sure he himself was next on the Central Intelligence Agency's list; he was confirmed in this fear by the particular virulence at that time of the clandestine broadcasts, which he described as a nail being driven into his brain.

8. Finally, there have been problems in personal relations. With one or two distinguished exceptions, Sihanouk does not like or understand Americans. Although fundamentally oriental, Sihanouk is also in some measure a Frenchman, being French educated, French speaking and a respecter of French culture, manners and methods of thought. The oriental in him is readily offended by American informality; the Frenchman in him despises what is interpreted as American political immaturity and cultural poverty. The French have always been careful, even in the days of the Protectorate, to treat Sihanouk with the deference and flattery to which an oriental monarch, especially a Cambodian god-king, feels justly entitled. According to his own account, however, Sihanouk has never been treated by the Americans with proper respect. Sihanouk never forgets the smallest slight, whether accidental or intended. Time and again in his speeches a list of familiar grievances crop up: how he was greeted on arrival in the United States on an official visit only by an Under-Secretary of State; how in New York where he addressed the General Assembly of the United Nations he had been jostled aside by policemen to make way for Mr. Khrushchev. "Questions of honour", Sihanouk once said,

"are much more important for a well-born Asiatic than money."

9. I regret to report that in the field of personal relations, the early representatives of the United States in Cambodia did little to redress the balance. Since Cambodian independence, a succession of American Ambassadors have consistently failed to establish effective human rapport with Prince Sihanouk. About their idiosyncrasies there is current in Phnom Penh a series of remarkable legends. The first Ambassador of the United States to the Cambodian Royal Court appeared at the palace to present his credentials appropriately dressed in silk hat and trimmings, but accompanied by two large dogs —animals for which Asians do not share the regard of the Anglo-Saxons. The same Ambassador subsequently appeared at the airport to greet (or bid farewell to) the Head of State clad only in sports shirt and shorts. The next man is said to have carried everywhere with him an ornamental stick: a stick, however, is associated in the Cambodian mind with arrogance and aggressiveness. A third is reported to have had an unfortunate manner which got on Prince Sihanouk's nerves; towards the end of his service in Phnom Penh the Ambassador was in the habit of closing his eyes and muttering the phrase "How I hate that man". Mr. Sprouse, the last of his line, was a major improvement on his predecessors; but during his service it came to Sihanouk's attention that the princely voice, shrill and staccato, had been imitated by junior staff down the public corridors of the American Embassy, and the princely person likened to "a little monkey."

10. The present outlook for Cambodian American relations is discouraging. In recent months Sihanouk has criticised the United States with increasing bitterness and intensity. He is at present doing so almost to the exclusion of all others. Nine months ago it was the British who were the villains of deepest hue, because of what was seen as

their wilful sabotage of the prospects for a Geneva Conference. Today, it is the Americans who are to blame. Last year, the South Viet-Namese and the Thais came in for swingeing attacks. Now it is the United States which is held responsible for their policies, the Viet-Namese in particular being seen as the unwilling instruments of American folly. The Prince apparently so fears and suspects the Americans, that an evil construction is placed on almost everything they do or say. He does not admit to any conviction that they are sincere in their professions of readiness to live with Cambodian neutrality. For Sihanouk, the temptation to throw in his lot with North Viet-Nam and the National Liberation Front, and finally to sever diplomatic relations with the United States, increases with the news of every successful skirmish by the Viet Cong, and with every fresh attack on his frontier posts and villages by the armed forces of South Viet-Nam.

11. In what is written above, I have tried to put myself into Sihanouk's shoes and to express what I judge to be his own peculiar viewpoint. I am aware that this raises the delicate issue of whether Sihanouk's complaints are justified and if so, what can be done to put matters right. Having posed the question, you, Sir, will do doubt expect me to attempt some answer. I pass beyond the proper bounds of this despatch to do so.

12. A great deal of Sihanouk's thinking about the United States seems to me mistaken and even nonsensical. Like so many others round the world, Sihanouk has exaggerated American characteristics and created for himself a caricature which bears no relation to reality. Whatever may be the explanation of the Dap Chhuon affair, there is no reason to suppose that the Americans have ever attempted to overthrow Sihanouk or to interfere in any inadmissible manner in Cambodian politics. I do not believe that they have afforded covert support to Son Ngoc Thanh and the Khmer Serei movement in their anti-

Sihanouk activities. The State Department, long haunted by a spectral Mr. John Foster Dulles, may possibly have been slow to move out of the bi-polar, black-and-white world of the middle 'fifties. But today there is no quarrel with Cambodian neutrality; indeed, the Americans were doing their best to support it until Sihanouk put an end to their more active endeavours.

13. Can American-Cambodian relations eventually be improved? The prospects as seen from here are not good. As I have reported separately over recent months to your department, Cambodian neutrality may not be able much longer to survive the present stresses and strains in Indo-China. The apparent steady erosion of the Western position in South Viet-Nam is one factor. The growth of Chinese influence inside Cambodia is another. Moreover, the United States would have to devote much more time and trouble than heretofore to the one man who matters in Cambodia, namely Prince Norodom Sihanouk. This would require great political skill and psychological insight. The Americans no doubt possess these qualities, but they cannot deploy them to any effect in Phnom Penh as long as wider considerations oblige them to do nothing which could cause offence in Bangkok or Saigon.

14. Nevertheless, the elements for a deal with Sihanouk still exist. Emotionally, most observers agree that the Prince is through with the Americans. There is little prospect that relations with him could ever again exist on a cordial footing. But Sihanouk is a political animal whose heart does not always rule his head. He has professed his readiness to preserve "correct" relations with the United States. Although he appears determined that the Americans should neutralise, and withdraw in good order from, Indo-China, he wants them to remain in Thailand and the Philippines, and anywhere else in the region where they may be welcome, in order to keep the balance of power with People's China. The Cambodian Government is

now experiencing acute financial difficulties as a consequence of the intemperate rejection of American economic aid; the possibility that he might be able to wheedle back this aid (without strings) no doubt sharpens any inclination which Sihanouk may feel once more to mend his fences (and sit on them). If (and this is perhaps a big "if") peace could be restored to South Viet-Nam, the clandestine radios silenced, and the few Cambodian dissidents such as Son Ngoc Thanh pensioned off quietly to the south of France, the major causes of friction between Cambodia and the United States would have been removed.

I have, &c.

Leslie Fielding

(Chargé d'Affaires)

Response of Foreign Secretary, Mr. Patrick Gordon Walker, passed on by his Private Secretary, December 29, 1964

Dear Leslie

The Secretary of State spent part of his Christmas holiday reading the print version of your dispatch No. 59 of November 25. ["The Americans, as Sihanouk Sees Them".] He was most interested to read your report, which he thought was a very good one, and has asked me to send you his thanks.

Yours ever,

Tom Bridges

CAMBODIA: ANNUAL REVIEW FOR 1964

Mr. Fielding to Mr. Gordon Walker

SUMMARY

1964 was a bad year for the West in Cambodia. The influence of the United States and Great Britain was greatly reduced; their Embassies were attacked and partly sacked by the mob. Relations with South Viet-Nam were also bad. The Communist Chinese made corresponding gains. But Sihanouk failed to get written undertakings from the Communist Viet-Namese to respect Cambodian territorial integrity. He will therefore continue to press for an international conference to neutralise Indo-China. The general outlook for 1965 is not good, although a deal with Sihanouk by the West is still possible.

Confidential	British Embassy
No. 2	Phnom Penh
Sir,	12 January, 1965

I have the honour to submit a brief review of Cambodia for 1964, together with a calendar of events.

2. It was a bad year for the West. The influence of the United States and of Great Britain in Cambodia was reduced almost to zero, while that of the Communist Powers, notably of People's China, mounted steadily up the gauge. Prince Sihanouk, the dynamic if volatile Cambodian Head of State, found it difficult to maintain his delicate neutralist balance between East and West.

3. Cambodian relations with the United States and South Viet-Nam reached an all-time low. A series of deplorable frontier incidents served to reinforce traditional

Cambodian hatred and distrust of the Viet-Namese. The most inglorious, but not least typical, of these episodes was the combined infantry and air attack by South Viet-Namese forces in the pursuit of alleged Viet Cong guerrillas on the 19th of March against the defenceless Cambodian village of Chantréa. (Seventeen peasants were killed and fourteen wounded.) The apparent successes of the Communists in the war in South Viet-Nam further increased Sihanouk's impatience with the policy of the United States in Indo-China. In consequence, Sihanouk rejected every conciliatory feeler put out by Saigon and lost no opportunity to criticise and humiliate the United States throughout the year.

4. As a corollary of the above, Communist influence increased. Important Chinese military and economic aid was announced following Sihanouk's visit to Peking in October. Consignments of weapons were also received in the course of the year from the Soviet Union, Czechoslovakia and Yugoslavia. Communist attitudes and actions were publicised and defended in the Cambodian Press. The Cambodian Government welcomed the Chinese "bomb of peace" and spear-headed the attempt to get China seated at the United Nations.

5. Fortunately, not all was gloom. Sihanouk looked elsewhere for friendship to replace that of the United States and to act as a make-weight in his policy of balance. France has been treated with consideration and respect—in Sihanouk's words, as a "bridge" between himself and the West. The friendship of the Soviet bloc of countries has also been maintained despite, and perhaps because of, the Sino-Soviet split.

6. Sihanouk had other headaches of his own. Most important, he failed to obtain the guarantees and concessions for which he had been hoping from his Communist friends and neighbours. There were talks with

79

representatives of North Viet-Nam and the National Liberation Front of South Viet-Nam in March, August, October and December. At the end of the year, he was still without any written undertaking on their part in recognition of Cambodia's frontier line. As regards China, he was told politely but firmly during his visit to Peking that it was in the general interest that Cambodia should remain neutral for the present rather than become formally allied with Peking, Hanoi and the Viet Cong. To this extent, Sihanouk's bluff has now been called. For years, he has been threatening to go over to the Communist Camp if the West will not help him; he has now discovered that, at least for the present, the Camp does not choose to admit him.

7. Sihanouk had his money worries also. At the close of 1964, Cambodia was facing a serious financial crisis. The country can no doubt survive, at a cruel pinch, on a peasant-subsistence basis. But a programme of austerity has had to be introduced which will be little to the taste of the easy-going Khmers.

8. Relations with Great Britain were poor because we were unable (because of the misgivings of the Americans, Thais and South Viet-Namese) to arrange a Geneva Conference to endorse Cambodian neutrality and territorial integrity in accordance with Sihanouk's wishes. When this became apparent in the early spring, Sihanouk's fury frothed over. On the 11th of March, this Embassy was sacked by a mob acting on Government orders. In June, Her Majesty's Ambassador was withdrawn, so far without replacement. The rest of us are still in the dog-house.

9. The prospects for 1965 are not good. There is the risk that faced with another serious frontier incident, Sihanouk may dismiss the United States Embassy from Phnom Penh. If Saigon goes further and cuts the Mekong in retaliation against alleged Cambodian connivance with the Viet Cong,

there will be the risk of open hostilities between the two countries and a serious regional flare-up to follow. Sihanouk may himself precipitate such a crisis by finally deciding to give diplomatic recognition to North Viet-Nam and the National Liberation Front, in the judgment that the pro-Western regime in Saigon has only a few more months to live, and that it is about time that he put himself on a friendly basis with Viet-Nam's future masters.

10. On the other hand, the Prince is no Communist and still clings to his preference for a neutral and nationalist Cambodia. We must expect him to continue to treat China as Cambodia's "Friend No. One"; to attempt to negotiate some sort of gentleman's agreement for the future with the Viet-Namese Communists; and to attack the Americans for their present policy in South Viet-Nam. But he will also campaign vigorously for the neutralisation of Indo-China under guarantees to be agreed at an international conference. If Great Britain were able and willing to convene a Geneva conference, Sihanouk would seize with both hands his chance to stay neutral with the blessing of all concerned.

11. In our future dealings with Sihanouk, however, we would do well to be hard-headed. There is much that is admirable and deserving about Cambodia and her Prince. Given luck and good judgment, Cambodia could probably be secured to our advantage as a viable buffer State between Thailand and North Viet-Nam, Malaysia and China. But we learned in 1964 that effective action to this end is only possible in the closest consultation and concert not only with the Americans but also with the Thais and the South Viet-Namese. There is no narrow British interest in Cambodia, only a Western one. If, after frank discussion, our allies and friends do not agree with us on what ought to be done about Cambodia, we may have to leave Sihanouk to make his own way through 1965.

I have, &c.

Leslie Fielding

(Chargé d'Affaires)

Letter to Mr. Fielding from Head of South-East Asia Department, FO, January 25, 1965

We were glad to have your annual Review, Despatch No. 2 of January 12, which we have read with great interest.

2. The record of the last year's events indeed makes depressing reading. The fact that the Australians share to some extent France's special relationship with Cambodia (paragraph 5 of your despatch) is welcome news and this may prove useful if circumstances ever enable us to mend our fences with the Cambodians. We have gained a useful breathing-space by China's refusal to admit Sihanouk to the hallowed Camp, but nevertheless I do not find much comfort in the fact that the Soviet bloc countries have maintained ties of friendship with Cambodia. It is worthwhile reminding oneself that the leaders of these countries believe implicitly in the eventual triumph of Communism and even if they do not actively promote this end in Cambodia they are most unlikely to do anything to check it. And meanwhile a frustrated and ill-tempered Cambodia can be (for their purposes) a useful irritant to the Western powers.

3. Looking back on it all, however, I still think we were right to make the effort of seeking an understanding with Cambodia. I think, too, that the implications of your final paragraph are a little unfair. We *did* consult the Americans and they agreed to our initiative *vis-à-vis* the Cambodians. If Sihanouk had been willing to meet us half-way, I have no

doubt that we and the Americans would also have been able to secure the necessary minimum of Thai and Viet-Namese cooperation. But Sihanouk was only interested in unconditional surrender and that was more than anyone could stomach.

(J.E. Cable)

DOMESTIC DISCONTENT IN CAMBODIA

Mr. Fielding to Mr. Stewart

SUMMARY

Cambodia is traditionally stable. Under siege from the Twentieth Century, however, she is undergoing change (Paragraphs 2-4).

There is growing Left Wing discontent, particularly among students (Paragraphs 5-8).

The Right Wing establishment, although fundamentally less formidable, has its grievances (Paragraphs 9-10).

Nevertheless, there is no immediate prospect of serious opposition to Sihanouk; and if he were to be removed suddenly from the scene, Cambodia might well go to the dogs. There is therefore at present no satisfactory alternative to him (Paragraphs 11-15).

Secret	British Embassy
No.5	Phnom Penh
Sir,	27 February, 1965

Over the past year, there have been rumours of agitation and discontent in various quarters in Cambodia. The present troubles, although growing, have not yet assumed dimensions sufficient to threaten the personal position of Prince Sihanouk, the Head of State, or to undermine the fabric of Cambodian society. Nevertheless, Sir, I think it advisable that your Department should have by them the assessment which I have the honour to submit below.

2. In order to place this assessment in perspective, I should perhaps begin by drawing attention to the traditional stability and freedom from turbulence of Cambodian society. In general, there prevails a remarkable passivity and conservatism, a principal feature of the national character being what sociologists have termed a certain amiable inactivity. Most Cambodians are genuinely satisfied with a life in which there are for the most part no extremes of wealth and poverty. More than eighty per cent of the population are countrymen. Land is abundant, housing is no problem, and food, clothing and other simple necessities are easy to come by. A mediaeval sense of order and a rustic calm prevail in Cambodian village life. The almost universal religion, Buddhism of the Lesser Vehicle, has inculcated over the centuries a gentleness, a spiritual system of values and a lack of emphasis on material needs throughout a now settled but formerly warlike and acquisitive populace. Associated with the state religion, and accepted almost as firmly, is the monarchy. Although technically only a Prince, Sihanouk effectively enjoys the status of a Khmer god-king. His relations with the people at large, who know him as "Samdech Euv" ("Prince-Daddy"), are affectionate and in their way intimate. Some observers, Her Majesty's Chargé d'Affaires in Phnom Penh included, consider that Sihanouk's popularity and unquestioned pre-eminence have begun of late somewhat to decline from the peak of the nineteen fifties. But his political ability and personal standing are still great and should never be underestimated.

3. The Twentieth Century is, however, laying slow siege to this quiet, sequestered and in some ways idyllic society. Under the French Protectorate, Cambodia slept protected; independence was a harsh awakening into a mysterious and not entirely comforting new world. Alien political

ideals, little known before, now assert conflicting magnetic attraction: the ideals of international Communism and Western-style democracy, of national socialism on the non-aligned model or of President Sukarno's New Emerging Forces. Cambodia finds herself saddled with new economic requirements: for ports and petrol pumps, highways, hydro-electric schemes and factories. A new concept of gracious living having afflicted the tiny social *élite* of Phnom Penh, driving them to ruinous expenditure on fast cars, Scotch whiskey and home movies, Dior gowns, and air-conditioned mansions. Wireless, gramophone and cinema, air travel and studies abroad have brought within easier and wider reach a surfeit of new cultural riches, from Corneille to Camus, from Bach to the Beatles. The sails of Cambodian foreign policy also have billowed in the winds of change. In the East/West, North/South ideological conflicts, Cambodia has found it ever more difficult to preserve a neutral and independent position. Recent Despatches have described the decline of American and British influence, the rise in the prestige of Peoples' China, and the development by Prince Sihanouk of a "neutralist" policy the clear bias of which is away from the West. In short, most of Cambodia's habitual values, objectives and methods of work have had swiftly to take some account of the exigencies of modern times.

4. Inevitably, these changes have administered a series of rude shocks to the traditional fabric of Cambodian society. It is against this background of hasty and harrowing change that domestic discontent has made its appearance in Cambodia. A susurration of perplexity and dissatisfaction is faintly to be heard in several quarters of society. But definite discontent is chiefly to be found on the one hand among the students and the Left Wing intellectuals, and on the other at Court, among the bourgeois *élite* and at places in the bureaucratic hierarchy. (For the purposes of this Despatch, I am excluding from consideration the Chinese and Vietnamese communities,

who are not active in Cambodian politics, and whose attitude and potential have already been treated in my Despatch No. 57 of the 17th November, 1964).

5. The more important are the students, and the Left Wing intelligentsia who exploit them. Much the greatest grievance in this sector is that of unemployment. This problem has become acute as a result of the economic difficulties of the past year. Government expenditure has been slashed, and an effort is being made to cut down the grossly over-weighted bureaucracy. There is a constantly expanding group of educated young men who want white-collar jobs in Phnom Penh but cannot get them. Far too many pupils are being channelled through the *Lycées*. It is thought that about 15,000 Cambodians each year who have completed their secondary education promptly join the ranks of the jobless. This education, a second-rate version of the French Baccalauréat, will have been theoretical and academic but not in the least technical—enough to sustain intellectual pretensions but generally insufficient in itself as a preparation for the modern world, and vocationally totally inadequate. Educated Cambodians do not normally relish a career in commerce (of which the Chinese and Vietnamese expatriate community in any case largely possess the monopoly) and show little interest in technical training. Their invariable aim is to secure a post in the bureaucracy at Phnom Penh, with the prestige, dignity and possibilities of advancement and corrupt enrichment which such a position affords.

6. The frustration of those unable so to join the political and social *élite* is increasingly turning into disaffection. Almost all these students and ex-students have the radical orientation of the young; many of them have pronounced Left Wing views of the kind fashionable in non-aligned countries today; some of them have outright Marxist sympathies; a very few may be thorough-going Peking Communists. The influence of Communism tends to be

particularly strong among those who have studied abroad, notably in Paris; almost all the leading intellectuals of the Left acquired their political tastes at the Sorbonne.

7. The political sympathies of this group are not fundamentally with Sihanouk. The personality cult of the god-king, the absolutism (if benevolent) of his autocracy, the monolithic one-party system of the Sangkum, and the absence of a free press, all appear incompatible with the fresh and exciting political ideals which they have embraced from abroad. Paradoxically, the Prince has himself in some measure helped these ideals forward. For the past two years, press and radio have maintained a steady and at times virulent flow of fellow-travelling propaganda. The Cambodians are not on the whole a critical or sophisticated crew, and what is often repeated tends eventually to sink in.

8. Student disaffection has asserted itself steadily in recent years but has tended of late to find increasingly overt expression. In 1960, three Left Wing newspapers had to be closed down for attacking the Prince's education programme, and at one stage Sihanouk (who was then Prime Minister) handed in his resignation in protest against Communist criticism. In 1961, Sihanouk launched a propaganda campaign against Marxist and anti-patriotic youth. In 1962, a Communist cell was uncovered and its members convicted of treason. In 1963, student riots, fanned by Left Wing agitators, took place at Siem Reap, in which the Minister of Education was frog-marched through the streets and anti-Government sentiments were uttered. In 1964, a number of spontaneous and unauthorised demonstrations took place ostensibly directed against the West, but in fact expressing a dangerous degree of independence from, and possible hostility towards, Sihanouk's tutelage. During one anti-American demonstration in May, there were shouts of "Down with Sihanouk". In the autumn of 1964, a sustained Left Wing

campaign for a break in diplomatic relations with the United States brought considerable and unwelcome pressure to bear on the Prince; if the Americans had not created a diversion by proposing talks in New Delhi, the campaign might well have succeeded. Student pamphlets circulated in January of this year ingeniously accused the Prince of having sold his country to the French.

9. The alternative main focus of discontent is to be found in the upper crust of Cambodian society, among the Royal Family, members of the established bourgeois *élite*, elements in the official hierarchy, and that part of the Cambodian Establishment which still looks to the West for political inspiration. The disruption and near bankruptcy which followed years of State extravagance, and which were given edge by Prince Sihanouk's ill-considered economic reforms and the simultaneous and abrupt termination of United States aid in the autumn of 1963, have made themselves felt most sharply among the rich, whose persons and pockets have not welcomed the current programme of austerity. Relations between the Queen Mother and Prince Sihanouk have been strained for some time, because the latter's policies and actions have curtailed some of the former's business interests. The severe reduction in imports, notably in the luxury sector, has threatened the living standard of the wealthy Cambodian minority who live up to European standards in Phnom Penh. Almost equally important as a stimulant of dissatisfaction among the group described above is their widespread disapproval of the way in which Cambodia's policy of neutrality has developed under Prince Sihanouk's leadership. The extreme nature of Sihanouk's quarrel with the United States, the accelerated drift towards the Communists, and the increase in China's influence, all have caused disquiet. There are also indications of a vaguely felt loss of confidence in the Prince personally and of resentment against what is considered as the increasing

arbitrariness of his actions and his growing disinclination to accept advice.

10. Nevertheless, it is significant that Right Wing discontent has rarely found overt expression. Prince Sisowath Monireth, the man who would have been king if the French had not instead chosen his nephew Sihanouk, has a soldierly and outspoken personality with from our point of view many of the right ideas. But he has had no real experience of responsibility in politics, and appears to lack the necessary consistency and self-confidence. As he grows older and more disheartened, his appetite for power grows less; for the past few years, although maintaining some contact with army leaders, he has largely withdrawn from public life. He does not seem to be the man to initiate a Palace Revolution. Prince Sisowath Sirik Matak, the competent Minister of Education, and his younger brother Prince Sisowath Essaro, are believed to be privately out of sympathy with Sihanouk's policies. Neither seems likely, however, to take positive action as long as Sihanouk maintains his present position of power. General Nhiek Tioulong, the only other obvious "strong man", a politician and former Prime Minister of considerable distinction and strength of character but now ageing and dispirited, is visibly knuckling under to the Prince in the hope of better times to come. He does not appear to like the Americans or seem likely to be tempted, at least in present circumstances, openly to oppose Sihanouk's will. Douc Rasy, the Editor of the only discreetly pro-Western newspaper in Cambodia, is a brave and out-spoken man, but a theorist and scholar rather than an effective political leader. The remainder, including various bureaucrats and ex-ministers, while expressing some misgiving in private, have neither the ability nor the desire to go and bell the cat.

11. A number of powerful elements are significantly missing from the pattern of discontent described above.

The Army, the only organisation which could change the power structure by force, appears to be a-political. General Lon Nol, the Minister of defence and Commander-in-Chief, is believed to have discreet Western sympathies; something of an enigma, the eye of the Prince is never far from him; but, hitherto, he has kept out of politics and remained scrupulously to outward appearances loyal to Sihanouk. There are vague stories of disaffection among a few junior officers in the provinces; but they hardly count for much. The troops themselves are mainly peasants, with an unquestioning devotion to the Prince. If a military coup were to be mounted in present conditions, the officers might well have to act without their men. The much smaller police force is subservient. So also is the paramilitary branch of the official youth movement (J.S.R.K.). There is no all-powerful security organisation; at least four agencies are responsible for intelligence, and none predominates. Ideological Communism has so far failed to make substantial inroads among the Khmers. There is no Communist-inspired terrorist or bandit movement at large in the countryside. The Viet Minh were checked by the Cambodians, and withdrew in 1954 to North Vietnam in accordance with the Geneva Agreements, never to reappear. The local Communist (Pracheachon) Party, although legally tolerated, has a tiny membership and no significant political influence. Almost equally impotent is the body of non-Communist dissidents, the Khmer Serei, who live in exile in Thailand and South Vietnam. Led by Son Ngoc Thanh, a former Prime Minister and founder of the Peoples' Democratic Party, the Khmer Serei engage in propaganda and subversive activities. But they have failed to ferment disaffection inside Cambodia. Their activities greatly incense Prince Sihanouk, but they do not threaten his security.

12. Against this background, you may ask, Sir, what is the future likelihood that opposition will assume an organised and effective form? At present, this eventuality

seems remote. The extreme elements on the Left will no doubt be discouraged from pursuing drastic courses as long as Sihanouk's relations with Communist China remain as good as they are at present. It is not in the interest of any Communist power to mount a coup against Sihanouk so long as he pursues his present line in foreign affairs. Extreme Left Wing personalities, such as Hou Youn and Kieu Samphan, although in the past openly critical of the Government, seem to have no desire for violent change. Chau Seng, the former Minister of Agriculture, being venal and a coward, is no Oliver Cromwell. The Left are, moreover, young, inexperienced and brash; agitation and the exposition of theory come more easily to them than responsible action and solid government. The Right Wing, while much more experienced in governmental matters, have no ideological unity and remain, as illustrated above, a collection of dissimilar individuals. Neither has any great influence in the Army or with the police. The leaders of both are, moreover, under close surveillance from the Cambodian security authorities; there are rumours of brutal suppression among the students, who are being narrowly watched; it is said that very little of importance happens in Cambodia that does not come to the Prince's attention. Neither Left nor Right can contest the wide degree of support among the populace at large which is still enjoyed by the person of the Prince. Above all, at least for the present, no-one has the moral fortitude to oppose Sihanouk and no-one has been able to develop and display the qualities which could make him an acceptable alternative leader to the Prince. With his remarkable sense of manoeuvre, Sihanouk has been able to play off one man against the next, Left against Right, and the National Congress and the Assembly against his own Cabinet. To Sihanouk, not without design, there is no apparent political successor. The present level of discontent, while higher than ever before under Sihanouk, is today therefore still below the danger point.

13. This situation would, of course, alter completely if Sihanouk were to disappear unexpectedly from the scene. His health over the past year or two has left something to be desired, and he conceivably might one day fall very sick. Alternative, he might, in certain circumstances, suffer a nervous breakdown through overstrain; a highly- strung man, there is a record of mental instability in his family background. (These intimate factors are important and will be discussed more fully in a separate Despatch on Sihanouk's personality). It is also possible, although this contingency seems remote, that he might be assassinated by some disgruntled individual. Unity round a strong leader, is however, at present essential for the survival of the Khmer nation. If Sihanouk disappeared, a stable successor Government would no doubt be established in the short term, but might not prove viable in the longer run. In any interim arrangement, the Right Wing would probably predominate; someone like Prince Monireth or Prince Sirik Matak, supported possibly by Generals Lon Nol and Nhiek Tioulong, would no doubt take over. But the apparent absence of any figure with the dynamism and the leadership of Sihanouk, the likely development on all sides of personal rivalries and factionalism of a kind which characterised the early years of national independence, the probability that Communist subversion directed from outside the country would be let loose, and the possibility that Cambodia's neighbours, Thailand and Vietnam, might exploit her weakness to seek their own territorial advantage, all could combine to bring political stability and unity to an end. Cambodia might then well fall under extreme Left Wing or Communist control; alternatively, she would probably become the sick man of South-East Asia and hence a general threat to the peace of the area.

14. If, as we must expect, Sihanouk remains in power, what are the future prospects? A good measure of the present discontents will probably never be eliminated. Modern ideas and techniques are steadily penetrating

Cambodian society. In the process, as in almost every other under-developed country, they are effecting changes which will inescapably prove painful. Pandora's box has been opened. Much depends on the general political situation in Indo-China and also on the development of Prince Sihanouk's personality. If his present trend towards ever more arbitrary personal rule is maintained, and if international tension in this area continues to impose severe stresses both on the Prince and on the politically conscious among his subjects, it seems likely that discontent and disaffection will grow. The Left Wing may then pose serious problems. If, on the other hand, international agreement were to be reached over the future of Vietnam and Laos, Prince Sihanouk to be given the political assurances he required and the Cambodian economy to be restored (possibly with western help) to a more healthy condition, the situation might prove manageable. In such circumstances, Sihanouk, who is an agile and inspired politician who still knows a trick or two, would probably continue to hold things together, and Cambodia might remain for some time to come, what she has been in sharp contrast with Vietnam and Laos throughout the past ten years, a haven of relative peace and stability in Indo-China, and a tolerably effective if unorthodox buffer against Communist expansion.

15. To sum up, domestic discontent, political economic and social, is on the increase. Cambodia, however, remains a stable society and the situation is still under control. In the short term at least, Sihanouk is likely to survive; there appears, in any case, to be no satisfactory alternative to him.

I have, &c.

Leslie Fielding

(Chargé d'Affaires)

<u>Letter to Mr. Fielding from Assistant Head of South-East Asia Department, FO, 30 March, 1965</u>

In the midst of our preoccupation with the Viet-Nam crisis it was pleasant to read the entertaining survey of domestic discontent in Cambodia contained in your despatch No. 5 of 27 February. We are having this despatch printed for the volume.

2. You emphasis once again that Sihanouk is the best that we can hope for in Cambodia. Neither of the conceivable alternatives on left or right wings are very attractive. The left wing would have obvious disadvantages while it is difficult to imagine the communists allowing the right wing to govern long in tranquillity. However, as both you and I seem agreed, the forces which you suggest are working for the destruction of Sihanouk are not likely to take effect for some time and so the alternatives are, mercifully, still only hypothetical.

(D.F. Murray)

THE PERSONALITY OF PRINCE SIHANOUK: SOME FIRST IMPRESSIONS

Mr. Fielding to Mr. Stewart

SUMMARY

Prince Sihanouk is the one man in Cambodia who matters (Paragraph 1).

Beneath the façade of French culture, he is essentially an Oriental (Paragraphs 2-3).

The Royal Court, its ladies and its superstitious practices (Paragraphs 4-7).

Sihanouk's faulty upbringing, somewhat feminine characteristics and great egotism (Paragraphs 8-10).

Sihanouk's personal brilliance, political flair and intense dynamism (Paragraphs 11-15).

How he treats Ambassadors and the Gentlemen of the Press (Paragraphs 16-18).

The Prince's physical and mental health, seen against his heredity; they are not over-promising (Paragraphs 19-22).

Sihanouk may be growing more isolated and arbitrary (Paragraphs 23-25).

Secret   British Embassy
No.6   Phnom Penh
Sir,   2 March, 1965

Cambodia is a one-man country. It is dominated by the personality of Prince Norodom Sihanouk, the Head of State. In many respects, the life story of this extraordinary man has been one of brilliant success. He is the father of national independence, which he obtained from the French without bloodshed; he has been the principal architect of the contemporary unity and stability of the Khmer nation; in an Indo-China riven and at war, he has kept Cambodia a haven of peace. His popularity among his people has hitherto proved great, his prestige is as yet without serious challenge. Yet goaded Western observers have sometimes termed Sihanouk unpredictable, erratic, unstable, even mad. In what follows, I have the honour to submit some first impressions of the personality of this fascinating man. If the Despatch is deemed to be overlengthy, or to contain material of a kind too indelicate or trivial to be submitted for the attention of Her Majesty's Principal Secretary of State for Foreign Affairs, I beg, Sir, to be excused. The object has not been to write a learned biography, or to rival the columns of the "News of the World", but merely to draw attention to those personal characteristics of the Cambodian Head of State with which it is advisable for anyone who has dealings with this country to be familiar.

2. The image which Prince Sihanouk presents to foreign diplomatists is occidental and suave. To outward appearances he is a Frenchman, speaking fluent French, respecting French culture. Sihanouk is turned out by a Paris tailor, drinks champagne, eats European food, and drives high-powered Western motor cars. Although now less active, in his younger years he has enthusiastically pursued most of the favourite sports and pastimes of Western man: riding, water-skiing, basketball and football. Within the marble precincts of his Residence at Chamcar

Mon, there is even to be found a Royal night club, cool, cavernous and dimly lit, in which the guests are seated on gilded red plush chairs while the Prince conducts his own dance band, or takes the saxophone lead in one of his own jazz compositions.

3. Important though Western influence over Sihanouk may have been, however, it should be remembered that he remains in essence an Asiatic. It was against the Eastern background described below that the decisive influences of environment and heredity cast the mould of the Princely personality. Subsequent contacts with the West and with the outside world generally have never really touched the core of the oriental inner man.

4. Norodom Sihanouk is descended from both the Norodom and Sisowath branches of the Royal Cambodian Family. Although not in his early youth destined for the Throne, he was raised, and now flourishes, in a mediaeval Royal court, the Byzantine qualities of which have been but little tempered by modern realities. In and around this Court are to be found a remarkable collection of amiable hirelings, good-for-nothings, gangsters and frauds of various nationalities. Prince Sihanouk does not entirely approve of all that goes on about the Palace, but cannot bring himself to call it greatly to order; it is, after all, his own home. The Court is, moreover, in a sense a part of his *mystique*. Among his own people, Sihanouk enjoys in fact if not in name the prestige of the Cambodian god-kings whose apogee of fame was reached in the Eleventh and Twelfth Centuries, and whose magnificent temple tombs stand to this day at Angkor. He likes to be addressed, even by Europeans, deferentially as "Monseigneur". Even the most distinguished Cambodians approach and address him in a sort of half-crouch; the more humble actually kneel on the ground and, (if faced with his displeasure), prostrate themselves in the dust.

5. Sihanouk's mother, Queen Kossamak, Symbol of the Throne, is the principal lady at Court, where she presides at the centre of an intricate labyrinth of petty intrigue. Until recently, when she fell sick, her main pleasures were to supervise the Royal Ballet School, play cards late into the night, and direct from the Royal Palace a variety of shady transactions designed to add to her private fortune. [Remainder of Paragraph 5 and all of Paragraph 6, deleted by the FCO].

6. Sihanouk is intensely superstitious. Although engaged in equipping Cambodia with all the appurtenances of a modern state, and despite having adopted with boyish enthusiasm such up-to-date means of locomotion as the helicopter and the sports car, he has retained a childlike respect for superstitious beliefs and spiritualistic practices. He regards as a talisman the earthly remains of his favourite daughter, Cantha Bopha. This princess, who died at the age of twelve, accompanies Sihanouk wherever he travels abroad; her ashes, in a small jewel box, always stand beside his bed each night. Prince Sihanouk also pays close attention to, and treats with awed respect, the messages conveyed to him from the 'Tevodas' (supernatural Guardian Powers) by the soothsayers traditionally attached to the Court of the Cambodian monarch. Particular importance is believed to attach to messages received through a Palace medium allegedly in touch with the spirit of Princess Nucheat Khatr Vorpheak. In 1834, this lady was at a tender age devoured by a crocodile at Oudong. Her body was miraculously recovered from the belly of the beast at Kratié, some hundred miles away. The *stupa* at Sambaur which contains her ashes was restored by the Prince in 1956 in gratitude for her help. Among her successes had been an accurate forecast of the success of his 'Royal Crusade' for independence from the French Protectorate. The Palace 'Horas' or soothsayers always fix a propitious departure date for Royal journeys abroad, while periods considered auspicious for Cambodia are marked

out for Royal decisions. Palace officials are indeed sometimes inclined to advise those in search of enlightenment in regard to the Prince's plans that they should go and consult the Horas. The Prince laughs at these superstitions in public but does not fail discreetly to respect them. He received supernatural advice to proceed earlier than arranged on a recent State Visit; he therefore felt obliged to set out from Phnom Penh three or four days in advance, filling in the time by travel within Cambodia.

7. Sihanouk's Courtly upbringing was sadly neglected and at fault, and in the formal sense he has received only an indifferent education. The much cosseted child of his mother, he attended a girls' school in Phnom Penh, appropriately attired, until the age of five. As a princeling without great pretensions or prospects, he was thereafter taught his lessons at a French-run primary school for boys. His secondary education, which did not reach as far as the Baccalauréat, was instilled at a *Lycée* in Saigon. Subsequently he was for a brief time at the French cavalry school at Saumur. He was a reasonably diligent but not especially distinguished pupil. Indeed, others were passed over, and Sihanouk was placed on the Throne by the Colonial Power, largely because the French thought in their error that he would prove a feckless and amenable ruler. Since achieving political power, Prince Sihanouk has travelled widely, but it is open to doubt how profoundly he has understood many of the countries that he has visited. Travelling literally *en prince*, staying at the best hotels, ushered here and there, conferring with foreign statesmen, he has not always been able to get much below the surface of things. The United States, and the ideals and processes of thought of the American people, have for example always been an enigma to him. He does not like Arabs, despises black men, and dismisses Latin Americans. Nor does he very much care for the Russians. He understands, of course, his fellow Orientals in South East Asia, but

among other peoples perhaps only the French are anywhere near his wave-length.

8. In many respects, Sihanouk remains the pampered and feminine child his mother created. Thus he is entirely dependent on others in the daily business of living and is always dressed from top to toe by his valet. He has no close men friends and his leisure hours are spent almost exclusively in the company of a seraglio of comforting and complaisant women. The French deliberately encouraged these tastes in the young king in order to keep him amused and out of politics. Sihanouk, whose amorous intrigues were formerly the talk of Phnom Penh, is still a lover of young girls. He is, however, inconstant in his affections. He always abandons the mothers of his children when their beauty fades and they lose their figure. This is perhaps a human failing. Less laudable, if equally indicative of a mixed-up youth, is Sihanouk's conduct as a father. Although affectionate to his daughters, Monseigneur's egotistical nature prevents him from taking much interest in their well-being and education, [passage deleted by FCO]. He is always accompanied by one or more of these Princesses on his travels, but their presence must chiefly be ascribed to his need of feminine company and to his superstitious belief that they bring him safety and good luck. The Prince's neglect of his sons is positively callous. Prince Norodom Naradipo, designated by Sihanouk as his possible successor as Head of State and now a schoolboy in Peking, spent the first five years of his life at an overcrowded and impecunious Roman Catholic orphanage in Phnom Penh; two others of his sons have been relegated to schools for the *Enfants de la Troupe*, where orphaned sons of Cambodian soldiers are educated and taught a trade under strict military discipline. Finally, Sihanouk's faulty upbringing is also reflected in the urchin-like side to his character, which leads him to intemperate and on occasion indiscreet public utterances inappropriate on the part of a Head of State. No foreign country, except perhaps China, is

immune from impudent verbal attack; and almost any Head of state, particularly if Asian, is liable to be rated in the language of a Billingsgate fish-wife if the Prince so feels the urge.

9. His complete egotism is indeed perhaps the dominant strain in Prince Sihanouk's character. His public speeches and private conversation is larded with the first personal pronoun. A conversation with Sihanouk is not a dialogue but a monologue in which his interlocutor is fortunate to be able to interject "*Oui, Altesse Royale*", or "*Non, Monseigneur*". This frame of mind has resulted inevitably in the creation of a sort of dream world, in which appearances are sometimes mistaken for reality, and the shadow for the substance. The success which Sihanouk has often achieved by apparently rash initiatives has filled him with a misplaced self-confidence in his ability to walk the international political tight-rope and has unjustifiably fortified his belief that his natural flair will safeguard him against the tumbles predicted by foreign observers.

10. Nevertheless, there is no doubt that Sihanouk is in many ways a man of great personal brilliance, approaching the proportions of genius. He is endowed with an extraordinary range of gifts and a passionate desire to excel in them. As an athlete, musician, bon viveur and wit, he has earned the description of "playboy". But he is also a gifted linguist, a nimble and eclectic brain and a dynamic leader of men. He has great charm of manner and zest for life. These characteristics are combined with child-like lucidity but basic shrewdness, natural pugnacity yet kindness of heart. Genius, particularly in a god-king, carries its own penalties. At home he is intolerant of opposition and hypersensitive to criticism. Abroad, he requires red carpet treatment and is quick to respond to slights, whether real or imaged. Exigent in the extreme of the loyalty of others, it might be said of Sihanouk as it was of Jehovah that he is indeed a "Jealous God". He is,

however, an ardent patriot possessed of intense national pride, and a genuine concern for the lot of his people. The reciprocal affection which binds him to the Cambodian countryfolk is probably the most attractive feature of the regime. It has been perhaps misleadingly said that Sihanouk is incorruptible. He holds the purse strings of the state and surrounds himself with every comfort and luxury his heart desires. But he does not believe himself to be extravagant in the exercise of privileges, which he considers to be no more than his due. In some mystic way, he regards his country as an extension of his own person. *L'Etat, c'est moi.* Sihanouk knows little self-discipline and there is within his nature a vein of arbitrariness, even of cruelty, which is now coming somewhat closer to the surface. But the tremendous physical and nervous energy which he applies to the affairs of state betoken a degree of devotion to his elected duties which must be rare in someone with his background and conditions of life. There is a Messianic quality in his living. He is convinced that he has been divinely invested with the mission of assuring Cambodia's national survival.

11. Sihanouk also possesses unquestioned if unorthodox political flair. His audacity and skill in domestic stratagem is particularly striking. When King, his unpredicted and eccentric manoeuvres to obtain independence completely flummoxed the French. Having obtained this independence, in 1955 he surprised everyone by renouncing the Kingship, an act without precedent in Cambodian history. Sihanouk claimed that he wanted to show that he did not cling to power, authority and privilege for his own person, and complained that while King he has been able only to "to see the flowers and hear the lies". In fact, he has subsequently never ceased to enjoy Royal authority and privilege (and also to be fed lies by his courtiers and advisers). His abdication was nothing more than a formality coolly calculated to relieve him of certain ceremonial and other burdensome duties of the Throne

and thereby to free him for the exercise of far greater power in the political areas. A favourite technique in the exercise of this power is that of "divide and rule". The Cabinet, including the Prime Minister, is chosen by the Head of State. The Assembly is controlled by Sihanouk's monolithic and monopolistic political party, the Sangkum, which won all the seats in the elections of 1955, the year of its creation—and has retained them ever since. As a further precaution, a popular National Congress was created in 1958, to "guide" the Assembly and to "advise" the Cabinet. Each can now be played off against the others. A mass youth movement, the *Jeunesse Socialiste Royale Khmère*, created in 1957, is associated with the Sangkum and firmly buttresses the authority of the Head of State. The Constitution has been tinkered with for the same purpose, since Sihanouk descended the Throne; the Commander-in-Chief of the armed forces has been made responsible direct to the Head of State, in whom Royal powers have been vested. The Prince is one of the few men who can keep a cake and eat it at the same time.

12. Sihanouk's success story is, of course, due to more than pure political legerdemain or the mystic attributes of Cambodian Kingship. Sihanouk's Royal blood and divine descent may have smoothed the path to political success, but they certainly do not ensure it. His exceptional energy, his patriotism and genuine concern for the peoples' welfare, his personal contact with all parts of the kingdom, the undeniable magnetism of his personality, have established for him complete ascendancy over the minds and affections of his simpler subjects. Sihanouk once said that the need to "come to the aid of the little people, the indigent and the countryfolk, imposes on a statesman .... the obligation of living constantly in close touch with them". The business of maintaining close touch is, of course, itself a technique. A Princely visit to a provincial city is carefully prepared. Pavilions are set up, bands play, flags fly, troops, school children, youth movement and

militia parade and finally, at the peak of excitement, Sihanouk himself arrives in a helicopter or an open Cadillac, to thunderous cheers. There is a long speech, spiced with earthy anecdotes, in which Sihanouk expounds everything from world politics to local affairs or details of his private life. The speech usually ends with the announcement of a large gift of money to some local institution. The Prince leaves distributing small presents, souvenirs or wads of bank notes to the crowd, who have been bursting to run forward and touch him or kiss his hand—and usually at some point succeed in doing so, irrespective of the efforts of the Princely bodyguard. Asked on one occasion to explain his popularity with the people, Sihanouk simply replied "I give them things". But the real secret of his public relations is that the principal gift is himself: his time, attention and physical presence.

13. In matters of policy, Sihanouk's head rules his heart. He does not generally permit his own personal likes and dislikes to influence him in major issues. Sihanouk looks down on Prince Souphanouvong of Laos and has described him as "unwashed": this has not prevented from courting the Pathet Lao. He probably thinks that the person of President Sukarno is repellent; yet Sihanouk still respects the Bung and seeks his friendship. Traditional Vietnamophobia does not prevent close contacts with the Government of North Vietnam or the National Liberation Front. Sihanouk's tactics are often unpredictable, being based on political flair, intuition and sheer opportunism. But his strategic thinking is based on cold, hard, long-term and somewhat pessimistic assumptions and assessments. He is beholden to no country, not even France; gratitude, kinship or other intangibles form no part of his political vocabulary. If his chilly calculations are in any way touched by human emotion it is by Sihanouk's sense of historic doom. Monseigneur is fascinated by the abyss; in the end, he sometimes appears to feel, the Khmer Kingdom and its Prince will never fade away or whimper into insignificance;

all will be consumed in one mighty and spectacular *Götterdämmerung*.

14. Sihanouk galvanises the Government. He is capable of working eighteen hours a day on matters of state. Although a late riser, he generally works far into the night. He has more energy than his entire Cabinet put together and perhaps three or four times that of the average European living in the tropics. He said recently with wry humour that his functionaries were always greatly relieved when he was out of the country on some state visit; they could then simply go to sleep. There is a great deal of truth in this, the climate and the Cambodian character being what they are. Other than Sihanouk, it would no doubt take a Chinese Commissar, employing the most ruthless Stalinist methods, to keep things moving. But Sihanouk also grinds his Government down. His egocentricity prevents him from delegating authority. He interests himself in the minutest detail, and applies himself to as much of it as his working day will permit. His Cabinet Ministers are for the most part mere ciphers, wielding little individual responsibility. Sihanouk has grabbed all the hats and wears them in turn, those of Commander-in-Chief, Administrator, Supervisor of Ministers, Leader of Delegations, Head of the Sangkum, and principal speaker at the National Congress. He behaves like a *prima donna*, threatening to resign and walk off the stage at the slightest breath of a suggestion that all may not be well. Everything he does has to be hailed as a brilliant success. In some ways this can be bad for business. The bureaucracy, traditionally immobile, continue to fight shy of responsibility, and since everything has to receive Sihanouk's personal approval, urgent decisions are sometimes long delayed.

15. Ambassadors do not find Prince Sihanouk easy to handle. They are usually treated, in externals, with great respect and attention; the Prince makes a great fuss of Diplomatic Heads of Mission. Numerous are the social

occasions which he organises for them; and he is always the perfect host. (I myself regularly see a lot of him, at close quarters). But in essentials, he treats us all as he treats his ministers, like office boys, and then gives them the blame if things go wrong. Any kind of privileged conversation with Sihanouk is almost impossible; one's confidences are liable to be passed on at once to the next visitor, or broadcast in the Prince's next speech. Sihanouk has an urge, whenever he sees a microphone, to rush over to it and pour out with quite appalling frankness whatever may be at that moment on his mind; in this regard he is no respecter of Secrets of State or of confidential diplomacy. In his speeches, personal attacks on diplomatists at his court, and even on foreign Heads of States, are not infrequent occurrences. No apologies are ever made and protests are only counter-productive. Sihanouk is very sensitive to any suggestion of foreign interference in what he regards as Cambodia's domestic affairs. He in particular considers that the speeches which he delivers in Cambodian, sometimes as many as five or six a week, and rarely less than one, are intended for the ears of his own people only; foreigners are not expected to know Cambodian or to concern themselves with what is said in that language. An official French text, bowdlerised and abbreviated, usually appears a few days later. This is the "official" version for the outside world and comment by diplomats must be addressed to this alone.

16. Curiously, foreign journalists are often better placed to approach the Prince and secure his confidence than are the official representatives of foreign governments. Sihanouk likes journalists, and enjoys talking with them frankly and at length. In earlier years, he was a journalist himself in the sense that, while in office, he wrote lengthy articles for the local press. Sihanouk reads his press cuttings with avidity and complains bitterly if Cambodia is criticised; he makes no distinction between the relative standing of newspapers and can detect in the back page of the "Somerset Observer" or the small print of the *Ciné-Télé-*

Review de Paris a world-wide plot of imperialist defamation. But journalists, unlike Ambassadors, are invariably forgiven; after a few months, even outright critics return to grace and are vouchsafed further audiences.

17. The explanation for this paradox may perhaps be found in Sihanouk's experience in the formative years of his life under the French Protectorate, during the last twelve years of which he was King. Sihanouk once said of this period that "I knew what it was to suffer insults. I tell you I suffered a life of a servitor; and because I know what that is, I do not wish to be anyone's lackey". He may therefore still tend to regard the diplomatic envoys of the Great Powers at the Cambodian Royal Court as if they were something like the French colonial administrators and dignitaries who effectively ruled his kingdom and told him what to do. He dislikes confidential diplomacy, because the secrecy of his negotiations with the French for national independence in 1953 led to serious misunderstanding among the people. Sihanouk was accused of treason and of playing the French game: charges which he sorely resented and has never forgotten. He sees the press on the other hand as an outlet to the world. It has been mainly through the international press that Sihanouk has drawn the attention of world opinion to his personal predicaments and those of his country. In so doing, he has by-passed the channels of diplomacy, and appealed to peoples over the heads of their governments.

18. In concluding this Despatch, I must give you notice, Sir, of certain clouds which loom on the personal horizon of the Prince and which might, if they further advanced, obscure the brilliance of his achievements and eventually bring his day to a gloomy close. I refer to Sihanouk's state of physical and mental health. His constitution is under stress and his moral character already exhibits subtle tokens of possible decline. Nothing spectacular may happen for several years to come. But, metaphorically

speaking, the cancer is there and may one day turn out to be malignant.

19. To approach the delicate question of Prince Sihanouk's health it is necessary to take a look at his heredity. The Norodom branch of the Royal Family possesses certain well-defined characteristics. Gifted for the arts, versatile and in some cases intelligent, they yet inherit, possibly due to inbreeding, a strain of eccentricity. [Passage deleted by the FCO.] One of Sihanouk's own children (by his aunt) has had a nervous breakdown. The cupboards at Court have always been crammed with skeletons. A discreet veil has, for example, been drawn by historiographers over the precise date of decease of Sihanouk's maternal grandfather, King Sisowath Monivong. The old man died from an overdose of aphrodisiacs locked up in his bedchamber in a mountain retreat; it was days before the Court knew what had happened, and were able to bring him back to the capital for a proper funeral. [Passage deleted by the FCO.]

20. To come to our subject, Sihanouk himself is highly strung. (The constant eating referred to below is itself a neurotic symptom; he recently told me that he eats because he finds it comforting). He is rumoured to sleep very badly and to be troubled by nightmares; he dislikes the dark and will never sleep in a room alone. Sihanouk has an obsessive fear of death (which the Horas have foretold will be a violent one); the idea of doom and destruction has a chill but unfailing fascination for him. The physical state of Sihanouk's health has, moreover, in recent years caused some anxiety to his doctors. At the time of writing, the latter have even felt it necessary to insist that he should spend several days each month in hospital for rest and observation. His father was a diabetic and it is know (although no-one will officially admit it) that Sihanouk from time to time takes mysterious injections. There is, in addition, an incipient heart weakness. This arises from his

being overweight (Monseigneur gorges himself with cream puffs and *pâté de foie gras*), from not taking regular exercise, and from working extended, irregular and utterly exhausting hours. The degree of energy which the Prince exhibits is quite extraordinary for a Cambodian and for this hot, sticky and enervating climate. Perhaps it is due to some glandular abnormality. However that may be, Sihanouk clearly cannot continue indefinitely to burn the candle at both ends.

21. It may be significant that the Norodom defects of character have tended, historically, to become more pronounced in later life. In recent years, these have been displayed in Sihanouk by an almost megalomaniac urge to sponsor grandiose projects bearing little relation to national resources or even requirements, by an increasingly childish resentment of criticism in any form, by defective political and moral judgement and by growing isolation from and indifference towards his closest advisers. In a word, he is tending to become dangerously arbitrary and authoritarian.

22. It is perhaps the tendency to isolation which is the most worrying. Few people these days have any real influence on Sihanouk and he seldom if ever consults anyone, except to seek endorsement of views already formed. His father, the late King, was in some ways a restraining influence and commanded filial piety. But the King has been dead for nearly five years. With his mother, Queen Kossamak, Sihanouk has for long been on bad terms. Penn Nouth, a trusted adviser from the earliest days, is now elderly and somewhat infirm. The older and established politicians, such as Tep Phan and Nhiek Tioulong, are discarded or out of favour; or at least, like Sonn Sann, no longer in the full confidence of the Prince.

23. Certain recent events selected at random may serve to underline the subtle changes which observers can now

detect in Prince Sihanouk. In the autumn of 1963, an emissary of the Cambodian opposition in exile, Preap Inn, entered Cambodia to parley with the Government. He was given a safe conduct by the Governor of Takeo Province. For political reasons connected with the tension then obtaining between Cambodia and Vietnam, Sihanouk decided to arrest him. The man, with his companion, was arraigned before a National Congress and mercilessly bullied. The companion, who caved in and gave the right answers, was set free. Preap Inn (who defended himself with dignity) was screamed down by the Prince, who disallowed the safe conduct and had the man shot. The proceedings had been broadcast. The bearing of Preap Inn, and the arbitrary cruelty of the Prince, were not lost on the Cambodians at large, many of whom murmured against the sentence. It was at this time that, following a series of screeching and hysterical speeches in which he seemed to be close to losing his mental balance, Sihanouk announced the abrupt rejection of United States economic aid and launched, without the slightest advance consultation with his Cabinet, a range of inept measures of state control. There were objective circumstances which precipitated the crisis; but Monseigneur's state of mind was his own. (Since this episode, he has never fully regained his former *joie de vivre*; only the other week a humble serving woman was heard to say that she did not know what had come over her Prince: his speeches were so packed with woe and nothing seemed to please him). In March 1964, at a work session with his advisers late in the night, Sihanouk decided that mobs should be sent out to sack the British and American Embassies; a highly effective operation was mounted by the Government the following morning, mercifully without injury or loss of life. The decision was a foolish one; in a more balanced frame of mind, Sihanouk would have realised that mob attacks could not modify the policies of the British and American Governments; could only alienate the sympathies of those in these countries who wished Cambodia well; and would give the student mob a taste for action which they might one day wish to satisfy at the expense of the Government. The principal architect of the attacks was Kou Roun, a police thug and a somewhat sinister figure. In recent months, this man has wormed his way further into the Prince's company if not his confidence. Monseigneur's appetite for luxury and comfort, formerly under some sort of control, are now showing signs of some slight enlargement. In order to meet Cambodia's acute budgetary difficulties, Sihanouk has proclaimed a regime of austerity. Redundant officials are being sacked, luxury imports slashed, air-conditioners and even fans switched off in Government offices. For a month or two, Sihanouk conformed, after his fashion, to the austerity pattern. But he is now said to be back busily planning more luxury villas for himself, purchasing new motor cars, and generally throwing the state revenues around. Finally, notwithstanding the financial straits of the nation, there seems to be have been no retrenchment in Sihanouk's plans for the expansion and embellishment of Cambodia. Anything other Heads of State can achieve, he can do at least as well. New projects and instructions for schools, hospitals, factories and roads, far beyond the resources of his compatriots to realise without halting other work already in hand, continue to flow from the Princely Palace.

24. There is therefore reason to believe that Sihanouk's character may be undergoing a subtle deterioration. All power tends to corrupt; absolute power corrupts absolutely. The truth of this dictum can be demonstrated in the Prince's life. Moreover, breeding will tell and Norodom Sihanouk bears no unblemished escutcheon. At forty-three years of age, he is no longer the charming and open youth who ascended the Throne at the age of nineteen, nor the still flexible political genius who descended from it at the age of thirty-three. In the earlier years of Sihanouk's rule, Cambodia had known an Antonine period of peace and prosperity. Sad though I am to say it (for I have felt the

charm of this extraordinary man and consider myself privileged to have known him) and unfortunate though this may be for the West (for if Sihanouk fails to uphold his country's independence from Communism no other Cambodian leader seems likely to do better), it seems less than certain that Sihanouk will live out a reign of perpetually golden and glorious years.

25. If I had to summarise in a few sentences my view of this most complex, unusual and fascinating man, I would do so as follows. Sihanouk is more than an Oriental, he is a Cambodian god-king. This means that he is in all matters a semi-divine autocrat, brooking no opposition or interference, imposing his own wishes, demanding absolute loyalty and admiration. He is also a man of dynamic genius. The effect of this is that he has asserted in his own right and by his own efforts absolute mastery over the minds of almost all his subjects, complete control over the government and uncontested political dominion as the national hero and leader of Cambodia. His genius is not, however, entirely a good one. His unmitigated absolutism carries the seeds of its own dissolution. His health, mental or physical, may weaken under continued stress. Some slight symptoms of personal decline are already apparent to the patient observer. But his momentum is great and may still carry far. British diplomacy must, therefore, continue to take full account of him. It was this belief which conceived the present Despatch.

I have, & etc.

Leslie Fielding

(Chargé d'Affaires)

Letter to Mr. Fielding from Assistant Head of South-East Asia Department, FO, 5 April, 1965

As James Cable is still away I am writing to thank you for your despatch No. 6 of 2 March about the personality of Prince Sihanouk.

2. We have all read with fascination your fine account of Prince Sihanouk's rather Gothik court and personality[9]. It is, of course, most important to have a detailed understanding of the character of the Head of state in a one-man country like Cambodia.

D.F. Murray

---

[9] See "The God King of Cambodia" pp413-416, below.

THE PROPOSED GENEVA CONFERENCE ON CAMBODIA: A POST-MORTEM

SUMMARY

Mr. Fielding to Mr. Stewart

In April 1965, the British and American Governments decided to support the convening of a Geneva Conference on Cambodia. In doing so, they hoped to prepare the way for possible talks on Viet-Nam (para. 2).

The Chinese were not ready for talks and in effect told Sihanouk he could not have the Conference (paras. 3-5).

Sihanouk acted on Chinese advice but later regretted it and reverted to a more neutral posture (paras. 6-9).
The Russians acted throughout with excessive caution (para. 10).
The exercise, though abortive, was worth attempting (para. 11).

Confidential	British Embassy
No. 24	Phnom Penh
Sir,	September 7, 1965

In the spring and summer of this year, a Geneva Conference on Cambodia was proposed, debated, deferred and finally it seems dismissed. The original initiative came from Prince Sihanouk, the Cambodian Head of State. His suggestion was taken up by the Western powers, who hoped thereby to promote a dialogue with the powers of the East which might eventually embrace the problem of Viet-Nam. It was brought to nothing by the Chinese, who did not want any form of talks, and by the Soviet Union, who, although favourable to a Conference, in fact crippled it by their extreme caution. No new initiative is at present in sight; Cambodia still lacks the international assurances which should by rights be hers. I have the honour to offer the following general post-mortem. A detailed autoptical analysis of events in calendar form is in the Annex.

2. Prince Sihanouk has advocated the neutralisation of Indo-China by international agreement since 1958. Since 1962, he has in particular repeatedly and earnestly petitioned for the independence, neutrality and present frontiers of Cambodia to be recognized and endorsed by a Geneva Conference. In 1964, he would have secured the latter, but for reservations entertained by the United States Government, who feared adverse effects in South Viet-Nam. In March 1965, however, when the Cambodian Government again petitioned the Co-Chairmen of the Geneva Conference, the climate of opinion in the West had become generally more favourable. The Americans wanted to look into the possibility of an honourable settlement by negotiation in Viet-Nam and the British wished to open up every path for exploration. When the U.S. Government announced their readiness to attend a Conference on Cambodia, and the British Government informed the Soviet Government that the Conference might forthwith be convened, the two allies were chiefly inspired by the hope that once the affairs of Cambodia had been satisfactorily settled the Conference might move on to discuss Viet-Nam. Failing this, informal contacts and a discreet dialogue might in any case be entertained with the Chinese and North Viet-Namese leadership in the corridors and hotel bars of Geneva. There is reason to believe that these hopes were also at this early stage shared by the Cambodian Government itself. The prospects of all-round success therefore seemed fair.

3. The Chinese were slow to react to these moves. At the Indo-Chinese Peoples' Conference held in Phnom Penh at the beginning of March, the Chinese camp had raised no

objection to resolutions calling for a reconvening of the 1954 Geneva Conference to consider Cambodia (my Despatch No.9 of 23 March, 1965). On 17 March, Marshal Chen Yi publicly endorsed the approach of the Cambodian Government to the Geneva Co-Chairmen. It was not until mid-April that the Chinese leadership appeared to realise that, contrary to the outcome in previous years, the British were now likely to agree to a Cambodian Conference and to carry their American allies with them. Faced with the real prospect of having to sit down at the same table with the Americans and with representatives of the Saigon Government, the Chinese took urgent evasive action in the hope that they could call the whole thing off before the Co-Chairmen actually issued the invitations to a Conference.

4. Messrs. Chou En-lai, Chen Yi and Pham Van Dong accordingly jumped on Prince Sihanouk at Djakarta, where they met for the 10th Anniversary celebrations of Bandung. They apparently said that the Chinese and North Viet-Namese had no wish to meet the American war criminals; that it was in any case the National Liberation Front and not the Saigon puppets who should represent South Viet-Nam at any conference; that the British and Americans had not the slightest interest in Cambodia's problems and would forget them once a Conference got talking about Viet-Nam; that, in short, the whole idea was a put-up job by the imperialists who wanted only to trick Cambodia and escape an ugly defeat in South Viet-Nam. Was a new Geneva Agreement really called for? Cambodia's only true friend was China; it was on China's assurances of friendship and support that Cambodia should rely. But friendship was a two-way matter.

5. After this highly successful performance, the Chinese never let up for one moment. On almost every occasion in the following weeks on which the Cambodian Government expressed some criticism or other of the "Anglo-Saxons", an immediate public endorsement followed within hours

from Peking. Mr. Chou En-lai even sent a personal message discreetly protesting about Sihanouk's letter of 15 May to the British Prime Minister (See Annex). It was a slick operation, carefully orchestrated from Peking, in which the Chinese drew effectively on the goodwill they already possessed and made full use of their informers and "agents of influence".

6. The extremely tough, negative line taken by the Chinese must have been a grave disappointment for Sihanouk. Out of deference to Chinese wishes, however, and still under the spell of Mr. Chou En-lai's mesmeric personality, Sihanouk came back from Djakarta dutifully bent on a hatchet job. In two sensational speeches, he accused the "Anglo-Saxons" of seeking to turn his honest proposal to their dingy self-advantage in Viet-Nam. The situation had evolved; the Saigon regime was no longer a genuine government; neither Saigon nor Washington were therefore wanted at the Conference; nor would he grant a personal audience to Mr. Gordon Walker, the Special Representative of the UK Co-Chairman, on his forthcoming visit to Phnom Penh.

7. Happily, Sihanouk subsequently had the wisdom to modify the extreme position described above. The ban on American participation in the Conference was lifted first; later, it was left to the Great Powers themselves to decide whether the Saigon Government should also participate.

8. The development which perhaps most served to bring Monseigneur to his senses was the almost universal opposition which he encountered from the top drawer of the Cambodian establishment, none of whom (including the Foreign Minister) had apparently been informed in advance of Monseigneur's *volte face*. The Establishment have, for the most part, long entertained inner misgiving about Cambodia's apparent drift away from neutrality and friendship with the West and towards dependence on

People's China. The rapid deterioration of relations with the United States, terminating in the Prince's decision completely to break off diplomatic relations in mid-May, would in any case have raised murmurs of discontent. Having lectured his people for the previous three years on the theme that the main hope for Cambodia's national survival was a new Geneva Agreement, Sihanouk was now in effect saying that this prospect should be foregone, and Cambodia's vital interests thereby jeopardised, just for the blue eyes of the venerable Chou En-lai and elder statesmen Pham Van Dong. Goaded past endurance, Cambodian elder statesmen expressed their misgiving deferentially but directly to the Prince; while the Cabinet submitted a unanimous recommendation that Cambodia should revert to the terms of her original proposal of 15 March to the Geneva Co-Chairmen. Mr. Gordon Walker's visit and a series of discreet and devious moves by the Foreign Office and this Embassy exploited the situation to the full. Possibly for the first time in his entire political career, Sihanouk found himself deprived of the initiative and out of step and sympathy with most of his own *élite*. As the memory of his traumatic encounter at Djakarta grew less vivid, and his basic and sincere desire for a Conference re-asserted itself, Sihanouk became less and less keen on his role as whipping boy for the Chinese.

9. By an adroit manoeuvre, Sihanouk duly put the ball back in the court of the Great Powers. But by then the practical prospects for an early Conference had immeasurably receded. Sihanouk subsequently floated the idea of individual assurances of respect for Cambodian neutrality and territorial integrity, in which the Powers would sign unilaterally a declaration, accompanied by a map of Cambodia's frontiers. But this project seemed also to raise difficulties, not least with the Viet-Namese communists, who were not over-anxious to commit themselves to anything in black and white. At the end of the day, all the birds were deep in the bush, with none in

Sihanouk's hand. On 2 September, the Prince left Phnom Penh in a state of bafflement and depression to embark on a four-month official tour abroad.

10. The Russians regrettably acted with extreme caution throughout the crisis. In first proposing that the two Co-Chairmen should issue invitations to a conference, the Soviet leadership may conceivably have been bent purely on embarrassing the West, sharing the Chinese calculation that the British and American Governments would be unable to respond. But it seems possible that Moscow had a more positive intent. The Soviet Union still has a position of influence in Cambodia, a country which it would like to keep out of the Chinese orbit as far as may be. A Geneva Conference, co-chaired by the Soviet Union, and leading to a binding international agreement, could both reduce the political dependence of Cambodia on China's friendship and enhance the local prestige of the Soviet Union. More than this, I have little doubt that the hopes of London and Washington that a Cambodian Conference might furnish an oblique approach to the problem of Viet-Nam were also privately shared in some measure by Moscow, the more so since there was little else the Soviet Union could do to promote negotiations over Viet-Nam more directly. Unfortunately, Soviet feet very quickly turned cold when it became evident that China was opposed, and that Prince Sihanouk himself had apparently in consequence modified his *desiderata*. The Soviets prevaricated, and despite numerous British reminders, the invitations to a Conference never issued.

11. How does everyone emerge from this affair? China emerges triumphant as Senior Wrangler. Being clearly anxious to avoid discussions with the West of any kind whatsoever about any part of Indo-China, she has successfully torpedoed the proposed Geneva Conference on Cambodia, and done so without apparent serious damage to Sino/Cambodian relations. China, moreover, now has

some grounds for believing that, at least as long as Prince Sihanouk continues as Head of state, she can call the tune of Cambodian foreign policy on any international issue of real importance. There is therefore no change in the assessments in my Despatch No. 57 of 17 November, 1964. The Soviets, on the other hand, barely scrape Third Class Honours, having earned the maximum of embarrassment with absolutely nothing to show for it; they were outmanoeuvred at every stage of the game. The French have kept their powder dry. The *Quai d'Orsay* has been and remains in principle in favour of a Geneva Conference on Cambodia. But the French Government did little positive to help the Conference forward; indeed their main concern was to stay in Sihanouk's good books. The United States took a laudable if difficult decision in plumping for a Conference. My only regret is that initial hesitation delayed a positive response to the Soviet proposal long enough to permit the Chinese to beat a hasty retreat. Finally, the United Kingdom probably deserves a Beta Plus. Chinese intransigence has been probed and to some extent exposed; the Co-Chairmanship has been exercised somewhat, and thereby kept in some semblance of working order; we have been able to convince most of our Asian friends that a readiness to consider giving legitimate formal assurances to Cambodia was not necessarily "soft" or a "sell-out to the Reds". Finally, Anglo-Cambodian relations have been raised somewhat above rock-bottom. We may also have given Prince Sihanouk personally a salutary shock—one cannot fool all the people all the time, even to please one's Chinese friends.

I have, &c

Leslie Fielding

(Chargé d'Affaires)

CAMBODIA: ANNUAL REVIEW FOR 1965

Mr. Fielding to Mr. Stewart

SUMMARY

1965 was full of disappointments. Chinese intransigence sabotaged a possible Geneva Conference. Cambodia became more isolated. (Paragraphs 1-2.)

Prince Sihanouk met setbacks in both foreign and domestic policy. Dissatisfaction was voiced at home. (Paragraphs 3-4.)

But Cambodia still values links with the West and may seek to strengthen them. In any case the country seems likely to survive 1966 as a neutral unless the war widens in Viet-Nam. (Paragraphs 5-6.)

Britain could help Cambodia in unorthodox ways at minimal expense. (Paragraphs 7-8.)

Confidential   British Embassy
No. 1   Phnom Penh
Sir,   3 January, 1966

The past year in Cambodia, on which I have the honour to submit this brief review together with a calendar of events, was heavy with disappointment both for Prince Sihanouk and the West, but ended with some slight hope of a rapprochement between the two.

2. Almost all the developments of international significance were discouraging. The fanatical intransigence of the Viet-Namese Communists and their Chinese overlords crippled Sihanouk's Indo-Chinese People's Conference in March, and killed the proposed Geneva Conference on Cambodia in April. The Chinese bloc would not give ear to Sihanouk's talk of negotiations, neutralisation and compromise in Indo-China, and were resolved not to sit round the same table with the West even to discuss Cambodia, despite the fact that Sihanouk had sought earnestly for such a Conference for several years with Chinese support. Such was the importance to Sihanouk of retaining a cordial relationship with Peking that he accepted this with all the outward grace he could muster. Unfortunately, Monseigneur's decision to break off diplomatic relations with the United States in May and his quarrel with the Soviet Union in October (over the latter's insultingly last-minute 'postponement' of his state visit to Moscow) served only to make matters worse by isolating Cambodia and exposing her yet further to Chinese influence. This influence was fortified by promises of more military aid from Peking.

3. The Cambodian Head of State met frustration at every turn, and ended 1965 in a mood of both anguish and uncertainty. Along the frontier with South Viet-Nam, incidents were less frequent and less bloody than in 1964; but considerable tension was created by accusations and

denials (neither of them always well-founded) concerning clandestine use of Cambodian territory by the Viet Cong. Along the frontier with Thailand there were signs of developing uneasiness. Cambodia's Communist neighbours were, in one important respect, no more friendly than the "running dogs of United States imperialism". Peking, Hanoi and the National Liberation Front politely declined a Cambodian proposal that they should sign unilateral declarations of respect for Cambodia's present frontiers. Sihanouk therefore failed to make the slightest progress towards the principal object of his foreign policy.

4. On the domestic front Sihanouk was equally hard pressed. Cambodia's financial situation moved from bad to worse and standards of living in the capital among all but the lowest classes underwent further decline. Sihanouk remained firmly planted at the helm. But the political and economic disasters of the year stirred up a groundswell of dissatisfaction among the majority of the Cambodian *élite* and bourgeoisie which began to slap the timbers of the Ship of State.

5. Happily, certain beacons of hope shone through the fog. Sihanouk was at pains to maintain and even extend certain links with the West. Relations with France were excellent. Canberra's patient diplomacy bore triumphant fruit; Australia was paid the compliment of being asked to represent Cambodian interests in South Viet-Nam, and became clearly established as Cambodia's second Western partner. Japan and Germany held their own. Relations with Britain began to improve in September and were given further impetus by the quarrel with the Russians. At the close of the year a Cambodian Ambassador had presented his credentials at the Court of St. James's and the British Chargé d'Affaires at the Court of Queen Kossamak was beginning to emerge from social ostracism. By December there were even small signs that American firmness in Viet-Nam had been noted (with respect if not approval)

and that a *Drang nach Westen* might with luck gradually assert itself. Sihanouk evidently felt that he was getting too close to an orbit round Peking and had begun to fire some retro-rockets.

6. Looking forward, the great danger is that Cambodia will be somehow sucked into the Viet-Namese war. The authority given in December to American military commanders to strike Cambodian territory in self-defence could prove a step in this direction. Short of such involvement, however, in 1966 Cambodia is likely to remain a neutral country and the "oasis of peace" of which Sihanouk justly boasts. The Khmer nation are ethnocentric, homogeneous, proud and madly independent. These, rather than their more modest share of the virtues of statesmanship, organisation and hard work, are the characteristics most likely to see them through the coming year.

7. What future part should Britain attempt to play in Cambodian affairs? We should nourish no illusion that we can exercise direct influence over Sihanouk or make him depart from his own stark and pessimistic judgments in world affairs. Britain's friendship and cooperation may be desirable to the Cambodians, but it is not considered by them to be essential. In the short term at least, the Prince and his kingdom, like Burma, can probably muddle through and survive unaided. What we can do, however, is to let Sihanouk make use of us for his own ends where we judge them to be good. Within this framework, various modest proposals designed to bring about more friendly relations are under consideration by your Department; they are not expensive (the most ambitious would call for additional expenditure across the exchanges of only £12,000) and are, for the most part, gestures with a purely psychological appeal slanted towards the Head of State.

8. It is for you, Sir, to decide whether, set in the wider context, such an effort ought to be made. But if we do decide to have a go, then you should know that our diplomacy will have to be unorthodox and flexible to a degree which it will not be easy for us, the stuffy British, to attain. We shall have to suppress our sense of the ridiculous, summon up a full measure of imagination and be prepared to deal with Asiatics in an Asian fashion.

I have, &c.

Leslie Fielding

(Chargé d'Affaires)

THE FRENCH IN CAMBODIA

Mr. Fielding to Mr. Stewart

SUMMARY

What are the French up to in Cambodia? They are influential and there is mutual understanding between them and the Cambodians (paras. 1 – 4).

There is also *rapport* between the two Heads of State, President de Gaulle and Prince Sihanouk. Each finds the other to his advantage (paras 5 and 6).

But de Gaulle's personal influence, and that of the French generally, may be a wasting asset (paras. 7 and 8).

In their political dealings with us over Cambodia, the French have been difficult. They are now somewhat more forthcoming, perhaps because they think they can use us (paras. 9 and 10).

Nevertheless, French influence in Cambodia is ultimately an asset to the West and we should not exclude limited Anglo-French cooperation (paras. 11 and 12).

Confidential   British Embassy
No. 10   Phnom Penh
Sir,   9 May, 1966

What is the French presence in Cambodia? Will the influence of France endure and what is its value to the West? How can we exploit it? These are the questions which I have the honour to treat in this Despatch.

2. The following is my *aperçu général*. Among the former colonies and protectorates of France in Indo-China, Cambodia retains the most influential French presence French panache gives Phnom Penh unique style and distinction. Culturally, it pleases the French, and upholds the *mission civilatrice de la France*, that Cambodia should be Francophone and Francophile from the palace to the paddy-field. Politically, France has always been the deepest rooted, and is at present the dominant, Western power. In matters of high policy, Cambodia is a potentially useful pawn in President de Gaulle's world game.

3. At grass roots, the French as individuals are better mixers than other Westerners, despite the fact that they make few cultural or social concessions to their environment. The interpenetration of French and Cambodian in the government machine is remarkable. French experts are at hand in most ministries; French teachers abound in the *lycées* and universities; French military instructors train the Cambodian armed forces (despite the fact that the latter have much Russian and Chinese equipment). A collection of bizarre and sometimes

sinister French journalists manipulate the propaganda machine.

4. The Cambodians naturally reciprocate. The Khmer *élite* are French-minded; they like French food and clothes and pay at least lip-service to French culture; the best of them reason and debate in the manner of the *Hautes Ecoles*. The Cambodians know that French commercial practice is often sharp, but still like to do business with their former "protectors". After a century of French rape and Cambodian concubinage, the two feel comfortable together like Darby and Joan.

5. Recent French political purpose in Cambodia has been blatantly Gaullist, with the encouragement and at times the active cooperation of the Khmer Head of state. The underlying motive of *le Général* is to establish *coute que coute* an independent and assertive world status for France. He does not get on with Americans and wants to see them leave Indo-China. He also wants close relations with People's China. This rings all the bells with Sihanouk, a fanatical nationalist with a strong sense of grievance against the Americans and a conviction that only a friendly and placated China can bring about security in the region. So the *roi soleil* and the god-king join hands, each hoping to make greater use of the other.

6. More specifically, Sihanouk expects de Gaulle to give him diplomatic support and sorely needed economic aid and also to show the world that neutral Cambodia has Western as well as Eastern friends. De Gaulle in his turn sees the Khmer pocket kingdom as of value both in itself and as a potential bridgehead from which the French may one day be able to sally forth and reestablish themselves in Indo-China when other Western influences have been ejected or diminished. Above all, neutral Cambodia may one day underpin a regional "settlement" (or "sell-out"),

with de Gaulle as architect and France as prime Western beneficiary.

7. The strength of purely Gaullist influence should not, however, be exaggerated; it depends on the survival of two mortal men. If Sihanouk were to be removed from power by the Right Wing (his potential if not overt challengers), the latter would restore relations with the United States, leaving France almost as irrelevant as she is today in Saigon or Vientiane. The General himself may die or lose power at any time. Even without all this, mutual disillusionment may set in and indeed to some small degree already has. President de Gaulle's recent electoral performance surprised Sihanouk and gave him food for thought. The General for his part refers in private to le *pauvre Sihanouk* now that he knows him better, and the Elysée is said to have decided to give only the diplomatic minimum of new economic assistance.

8. The French position generally is, moreover, not as strong as it looks. The economy has been depressed by Sihanouk's policies. Business is not good and, although France has traditional commercial primacy, there has been no significant new investment by private French concerns for several years. Although the French Embassy would die rather than admit it, the French community has been steadily shrinking for the past two or three years. Socially, a certain distrust of the white man—a formerly unheard of phenomenon in Cambodia—is beginning to creep into the Khmer nature and will sooner or later make life difficult for the expatriate experts and mercenaries. Politically also, the French have cause for uneasiness. They have had little more success than anyone else in persuading Sihanouk to do other than his own wisdom has dictated. They do not like either the extension of Chinese influence over Sihanouk or the recent growth of Right Wing domestic discontent with his rule. French diplomats in Phnom Penh now speculate gloomily in their cups on how long Sihanouk

will keep his Rightists at bay and how long his likely possible successors might withstand Communist subversion.

9. How do the French in Cambodia see the British? Francis Garnier, one of the most passionate colonisers of Indo-China of the 19th century, had a burning hatred of Britain and there are still one or two of his ilk left around. We also have our share of friends and admirers. By and large, however, the general attitude today is relaxed and even indifferent. The French are more successful by far, and therefore surer of themselves, in Phnom Penh than elsewhere in Indo-China. Their first concern has been to stay in with Sihanouk and to devote themselves exclusively to their own national interests. During the past few years of local difficulty for *les Anglo-Saxons* in Cambodia, the French have sometimes seemed politically mean and dishonest. There has, however, always tended to be a conflict, as regards dealings with ourselves, between Gaullists and non-Gaullists, respectable professional diplomats and the less reputable *barbouzes* and old Indo-China hands. More recently, the former seemed to have gained the upper hand and it is fair to state that the French Embassy is now adopting a cautiously forthcoming attitude.

10. The new emphasis is probably due to the fact that the French—or at least the professionals who have to deal with stark realities to which Elysée-bred illusions do not hold the key—now doubt their ability alone to keep control of events. For their own purposes, the French object is to keep the present neutralist regime going, with Sihanouk still successfully perched on the East/West tight-rope. They believe we want the same. They have no illusions as to the means at our disposal, and no great respect for our savoir-faire in the country, but evidently consider that every little helps. These are therefore days in which M. Couve de

Murville urges the Cambodians to restore normal relations with the British.

11. Behind the tinsel of French vainglory and the (to us) sheer *méchanceté* of some aspects of Gaullist foreign policy, the influence of France in Cambodia is still at bottom an asset of the free world. France under de Gaulle may no longer represent the West, as we use that expression; but she is undoubtedly western with a small "w". Cambodia is not, and never has been, our affair; we have available no great resources to devote to the Khmers even if we should wish to make a major effort to support Cambodian neutrality and arrest the growth of Communist influence. The French on the other hand do have such a commitment and have in the past been prepared to honour it with men, equipment and money.

12. While cautious in future dealings with the French over Cambodia, we should therefore not overlook the area of common interest. For the present, we share the basic French objects (to completely different ends) and could benefit from French understanding and discreet support for our various diplomatic initiatives. I therefore recommend that we should pursue *ad hoc* any prospects of limited Anglo-French collaboration. There may be more scope for this in the future than in the past.

I have &c.

Leslie Fielding

(Chargé d'Affaires)

Letter to Mr. Fielding from Head of South-East Asia Department, FO, 28 July, 1966

I am afraid that in the hurly-burly of the last couple of months, I overlooked the fact that I had not written to thank you for your despatch No. 10 of 9 May about the French in Cambodia. It was interesting to read of Cambodia as yet another example of how attachment to the French way of life and to French culture manages to survive even the associations of a colonial past, and the Department is very grateful to you for taking time out from your own busy programme to prepare this report.

2. I agree with you that we should not overlook Cambodia as a possible area of common interest with the French, since our basic aims to maintain Sihanouk on his tightrope are the same; and that we should attempt to collaborate with them when it suits us. As you say yourself, Cambodia is not, and never has been, our affair, but we must be prepared to do whatever we can to contribute to the stability of Indo-China as a whole.

3. According to Prince Sihanouk's assessment of the future of South East Asia, China will be the main power and will be the greatest single influence on the future of Cambodia. The fact that General de Gaulle is also convinced of the need to accept China as a great power and of the need to establish good relations with her should go a certain way to cement their relations though in a way that may irritate the Americans and make our own position somewhat invidious.

(D.F. Murray)

PRESIDENT DE GAULLE IN PHNOM PENH

Mr. Fielding to Mr. Brown

SUMMARY

President de Gaulle's State visit to Cambodia was on the whole a brilliant success. (Paragraphs 1-2.)

Little constructive emerged about Viet-Nam, de Gaulle contenting himself with condemnation of the United States. (Paragraphs 3-4.)

Franco-Cambodian relations were, however, yet further strengthened, to the general advantage of the West. (Paragraph 5.)

The reception was lavish and the General tired but determined and triumphant. (Paragraphs 6-7.)

The Press found it all hard to believe, but the visit left a deep impression on the Cambodians. (Paragraphs 8-9.)

Confidential   British Embassy
No. 20   Phnom Penh
Sir,   12 September, 1966

1. I have the honour to report that President de Gaulle of France paid a brilliantly successful State visit to Cambodia from the 31st of August to the 2nd of September. 1966.

2. Although the visit probably failed to attract world attention to the degree which the French Government would have wished, it nevertheless served powerfully to reinforce the existing very close links between Cambodia

and France. President de Gaulle strengthened the Khmer Head of State's confidence in his policy of neutrality and fierce national independence. In doing so, the General struck a shrewd indirect blow at Communist influence over Cambodia.

3. International attention was mainly focused upon the significance of President de Gaulle's visit for Viet-Nam. Not without encouragement from the Elysée, the world Press had speculated that a major mediatory French initiative would be launched. In practice, little of immediate consequence emerged. President de Gaulle's speech in Phnom Penh on September 1, delivered a forthright, brutal and one-sided attack on the American position in Viet-Nam; but contained no offer of French good offices. The General appealed to the United States to undertake to withdraw from Viet-Nam within an appropriate and fixed period of time, but afforded no assurance that a reasonable settlement might thereby be reached. The President and his entourage had private talks respectively with the local North Viet-Namese Government Representative and with members of the National Liberation Front. But despite the arch and somewhat mysterious manner in which these contacts were presented to the Press, it now seems most unlikely that the French obtained any modification of substance whatsoever in the hitherto rigid policies of the Viet-Namese Communists.

4. General de Gaulle's pronouncement was presumably therefore made for the long term and in the calculation that, whatever the rights and wrongs of the matter, the Americans would eventually have to get out of Viet-Nam; France, if she meanwhile won the confidence of the Communists, could then intervene to make all whole. The text of this discourse can accordingly do little than at present gather dust in the archives of the Chancelleries concerned.

5. The main achievement of the visit was in the field of Franco-Cambodian relations. The French presence in Cambodia, as reported in my Despatch No. 10 of May 9, is deeply rooted, and there is great personal *rapport* between the two Heads of State. French policy is to support Prince Sihanouk, and Cambodia's neutrality and integrity. The State Visit magnificently served both purposes. The mere magic of the General's presence usefully reinforced Sihanouk's domestic prestige at a time when discontent and criticism of his conduct of State affairs had been perceptibly on the increase. But Monseigneur also obtained more tangible blessings from the General: a statement of respect for Cambodia's present frontiers contained in the final joint communiqué and agreement in principle on further French economic and military aid. France displaced China as Cambodia's "Friend Number One" and Western values generally began to look more respectable than they have for years hereabouts.

6. The arrangements for the President's reception were the most lavish and spectacular ever known in Cambodia. They are not likely to be surpassed in the future, until such time as the Queen of England should come to Phnom Penh. Three hundred thousand Cambodians turned out to greet President de Gaulle on his arrival. Half the population of Phnom Penh were present for his open-air speech on September 1. A fabulous pageant was mounted by floodlight before the brooding temples of Angkor. The French President and his wife were accommodated in the Royal Palace itself, a personal honour totally without precedent. The associated security precautions were on an equally grandiose scale. Dubious French locals were banished by the dozen to the distant seaside and almost every petrol station in Phnom Penh was drained in case someone should blow it up while the General rolled by. Armoured cars stood grimly at the street corners and steel-helmeted troops lurked in the leafy shade of the main boulevards.

7. President de Gaulle himself was a remarkable figure, standing on dais and tribune with Prince Sihanouk's head coming up to his waist. The General was not comfortable in the heat and looked old and drawn. Yet he forced himself through his heavy programme with great determination and dignity. At times, as he sat through long ceremonies muttering to himself and twitching his neck, he looked like a large and horrid Rumpelstiltskin. But he clearly had no intention of stamping his foot and disappearing into the bowels of the earth. This was President de Gaulle's first visit to Asia and he had chosen as a matter of policy to make his first stop in Cambodia. He so charmed and impressed Prince Sihanouk that the latter could not keep still for excitement, constantly wriggling and bobbing his head. And when the General spoke, with a rasp, of "foreign intervention" and an "armed expedition without benefit or justification" in Viet-Nam, he communicated the authority of the father of all prophets and patriarchs.

8. Much of the international Press found most aspects of the scene during the State visit frankly incredible. They gaped at the golden palaces and glittering processional lictors. They gasped when at a giant rally an Ode of Welcome was declaimed in affected French by a representative of the Cambodian masses (Her Royal Highness Princess Norodom Viryane):

> "L'Occident et l'Orient tournent ver lui les yeux,
> Attendant réconfort, sympathie et soutien;
> Il écoute les peuples, il accède a leurs voeux
> Et fait de l'amitié leur authentique lien".

Der Spiegel later wrote that each Head of State had spent all his time saying how marvellous was the other.

9. Yet what the East hyperbolises is no less genuine than what the West understates. There is no question that the great mass of the Cambodian people welcomed Charles de

Gaulle with joy; concurred (in so far as they understood it at all) in his *Weltanschaung*; took comfort from his presence among them; and will cherish the memory of their wise old man from the West for several years to come. It was not without some justification that Monseigneur boasted: *"Vous vous trouvez ici, Mon Général, dans un pays souverain, Francophile—et très gaulliste"*.

I have, &c.

Leslie Fielding

(Chargé d'Affaires)

CONTROLLING CAMBODIA'S FRONTIERS

Mr. Fielding to Mr. Brown

SUMMARY

We have tried, but failed, to secure enlargement of the I.C.C. in Cambodia in order to help keep the Vietcong out (Paragraph 1).

The Cambodians genuinely wanted enlargement but were too slow in putting their case directly to the Communists (Paragraphs 3 and 4).

The Chinese bloc were against the idea (Paragraph 4), the Russians embarrassed but negative (Paragraph 5), the Indians un-embarrassed and lukewarm (Paragraph 6).

Anglo-American efforts were persistent and in close harmony (Paragraphs 7 and 8).

An enlarged I.C.C. could have been effective but was the victim of acute international tensions arising over Viet-Nam (Paragraphs 9 and 10). Meanwhile, we must make the best of what we have left (Paragraph 11).

Confidential   British Embassy
No. 21   Phnom Penh
Sir,   19 September, 1966

During the first eight months of this year, H.M.G. valiantly attempted to secure the enlargement of the International Control Commission in Cambodia (originally set up in 1956 by the Geneva Peace Conference; still very much in place; composed of Indian, Canadian and Polish officials), so that it might exercise more effective surveillance over Cambodia's Indo-Chinese frontiers and thus help deter possible clandestine use of Cambodian territory by the Viet Cong. This attempt dove-tailed with Canadian efforts within the Commission to the same end and with American efforts behind the scenes. It also corresponded with the wishes of the Cambodian Government. But the project, gently smothered by the Indians as Chairmen of the Commission, was finally brutally slain by the Communists. This worthwhile if abortive diplomatic skirmish is not likely to feature high up in the battle honours of the Foreign Office. But I have the honour in this Despatch to count the prisoners and review the casualty list.

2. The Cambodians supported the enlargement of the Commission sincerely. Prince Sihanouk has always liked the Commission. It effectively supervised the withdrawal of the Viet Minh after the Geneva Agreements of 1954 and he still sees it as the physical custodian of the understanding which East and West reached at Geneva to leave Cambodia to herself. He does not want the Viet Cong to make clandestine use of Cambodian territory; but he has not

been in a position to prevent it, given the size of his armed forces, the wildness and inaccessibility of much of the frontier and above all his anxiety not to fall directly foul of those he terms "the future masters of Viet-Nam".

3. Sihanouk's advocacy of a reinforced Commission was characteristically presented in an anti-Western guise to make it more palatable to the Communists. Less wisely, although he was aware that the British Co-Chairman had proposed as early as January to the Soviet Government that the Commission should be expanded, it was not until June that he plucked up the courage to make a direct appeal to the Russians for their assent. Sihanouk had hoped that "The Powers" would somehow fix it up between them, leaving it to Cambodia to take life vows to an enlarged Commission out of devotion to Geneva's holy word and with an apologetic gesture to her Communist boy-friends. This hope proved vain and delay was damaging.

4. The Viet-Namese Communists and the Chinese were opposed to enlargement because they thought it could hamper the Viet Cong fighting machine. For several months, they kept their fingers crossed in the hope that the Soviet Co-Chairman would be able to stall the British and that Sihanouk would eventually lose interest. Finally, however, they were forced into adducing various spurious objections, principally to the effect that an enlarged I.C.C. would be the "agent of American imperialism". This shocked the Cambodians, who had hitherto assumed that they could do what they liked in their own country, provided that they kept within the letter as well as the spirit of the Geneva Agreements.

5. The Soviet Government found themselves in an embarrassing position. They, too, played it as long as they could, attempting to obscure the issue with propaganda. It is just possible that the Russians could have agreed to an enlarged Commission, if other things had been equal; they

have almost as much reason as the West to want to insulate Cambodia from the Viet-Namese war. But Soviet-Khmer relations have still not fully recovered from the row over Sihanouk's state visit in October 1965. For wider reasons also, Moscow cannot fail to put Hanoi well before Phnom Penh when the chips are down.

6. The Indian attitude was passive and in some ways rather pathetic. In recent years, the Indians have supplied nonentities as Chairmen of the International Control Commission in Cambodia. The present incumbent, a wily but low-powered Hindu, pooh-poohed for months the Cambodian Government's various requests to the Commission for more control and (despite Canadian protests) acquiesced in Polish moves to ensure that they never even reached the agenda. Back in New Delhi, the chief hesitations about an enlarged Commission were expressed in financial terms. But there is little doubt that it was basically on political grounds that the Indians declined to play ball. They do not want to cross the Russians; are fed up with their present unrewarding responsibilities in the three Commissions; and see no national advantage in becoming more deeply committed in Indo-China. It is hard to blame them, now that Nehru is dead and the mandate of heaven withdrawn. But Indian conduct of the Control Commission's affairs has been a saddening spectacle of my service in Cambodia.

7. The chief interests involved, apart from Cambodia's, were those of the United States. The discreet American offer to contribute to the expenses of an enlarged Commission was statesmanlike. In making it, they did well not to brand the project too openly with the seal of their support, leaving it to the British Co-Chairman and the Cambodian Government to make the most of the moves.

8. British diplomacy was very persistent. The Prime Minister pressed the Soviet leadership hard and at length

in Moscow; the Secretary of State sent two messages to Mr. Gromyko (one of which is still unanswered); and this Embassy were in constant touch with the Cambodian Government at the highest level. In the event, the exercise was not totally without reward. The proposals to the Russians of January 1966 helped to take some of the diplomatic heat out of the situation which had been engendered by the American announcement of the month before, in itself no doubt militarily justifiable, that "hot pursuit" operations might in certain circumstances have to be launched into Cambodian territory in pursuit of Viet Cong forces. Advocacy of an enlarged Control Commission enhanced our standing with the Cambodian Government and finally prepared the ground for a resumption of more cordial diplomatic relations between London and Phnom Penh. Finally, the Communists were given *un mauvais quart d'heure*, and yet another wedge was driven between them and Prince Sihanouk.

9. This Despatch does not make very cheerful reading and prompts the question whether the Control Commission, even if it had been enlarged, would have effectively secured its objectives. It was clear all along that our plans could be put into full effect only with the agreement or at least acquiescence of Poland and the Soviet Union and only provided India was prepared to show some backbone and positive leadership. It was equally clear that, however numerous and well-equipped the Commission might be, it could never provide watertight coverage of the entire Cambodian frontier, a task which would probably have required several thousands of men. Nevertheless even one mobile team, fully equipped with jeeps and helicopters, and making constant unheralded descents at points along the frontiers, would have served a worth-while purpose.

10. For the future, we have learned one or two grim lessons. The issue in Viet-Nam has assumed such

proportions that it completely overshadows not only Laos but also Cambodia. The Soviet Government are putting into cold storage such as is possible of their Co-Chairman's responsibilities. India is likely to continue to prove a broken reed. China must be expected to decline to make any further financial contribution to the Cambodian Control Commission. The prospect for collective and constructive action to strengthen the neutral status of Cambodia in therefore, at present, pretty bleak.

11. Nevertheless, we must be thankful for small mercies. A Control Commission of sorts although drastically reduced in size since 1956 and now little more than a token force, still remains in being on the ground. At least a notional deterrent, it is a body which could be expanded in more propitious international circumstances. Its continued existence helps keep alive Prince Sihanouk's confidence in the Geneva Agreements. One day, like the phoenix, the I.C.C. in Cambodia may be lifted up from its own ashes.

I have &c.

(Leslie Fielding)

Chargé d'Affaires

CAMBODIA: SOME FAREWELL IMPRESSIONS

Mr. Fielding to Mr. Brown

SUMMARY

Cambodia is Sihanouk, a mercurial but outstanding figure. (Paragraph 2.) He has slowed down a bit but is still on top of his job. (Paragraph 3.)

Cambodian foreign policy is now less anti-Western; the Communists have been beastly to Sihanouk. (Paragraphs 4-5.)

There is domestic discontent, but it is not serious. (Paragraph 6.)

The Cambodians are likeable and their country is a natural buffer-State. (Paragraph 7.) We have been wise to keep a foot in the door. (Paragraph 8.)

A personal retrospect. (Paragraph 9.)

Confidential　　　　　　　　　　British Embassy
No. 23　　　　　　　　　　　　　　Phnom Penh
Sir,　　　　　　　　　　20 September, 1966

When I was invited at less than two weeks' notice to proceed to Phnom Penh in order to assume temporary charge of a sacked Embassy, no one foresaw that circumstances would require me to conduct the Mission for nearly two and a half years. For this reason, I did not trouble your third predecessor with my First Impressions of Cambodia. As some aspects of this country have always remained a mystery to me, the Valedictory Despatch which

I now have the honour to compose must still be considered more of a retinal sensation than a coherent picture.

2. As long as he remains Head of State, the Kingdom of Cambodia is Prince Norodom Sihanouk. He is at once the most attractive and most infuriating of Asian leaders. Attractive, because his profound concern for his people, his dynamism and sheer native wit make him a national leader of international standing. Infuriating, because of his extreme sensitivity to criticism, his resistance to well-meaning advice, the unpredictability of his day-today conduct of affairs and the urchin-like quality which prompts him to hand out mockery and abuse on all sides.

3. Fortunately, the Prince has visibly slowed down over the past two years. The intractable problems with which he is faced, the various reverses with which (perhaps for the first time in his life) he has been confronted, and the growth of criticism at home, all have left him a quieter and (hopefully) a wiser man. Some say he is becoming a burnt-out case. But my astrological faculties assure me that the Mandate of Heaven has not yet been withdrawn from the God-King. Norodom Sihanouk is likely to control the destiny of the Kingdom for as far ahead as we can see; our diplomacy must take the fullest possible account of him. For all his foibles, he is a good thing and there ought to be more like him in these parts.

4. Cambodian foreign policy is now moving tentatively along more Western lines. On my arrival in May 1964, Chinese propaganda was going full-blast, the Communists generally were riding high and the Anglo-Saxons were firmly in the doghouse, hemmed in by rioters and forbidden all social contact with the· Cambodians. Today, China is at least momentarily in eclipse and improved relations with the United States and Thailand are in the air. The Ambassador-designate will shortly set his seal on the normalisation of Anglo-Cambodian relations, in the hope

that it will not be too soon his turn to appear in Monseigneur's rifle sights.

5. Some of this was bound to happen anyway; Cambodia *habitually undulates with serpentine flexibility* across the field of foreign relations. But the Communists have only themselves to blame for the ground they have lost. The Viet-Namese muscled in on Sihanouk's Indo-China Peoples' Conference because they found it too neutralist; the Chinese vetoed his proposed Geneva Conference on Cambodia because they suspected it could lead to negotiations on Viet-Nam; the Russians cancelled his State visit to Moscow at a few days' notice because they found him too pro-Chinese; they all joined hands to sabotage the proposed enlargement of the Cambodian Control Commission because it might hamper the Viet Cong war effort. Sihanouk patched up his quarrel with Moscow, maintained his lines to Hanoi and kept his temper with Peking. But his confidence has been touchingly shaken by what he sees as *Chinese extremism* and intransigence. For Sihanouk today the East is not so much red as just bloody.

6. The domestic scene, outwardly calm, has *seethed beneath the surface*. The political *élite*, educated in or by the West to a man, have been restless at what they have seen as Sihanouk's growing isolation, feeling in their bones that it was surely not necessary to be at odds with everyone all the time. All but the humblest in Phnom Penh have felt the pinch of Sihanouk's rather eccentric economic policies and not least of his rejection of American aid. The top-heavy educational system is now in full swing as sorcerer's apprentice, producing ever more numerous useless graduates to fill the ranks of the disgruntled urban unemployed. Sihanouk's personal prestige has taken a few knocks in the eyes of all but the peasants in the countryside. Yet *there remains at present no individual rallying point for dissent, no common courage or conviction among the critics and no clear sign of a possible move* towards change.

Sihanouk's skill in handling his people gives daily proof that he is still the one man who can control the factions and unite the nation.

7. I have found that nation by and large a likeable lot. There is a strong mixture of Chinese blood, and more than a tincture of Siamese, in the veins of the upper class, whose lively but mixed-up members tend to be a little complex. But the underlying hysteria of the Chinese races is alien to the easy-going, dark-skinned Khmer. They are a more primitive and occluded people than their neighbours and one sometimes has the frustrated impression of dealing with a pack of amiable simians (just as they privately think of us as long-nosed wonders from outer space). But their ethnocentricity, pride and deep Buddhist persuasions are the roots from which Sihanouk's own policies of nationalism and neutrality draw their strength. Their country is a natural buffer-State on the long cultural and political frontier between the Indian and Chinese civilisations, between East and West in South-East Asia.

8. But Phnom Penh shivers to the shock of all kinds of conflicting ideologies and interests. Overshadowed by the Viet-Namese conflict, Cambodia is a field in which it is prudent that a modest British diplomatic effort should be deployed. We were wise not to break off relations after the Embassy was attacked by the mob in March 1964, and it has been worth it to have slogged on through the mud and blood towards at least the illusion of green fields beyond. There is no inherent hostility towards the West and certainly none to the British in this country. Sihanouk's tantrums are of a feminine nature; they can be soothed with manliness and a well-timed box of chocolates. It is perhaps less awkward for London than for Peking that Monseigneur should be a capricious mistress who will not be bought for money nor ever be taken the slightest bit for granted.

9. In retrospect, and on the human plane, the fare has been rich. Loyal allies (not least the Australians) and a small but enthusiastic staff; international intrigue; an exotic court complete with a ballerina princess in the limelight and the odd narrow-eyed Rasputin in the gilded shadows; the varying beauties of tropical nature, from the dark tiger-jungle to the white-sanded sea; the brooding solemnity of the Angkor temples and the fun-loving company of their modern Deva-Raja, Norodom Sihanouk. These have left me with no dull moments and few sad ones; I shall be sorry to step back through the looking glass into normality. It is all worth several books, but the Official Secrets Act and the chastity of diplomatic intercourse would prevent their publication. There remains a handful of grey despatches printed in the Indo-China volume. To be circulated to officialdom around 1972, this *magnum opus* will eventually be released to an eager public on what I calculate may be my 80th birthday. I hope that I shall still then in some sense enjoy the honour of being, as today, your obedient servant.

I have, &c.

Leslie Fielding

(Chargé d'Affaires)

<u>Letter to the FCO from Michael Palliser, Private Secretary to Mr. Harold Wilson, 18 October, 1966</u>

The Prime Minister has seen in print Leslie Fielding's farewell despatch from Cambodia (Phnom Penh Despatch No. 23 of September 2) and has commented:-

"First class—it tells me more than a hundred telegrams. Where is this chap going now?"

I thought you would like to know of this comment; and perhaps you would give me a ring about Fielding's next appointment.

<u>Reply from the FO, 21 October, 1966</u>

Many thanks for your letter of 18 October passing on the Prime Minister's comment on Leslie Fielding's farewell despatch from Phnom Penh.

Fielding is being posted to Paris as one of the two First Secretaries in Chancery. As you know, this a job on the way to stardom.

5. DESPATCHES FROM PARIS

LA FRANCOPHONIE

Sir Patrick Reilly to Mr. Stewart

SUMMARY

In recent years, various suggestions have been made for the closer association of French-speaking peoples. The collective name applied to these ideas is *La Francophonie*. Although initially a purely cultural concept, Francophonie is now also spoken of in economic and political terms. We are likely to hear more of it in future (Paragraphs 1-3).

The concept has a certain appeal in France. Partly this is because of "culture shock" in the early post-war years. Frenchmen, deeply convinced of the superiority of their language and culture, found that the world had suddenly become English-speaking (Paragraphs 4 and 5). Great efforts were therefore required, under the impulse of the intense nationalism of General de Gaulle himself, to regain some of the lost ground (Paragraphs 6 and 7).

Although various francophone associations have been set up in France with some degree of official encouragement, the French Government's attitude to Francophonie has been outwardly reserved. The French are sensitive to the charge of neo-colonialism; they know the Africans (even those who openly support Francophonie) are not all of one mind; they are not sure what the ultimate membership and potential of Francophonie might be (Paragraphs 7-10).

Nevertheless, General de Gaulle probably sees Francophonie as potentially a useful field of influence for France (Paragraph 11).

The real international danger is that de Gaulle may try to make use of Francophonie to stir up trouble among French-speaking minorities in Europe. He will not advocate the territorial expansion of France: but might conceivably one day encourage separatism in Belgium, Italy or Switzerland in order to discipline his neighbours and maintain the dominance of France in Europe (Paragraphs 12 and 15).

What view should we take of Francophonie? There is much in it that is positive and worthy of admiration. But the fomenting of political discontent among minorities by France would evidently be against our interests and those of a united Europe (Paragraphs 14 and 15).

Fortunately, General de Gaulle seems likely at present to remain cautious in Europe and there are other goals which appeal to him more urgently. After his departure, Francophonie is likely, if it survives him, to assume a form we can live with (Paragraphs 16 and 17).

Confidential   British Embassy
No. 2/12/6   Paris
Sir   4 April, 1968

During the past two or three years, a word recently coined in the French language has been receiving wider and wider circulation. Its basic significance is cultural. But, while General de Gaulle remains President of France, the word is likely to acquire increasingly a political connotation; indeed, in the sense that the pen is mightier than the sword, it could be converted into a weapon of attack against the Anglo-Saxon world. In this despatch, I have the honour to discuss *la Francophonie.*

2. The word itself means literally "French-speakingness" and perhaps metaphorically "the French-speaking world". The coining was probably the work, over ten years ago, of the scholarly and deeply Francophile President of Senegal, M. Léopold Sédar Senghor, who has defined Francophonie variously as "humanism", as "a spiritual community" and as "the corner stone of universal civilisation". Other Africans have carried the idea further, envisaging Francophonie as an institution with economic as well as cultural content. The torch is at present being carried round. Africa by President Hamani Diori of the Niger Republic, who has been entrusted by the Heads of State of the *"Organisation Commune Africaine et Malgache"* (OCAM) to take soundings and prepare recommendations of a concrete nature. Some Frenchmen now see Francophonie as developing political identity as a Commonwealth *à la française.* Interest in Francophonie has also been aroused in French Canada and it may come in the course of time to exert a magnetic attraction over French minorities elsewhere.

3. The French Government for their part have hitherto maintained in public an attitude of some reserve towards Francophonie. Yet it is not unpalatable to the French authorities to hear francophone Africans like Senghor and Bourguiba, both men of some distinction, acclaim throughout the world the value of French civilisation, and to see French-Canadians such as Premier Johnson of Quebec turn again for comfort to France. We at this post are therefore likely to hear much more of Francophonie in the future. Great interest now attaches to whether General de Gaulle will decide to give shape to the amorphous.

4. What lies close to the root of this appetite in France is the political, economic and even cultural inferiority

complex with which the French nation emerged from the Second World War, defeated, divided and technically backward. It came fully home to the French that their language was no longer the chosen vehicle of expression of the international *élite*; the world had suddenly become English-speaking and French was steeply at a discount. While France quarrelled with her colonies, there sprang from the British Empire a series of independent, populous and faithfully Anglophone nations to assert their station in international life. Much more important, the United States of America, no longer in isolation but omnipresent in the world and very nearly omnipotent, brought the English language into many spheres which were not formerly British and fashioned that language into the key to modern science and technology. The shock within France was profound; the culturally articulate felt almost that they were being smothered.

5. There remained among many Frenchmen, however, the deep conviction that French culture was of universal significance and the French language technically an instrument of communication superior to other tongues. Deep in the French subconscious, the assumption was still to be found that France was in this sense special; that she stood in the succession to the Roman world; that she was endowed with a "civilising mission" and her culture was destined to "radiate" across the globe. According to this creed, France was a kind of "Middle Kingdom", like ancient China, which was entitled to special admiration and respect among the nations.

6. As France found a new international footing and came to acquire, under the Fifth Republic, both political stability and a growing measure of prosperity, the campaign for the defence and advancement of all things French gained momentum. Many thousands of teachers were sent abroad to help to maintain, within the zone of former colonial influence, the habit of speaking French. Efforts (so far not

very successful) were made to expunge from the language hundreds of neologisms, often pretty barbarous, of more or less Anglo-Saxon origin (*le franglais*). At the United Nations, supported by a clientele of francophone mini-states and a miscellaneous array of non-anglophones, France asserted with increasing effectiveness the equality of French with English; while within the European Economic Community she took care to ensure that French became the *de facto* working language. The chief driving force in all this was the intense nationalism of General de Gaulle himself.

7. Against this background, the idea of a world organisation based on the French language has proved in recent years an attractive theme of debate for certain intellectuals in France, as well as for Gaullist romantics. In more concrete terms, a politician like the former junior Minister at the *Quai d'Orsay*, Prince Jean de Broglie, foresees Francophonie as something "half way between UNESCO and the Arab League" which must be "political or nothing". As steps towards the ultimate realisation of Francophonie, associations have been formed of French-speaking universities, parliamentarians, lawyers and so forth, and committees set up for "francophone solidarity". With official or semi-official support, international conferences and seminars now take place regularly in Paris, assembling for various purposes French-speakers from as far apart as Haiti, Mauritius and Polynesia, Cambodia and Quebec.

8. Despite the evident visceral appeal of Francophonie to many Frenchmen, however, the French Government's present attitude of apparent reserve towards the creation of semi-institutional links with other francophone countries, and their refusal hitherto to take any leading part in proceedings, is soundly conceived in the interests of France. There have been signs of a more activist, if still pragmatic, approach to these matters since the General's visit to Canada: but it would undo the achievements of recent years if the French Government were to open

themselves to the accusation of seeking to institutionalise neo-colonialism. To rush things would moreover risk damage to the harmonious relations which France at present enjoys with almost all the French-speaking countries of the African continent.

9. Perhaps no-one in France is more sensitive than M. Couve de Murville (consistently a moderating influence in this matter within the French Government) to the divided approach of African Governments to Francophonie. Algeria considers the Evian Agreements to be her title to an especially close relationship with France that must not be demeaned by equation with that between France and the negro states. Algeria, with Mauritania, also has strong pan-Arab sympathies which extend beyond the bounds of the French-speaking world. Morocco prefers to regard herself as Arabophone rather than francophone; and would also want to think twice before being associated with her Algerian and Mauritanian rivals in a wider organisation. South of the Sahara, Guinea is inevitably shrill in criticism of Francophonie, if only because of the strained relationship between President Sekou Touré and General de Gaulle; but there is also reticence in Cameroon, where relations with France are good. Motives elsewhere tend to be mixed. There is a genuine wide-spread belief in the merits of French culture and the advantages of cooperation with France; but we are told that some of the weaker Heads of State advocate Francophonie because they think it flatters France and helps keep themselves safe and prosperous in their Presidential palaces. Others see it as a means of obtaining a greater say in how French aid to Africa should be apportioned among themselves. Yet others favour Francophonie as a kind of insurance policy against a "Cartierist" reaction in France following General de Gaulle's eventual departure, which might result in a loss of interest in and a reduction of economic aid to the former French African colonies.

10. Another reason for the caution of the French Government is no doubt a preference to wait and see whether it will be possible for Francophonie to acquire members outside Africa, for instance (very important) French Canada and (less important) Indo-China. In Europe too, there may be francophone gains to be consolidated at a time when the Belgians are asking themselves whether it is not conceivable that Wallonia might in due course become part of France. But for the present the French must still find it difficult to guess the potential of Francophonie.

11. If what General de Gaulle will be able to achieve with Francophonie cannot be predicted, it is nevertheless not difficult to guess what he would like to make of it. Francophonie would help give France back her "rank". It would constitute a further sphere of special influence for France in world affairs and would afford additional means for disruption of the activities and influence of rival powers. Despite French membership of the European Economic Community and despite the frequency with which the supposed interests of a united Europe are invoked in the justification of official French policies, there is more than a superficial resemblance between the political thought of General de Gaulle and that of past statesmen whose "European" credentials he has been the first to challenge. There is in Francophonie something of the "fraternal association of the English speaking peoples" of which Sir Winston Churchill was the advocate; something also of the concept of concentric spheres of influence entertained by Mr. Harold Macmillan. Seen from the Elysée, there would thus be France in the Economic Community in Western Europe, France in a special and separate relationship with the Soviet Union and the East European countries in the promotion of East/West understanding and cooperation; France as a Great Power at the United Nations, a permanent member of the United Nations Security Council; France linked by authority, aid and understanding to present and former overseas

territories round the world; and, finally, France as the head of a no doubt loosely-knit but clearly defined community of French-speaking nations and of the French-speaking minorities in all parts of the globe which seek her protection and leadership.

12. The real international danger in this admittedly somewhat Utopian Gaullist vision undoubtedly resides in the relationship which France under General de Gaulle might offer to French-speaking minorities. The damage which de Gaulle's policy has inflicted upon the federal structure and sense of national identity in Canada is notorious. Other minorities as yet unexploited lie within much easier reach—the Walloons of Belgium and the French-speaking pockets across the frontiers in Switzerland, Luxembourg and Italy. Open advocacy of some kind of "Greater France" of which the metropolitan frontiers should be extended towards the limits attained under the Napoleonic Empire, is extremely unlikely. The General is not thinking in such terms. So blatant a nationalist and expansionist design, against the trends and instincts of modern Europe, could in any case rebound to destroy its author. But some encouragement to separatism, if not the direct offer of incorporation into France, could still conceivably one day be proffered by the French President.

13. General de Gaulle probably cares little at heart for the *Québecois*; indeed, for most of his life he ignored and despised them. When he took up the issue of Free Quebec, it was chiefly to aim a blow, upon the American continent itself, against what he sees as American global hegemony. Similarly, his life-long contempt for *les petits belges* would not prevent him, at the right moment and for some wider purpose, from effecting a sortie into their internal affairs. If it should seem desirable to bring a new weapon into his armoury in order to maintain the dominance of France over her partners within the Common Market, the General

might well find the Aostans and Walloons a convenient means to hand; to subvert them successfully might enable him to discipline and discomfort the Italians and break up the Benelux bloc. As regards Wallonia in particular, the man who, at the conclusion of the Second World War, advocated the permanent annexation of the Saar and dreamed of the division of a defeated Germany into the collection of small principalities which had existed before Bismark, has not forgotten that Flanders was once French. Only the other day, in an address to the *Ecole de Guerre* centering on the "All-Azimuths" defence policy, he reminded his audience that France had been accustomed to fortify all her frontiers, "even Belgium".

14. In formulating our own attitude towards Francophonie, it is necessary to draw several clear distinctions. We cannot object to, and must indeed learn from and even admire, the truly prodigious efforts deployed by the French to protect and extend their own language and culture. French is the first foreign language of the British Isles, where there are more teachers of that language in secondary schools than there are, for example, in Germany; the cultural heritage and contemporary inspirations of France are therefore to that extent our own also. Nor, I submit, can we decently oppose, although our commercial interests might conceivably sometimes suffer, the creation of a loosely-linked international community of French-speaking countries. France, we must hope, will in the future be more with us than against us. The overseas mission of France is beneficial to the countries which are her "clients" and could prove an important constituent element in the policies of an outward-looking Europe of which we hope that, before long, Great Britain will also form a part.

15. Where we should be obliged to part company with France would be over the fomenting of political discontent among linguistic minorities in allied countries. This would

particularly apply to any French attempt to redraw the national frontiers of Europe. Canada will naturally want to solve her own problems in her own way and in any case would be supported in the hour of need by the colossal strength and influence of the United States. In Europe, a countervailing force to Francophonie exists in the European ideal itself; and there is also a latent hostility to the idea among France's neighbours which will have to be taken into account. It would be premature to consider what steps we should take if France were to set out deliberately to encourage the dismemberment of Belgium. But what is clear is that the deeper our commitment to participate in a European political community, the less will be the danger of the situation getting out of hand.

16. Is General de Gaulle likely to launch into a francophone adventure? As far as Europe is concerned, I would expect him to remain cautious as long as he has hopes of winning his neighbours over to his idea of "Europe from the Atlantic to the Urals". The storms provoked by his actions in Canada and by his policies towards the Middle East have moreover subsided in some measure because of the geographical remoteness of the areas concerned and of the indifference of much of the electorate to issues of foreign policy as such; whereas action in Belgium would be on everyone's door step and could break up a Common Market which is the basis for much of the recent prosperity of France. I would, however, expect General de Gaulle to continue actively to encourage Quebec to work with France in the wider field of Francophonie. The creation also of loose inter-Governmental institutions for Francophonie cannot be excluded if African opinion consolidates in its favour. The harnessing of francophones everywhere to the support of French interests is now established policy in Paris. I do not believe that in the immediate future the movement in Europe is likely to acquire more of a political character than that.

17. To conclude, much may turn on how long the General remains in office and what risks he chooses to run. I think, however, there are goals which appeal to him more urgently than does Francophonie. If it continues to develop and flourish after his departure, it is likely to be in a cultural form which we can live with rather than as a political hegemony which we would have to fight.

I have &c,

(D.P. Reilly)

(Ambassador)

GENERAL DE GAULLE'S FOREIGN POLICY

Mr. Soames to Mr. Stewart

SUMMARY

The despatch is an attempt to give an assessment of General de Gaulle's achievements, in the field of foreign policy 1958-69. (Paragraphs 1 and 2.)
The General's principal aim was to assert the power and influence of France and to promote French greatness as he saw it. (Paragraph 3.)

The chief means by which the General tried to achieve his purpose was by attempting to weaken the two super Powers. (Paragraph 4.)

This consideration lay behind much of his policy towards the Third World. But another factor was the consequential material benefits likely to be derived by France at the expense of others, (Paragraph 5.)

None of the General's policies was very successful except to a limited degree and mostly in a negative sense. This is true of his policies over Latin America, China, the U.N., Viet-Nam, NATO and international questions. "Francophonie" and the pro-Arab policy promised better but may not be easy to sustain. Above all his European policy failed to gain acceptance by other governments. (Paragraph 6.)

The General's view of the "English question". He thought that for the time being we must be kept out of Europe and if possible persuaded to go away for a while. (Paragraph 7.)

Europe was de Gaulle's main failure. He could not get his own vision accepted. All that he achieved was to inflict grave and perhaps lasting damage to post-war ideals of European unity. This sombre achievement may be the main legacy of his foreign policy. (Paragraph 8.)

The evolution of the General's policy after the May events of 1968. Apart from the improvement in Franco-American relations, change had not gone very far by the time the General left the Elysée. (Paragraph 9.)

The reason why the General's policies failed, apart from the negative achievement over Europe, was that he had an exaggerated idea of the strength of France. The main practical effect of his policies was to alienate France's friends and to put an excessive strain on her domestic economy. (Paragraph 10.)

The General's influence will persist to some extent both in France and in the world, especially his achievement in raising French self-respect and in spreading her influence abroad. But it is sad that the vision of this great man was so narrowly nationalistic and did not enable him to lay the foundations of a united Europe. (Paragraph 11.)

Confidential   British Embassy
No. 3/1   Paris
Sir,   10 July, 1969

Thousands of words have already been written about General de Gaulle's foreign policy—by himself in his memoirs, by several of my predecessors in this Embassy and by other very well qualified people. If I now add to all this, it is simply because, so it seems to me, a backward glance soon after the General's departure may succeed in giving a true, if fleeting, impression which deeper study might blur.

2. General do Gaulle spent eleven years at the Elysée, not as long as some previous rulers of France such as Louis XIV, or Napoleon I or III but long enough to make his mark. Even if we take away the first three or four years, when French foreign policy was still heavily mortgaged by the Algerian war, seven or eight years remained in which the General had the opportunity to play the "world game". Yet, in retrospect, in spite of the inimitable style and vigour of his various policies, it is hard to identify any positive achievement in the field of foreign policy except for the Algerian settlement itself. And this, after all, appallingly difficult though it was, amounted to a brilliantly executed, if expensive, political withdrawal, rather than to the creation of a genuinely new relationship between France and Algeria.

3. What was the General trying to achieve in his foreign policy? He was primarily trying to assert the power and influence of France, wherever and whenever opportunity offered, as a desirable end in itself to be pursued ruthlessly and single-mindedly. At different times he adopted different policies in order to fulfil this basic purpose and from time to time policies were given up, or modified, or

left on one side. But the fundamental purpose remained the same. This emerged clearly in the General's writings and was illustrated in countless sayings recorded by M. Tournoux and by French and foreign statesmen who conversed with him over the years. Indeed, a striking feature of these writings and records is that, although many of his specific policies have changed over this period, the basic concepts of General de Gaulle's political outlook and often, too, the language in which these were expounded remained virtually unaltered for some thirty years. As the General himself put it in the first sentence of his Memoirs, he has "a certain idea of France". The promotion of French greatness was undoubtedly his principal aim and his idea of the nature of this greatness informed all his actions in the international field.

4. The chief means which the General chose to promote this end of French greatness was his attempt to create a French-led Europe which would act as a third force between the two super Powers which must therefore themselves be weakened. It was in an effort to bring about this weakening that the General followed policies which were designed to harm either the United States or the Soviet Union, or both. This was an important element in all his major policies, for example his move to recognise China in 1964, his withdrawal from the integrated NATO structures in 1966, his attack on the dollar and his dramatic championship of Quebec separatism in 1967, and his encouragement of liberal and patriotic sentiments in Eastern Europe in 1968. Although the General often had other objectives in mind, he never lost sight of the fundamental importance of weakening the two giants so that the weight of France might become more significant. That his policy seemed sometimes more anti-American than anti- Russian was due to his view that the United States was by far the stronger and the more influential in France of the two super Powers, and therefore the more to be weakened.

162

5. In his policy towards the Third World, the General often gave the impression of tactical opportunism by his habit of attempting to spot a winner and then put money on it. Thus, on Viet-Nam he came to the conclusion at least as early as July 1965 that the Americans would not succeed in winning the war; French influence, such as it was, was then directed towards making this view come true. In the case of his pro-Arab policy, too, the General seems to have thought in mid-1967 that Israel bad overreached herself and that it was time to transfer French backing to the side that would most probably come out on top in the long run. But these were not mere tactical ploys: the General's steady and considered policy was of advocating the greatest possible independence in the Third World, in most cases thus weakening the domination or influence of one or other of the Great Powers and, in any case, winning some local popularity and gaining cultural influence and trade for France.

6. In sum, it cannot be said that any of the General's policies were very successful except in the negative sense, and even then only to a limited degree. Thus he succeeded, it is true, in irritating and hampering American interests at various times in respect of Latin America, China, the United Nations, Viet-Nam, NATO, and international monetary questions; but in none of these questions did he wholly succeed in blocking the policies which he had set out to oppose. Nor did he fare much better in his attempts to weaken the other giant. His eloquence in Poland and Rumania cannot have been more than a mildly tiresome element from the Russian point of view. As for the rest of the world, most of it has been offered the General's friendship on his own terms at one time or another but all seem to have disappointed him. China failed to understand him or take him seriously. Prestige successes in Latin America and Africa and the launching of "francophonie" throughout the world could not be fully exploited to the

benefit of France without devoting much greater resources to the task than could be afforded. The pro-Arab policy certainly promised good dividends, but it was a delicate affair and would have been difficult even for the General to sustain for a very long period. Most important and distressing of all, the General's concept of Europe failed altogether to make an appeal to the other Europeans. Although he was able to block progress in Europe on lines unacceptable to him, the General had not succeeded at the time of his departure in getting his own policies accepted even by the Germans whom he so much despised. Indeed, in spite of the reassuring Francophilia of Dr. Kiesinger and Herr Brandt, the Germans had lately shown disturbing signs of their old clumsy arrogance, thus causing the General to look once more at the possibility of turning to Britain. But in February 1969, the British, too, failed to respond to his advance in an acceptable way.

7. What was, in fact, the General's view of the English question, as he used to call it? This is not the place to analyse his attitude in detail, but the short truth about it is that we did not, at least for the time being, fit into his scheme of things. He refused to believe that we had changed in any significant or decisive way since 1945. We remained for him a maritime power endowed with admirably stable institutions, an island separated from the Europe of the mainland which must be created under French leadership. He probably envisaged us joining the European Economic Community one day, if it still existed, but only when we had become weaker and France stronger, so that we had to fit into a plan made in Paris. In the meantime it was clear to the General, at least until quite recently, that we must be kept out and if possible persuaded to go away for a while.

8. In terms of his own vision, Europe was de Gaulle's failure. He and his representatives succeeded remarkably well in promoting and sustaining French national interests

in the E.E.C. and in preventing any development, such as Britain's entry, which might have hampered France. French successes in the practical operation of the E.E.C. were substantial and many of them may well last. But the General made no real progress with the construction of the Europe of his own vision. Even without the disturbing factor of our repeated requests for admission, it would no doubt have been extremely difficult to construct a French-led Europe on the Gaullist pattern, since it conflicted with strong tendencies within each of the European countries, including France itself. Furthermore, it depended for success on keeping the Germans down. It was undoubtedly the resurgence of Western Germany, in spite of the continued Russian occupation of Prussia, that latterly caused the General to look again at the possibility of letting us into Europe somewhat earlier than he had hitherto envisaged. It is not clear how his policies in this field would have evolved if he had remained in power, but by the time he left the Elysée virtually no positive progress had been made. On the other hand, he had managed to exert a disconcertingly destructive and negative influence in European affairs. It must be said that his exaggerated and outmoded concepts of nationalism led him to inflict grave and perhaps lasting damage to the post-war ideals of European unity. Indeed, this sombre achievement is probably the main legacy of the General's foreign policy.

9. During the last year of his presidency, the General was clearly reassessing French interests in the world as a whole, for the position of France had been much weakened by the upheavals (the '*événements*') of May and June 1968. It was not long after this that he started to modify some of his anti-American policies, notably in monetary matters, and to work for the rapprochement with the United States which has now become a fact under President Nixon. As for the other Super Power, he recognised after the invasion of Czechoslovakia that since political evolution in the Soviet Union had evidently not gone as far as he had earlier

hoped, the time for dismantling Western defences or damaging the Atlantic Alliance was not ripe. He let it be known that there would be no question of France leaving the Alliance in 1969, as had been widely feared. However, he still kept his reserves about cooperation within the Alliance and continued to pursue his own dialogue with the Russians, purporting to act in this respect as the leader of Europe. Here again, in his relationships with the Super Powers, it is not clear how the General's policy would have evolved and what the practical consequences for the international situation would have been.

10. If we now look back on General de Gaulle's foreign policies, and making allowance for the fact that they were unfinished, it is hard to discern any positive or lasting success, apart, unfortunately, from his wholly negative achievements in Europe referred to above. The fact is that from 1962 onwards his antique vision of national grandeur and his personal arrogance led him to draw exaggerated conclusions about the strength and destiny of France. He cast her for the role of a great power in her own right, a role which most Frenchmen do not now desire or believe to be feasible. In pursuit of this chimera, he adopted Cardinal Richelieu's principle of trying to make temporary rather than lasting friends and of changing them from time to time ("*le zigzag de Richelieu*", as André Malraux described it the other day at a Gaullist electoral meeting) with the general aim of weakening in the long run any State significantly more powerful than France while building up the strength of France herself. But his France, unlike Richelieu's, had not the power to exercise a decisive influence on the march of events. The two giants saw through his artifices and, although a little shaken by them, survived in control of their respective alliances. The main practical effect of the General's efforts was to alienate to a considerable extent France's existing friends without making her new ones; and to impose excessive strains on the domestic economy by putting gold reserves before

growth and sorely-needed modernisation in the pursuit of his designs abroad. Moreover, he displayed increasing contempt for the average Frenchman as that practical individual showed increasing signs of growing tired of the pursuit of unrealistic grandeur. This was widely observed and resented in France. Thus the way was prepared for his fall. The salient events of 1968 in the French calendar: the May crisis, the Soviet occupation of Czechoslovakia and the devaluation crisis of November all drove home the hard lesson of the weakness and limited influence of France even after ten years of the General's rule.

11. It is already clear that the General's effort to make a great and independent power of France has failed, and that no possible successor will pursue it with the same zeal. That aspect of his mission must be set down as a romantic but unrealistic effort to turn back the clock of history. But it is unlikely that France will simply resume her place in the Atlantic Alliance like a returned truant. She will probably continue to pursue a rather independent course though remaining essentially with the Western side. To that extent, the General's influence will, I believe, persist. Then, too, in spite of stubbornness and perversity, General de Gaulle must surely be judged to have left his mark on France and on the world by his achievement in raising the self-respect of his countrymen and of French representatives throughout the world. He thus furthered the traditional French task of spreading their language and culture abroad. A good deal of this achievement will, I think, remain even if for the time being the French are tired of grandeur. Yet what a pity it is that this great man could not have been endowed with a less narrowly nationalistic vision so that he might have laid the foundations of a united Europe.

I have &c,

Christopher Soames

M. POMPIDOU'S FOREIGN POLICY

Mr. Soames to Mr. Stewart

SUMMARY

M. Pompidou has made foreign policy his private domain. (Paragraph 1.)

The style of this foreign policy is the index of the man. M. Pompidou has an intensely conservative and franco-centric view of the world; but is shrewd, courageous and pragmatic. (Paragraph 2.)
In taking stock of a field which is relatively new to him, M. Pompidou has had to face up to the limitations and failures which beset French power. (Paragraphs 3 and 4.)

He has decided to maintain a mixture of continuity and change, and realistically to concentrate French efforts nearer home (Paragraph 5). Priority goes to Western Europe; and he is prepared, under certain conditions, to see Britain join the Communities. (Paragraph 6.) Relations with the United States are to be improved but France will continue to be active in East/West relations. (Paragraph 7.)

Outside Europe, M. Pompidou will proceed pragmatically, extending French influence where it is already implanted. His policy recalls the Churchillian concept of concentric circles, The new Mediterranean policy illustrates what he is about. (Paragraphs 8-10.)

M. Pompidou is learning the ropes and much of his thinking is still fairly fluid. His attitude to the United Kingdom is rudimentary. (Paragraph 11.) But he is moving in a realistic direction to modernise France. He realises that his best chance of achieving this lies in constructive partnership with others. Therein lies some hope for both our countries. (Paragraph 12.)

Confidential   British Embassy

No. 2/1   Paris

Sir,   2 March, 1970

Since becoming President, M. Pompidou lies made foreign policy his private domain. His predecessor did likewise and indeed drafted the Constitution of the Fifth Republic so as to enable him to do so. The President is, however, still learning the ropes, still feeling his way cautiously forward in a field where he has few deeply seated convictions and no desire too violent and too widespread a break with the Gaullist past. But M. Pompidou sees himself as a strong President; whichever of his ministerial subordinates may conduct this or that aspect of French foreign policy, it is he who dominates and directs. The heart of this policy remains *une certaine idée* de la France, but with this difference—a realistic view is now held of the ends within the reach of France and a pragmatic choice is made of the means to serve these ends.

2. The style of this foreign policy is the index of the man. M. Pompidou was born South of the Loire, the grandson of a peasant and the son of a poor country schoolmaster. During the early part of his life he was sufficiently adventurous to have made his way to Paris; but only when he became Prime Minister did he begin to travel at all widely abroad. A brilliant student of letters who carried off all the prizes at the University, he nevertheless knows little German and no English and he habitually speaks no language but French. This background imposes certain handicaps upon the style of the President: inexperience of foreign affairs, a certain lack of vision and above all an

intensely conservative and Francocentric view of the outside world. But M. Pompidou brings to diplomacy his own high intelligence and courage and also the inbred shrewdness and even ruthlessness of the Auvergnat countryman. Two acute French commentators, André Fontaine of *Le Monde*, and Roger Massip of *Le Figaro*, have attributed to him "a peasant preference for patient negotiation rather than theatrical demonstrations"; and described him as a "statesman steeped in pragmatism preferring the more solid methods of dialogue and man-to-man encounter to strokes of audacity and defiance". But the best comment came recently from the lips of the President himself; in answer to a journalist who contrasted his foreign policy with what had gone before, M. Pompidou replied that he did not know whether his polity was more realistic but that it certainly corresponded better to his own temperament. (In fact, it is notably more realistic.)

3. In the early months of his Presidency, M. Pompidou called for the files and took stock of French foreign policy. He came fresh to the task, having been out of Government office for nearly a year and, during the preceding six years of his Prime Ministership, having been allowed but rarely to concern himself directly with diplomacy. He found that, whatever General de Gaulle might have been able to get away with in the Sixties, the Seventies were a different matter, presenting certain hard facts of life of which he, Pompidou, would be compelled to take full account.

4. Essentially, these were limitations on the power of his country abroad. There was first the underlying economic and social weakness of France of which the near-revolution of 1968 and the devaluation of the franc in 1969 had been outward and visible signs. Second, there was the rise in the star of Germany, apparent not only in her massive industrial strength (in itself already sufficiently alarming) but also in her growing political authority and sense of initiative. Then there were East/West relations. A dialogue

had been opened directly between the two super-powers without the benefit of the aid or advice of France and indeed entirely over her head. Despite the concessions she had made to the Kremlin, France had not succeeded in developing a genuinely influential relationship with the Soviet Union; and the invasion of Czechoslovakia had made clear the limits within which the countries of Eastern Europe would be permitted to evolve independently of Soviet Union. The definition of a new—and to the French in some ways a disquieting—*Ostpolitik* by Herr Brandt had moreover even further reduced the opportunity for France to play the role of honest broker for Europe. Within Western Europe there was the perpetual harassment inflicted by the British campaign to enter the Common Market. There was also the question of defence: the maintenance of an independent purely national nuclear and conventional defence system, politically highly desirable though it was, was imposing a growing burden on the French budget. Consequently, there was no conceivable chance of achieving the Generals dream of "all-round defence", of a France ready to take on all comers; nor was there much sense in so placing France that she could not benefit to some degree from defence cooperation with the countries best placed to afford it—notably the United States of America, but perhaps also one day Britain. Finally, beyond the confines of Europe, there were more failures and follies to be decently interred than there were triumphs to be upheld. The French position in the Middle East and ex-French Africa was good; but French policy towards Nigeria was in a mess, the Quebec episode was dangerously absurd, the French role over Viet-Nam had largely disappeared with the opening of the peace talks, while jejune Gaullist efforts to open a fruitful dialogue with Peking and assert an active presence in Latin America had best be passed over in silence.

5. Given the style of the man and the limitations with which he is faced, what is the content of M. Pompidou's

diplomacy? Seen in terms of Gaullist doctrine, it is a blend of continuity and change. The continuity has been observed partly for domestic political reasons and partly from conviction—not for nothing was he for ten years one of General de Gaulle's closest associates. As to change, M. Pompidou admits to two things—that today's circumstances are different and that "I am not a General de Gaulle". In practice, while M. Pompidou stubbornly believes in the universal validity of French culture and values, and while he still wishes to assert the rank and presence of France world-wide, he realizes that he can approach this task only step by step and he has said that he intends to begin in the areas geographically close to home or where French influence is traditional. The field of concentration is traced out liberally to include not only East and West Europe and relations with the two Super Powers, but also the Mediterranean, the Middle East and ex-French West Africa. In essence, Europe is the area considered vital to French national security and the surrounding region is where in the President's view France can realistically hope to win friends and influence people.

6. The point of departure is Western Europe. M. Pompidou is no fervent European, but he sees the Common Market as here to stay and he intends to give priority to making it work. He understands in this respect, what the General tended or tried to forget, that a nation's power and influence rest largely on the strength of its economic base. He is also prepared to see Britain join this Europe, provided that there is no trespass on vital French interests. In 1963, even after General de Gaulle's veto, and again in the course of the Presidential campaign in 1969, he said that we belonged there for historical and geographical reasons. He now realises that the Common Market's development, upon which he depends for both political and economic reasons, will continue to be frustrated so long as the question of the British candidature remains unresolved one way or the other. He is even today still not fully convinced that we

really want to join the Communities; or, alternatively, that our aim in seeking to do so is not fundamentally to change them. But he thinks that Britain could help balance Germany (a problem which is increasingly preoccupying both M. Pompidou and his Ministers). He suspects that our view of the future development of a political Europe is likely to be closer to that of the French than to that of the Five. He probably hopes also that, in the long term, there could be some beneficial Anglo/French understanding on defence, as well as in technological and other fields.

7. Everything else follows logically from the postulate of a Western European Community in which a dynamic position at the centre is to be assured for France. Relations must be improved with the United States because there are or can be solid bilateral advantages for France and because the needlessly bad relationship of former days had harmful side effects on France's relations with her European neighbours. M. Pompidou has made it clear that, while does not think an East-West conflict in the least likely, he still wants the Americans to maintain a significant presence on the European mainland. France remains as opposed as ever to the division of Europe into "blocs". The fact that Europe is still dependent on the protection and solidarity of the United States, and that the Americans recognise this, both requires that France should remain a member of the North Atlantic Alliance, and affords her the luxury, for the present at least, of not being integrated in the NATO command structure. In East/West relations, despite M. Pompidou's own deep-seated personal distrust of the Soviet leadership, the French Government must continue to be active. The President recognises that Europe extends east of the Elbe as well as west of the Channel. He knows that to be on the right side of the Russians helps him to make life that much more difficult for the Communist Party in France. And, in any case, France can do with some cash—the trade relationship with Eastern Europe, if heavy on credit, is considered to be potentially lucrative. She also

requires as much authority as she can continue to muster in a field in which, despite setbacks and disappointments, she has in the last made some impact. It would in French eyes be dangerous as well as undignified to play second fiddle to Germany, whatever words of encouragement M. Pompidou may find for Herr Brandt. Nor need the French Government accept such a subordinate role, given the skill of their diplomacy and their proven ability to play from weakness as well as from strength. And, so long as the European Community remains politically undeveloped, Russia too, like England, has her part to play in balancing Germany's new-found power.

8. Outside Europe, M. Pompidou will endeavour to assert a French presence for its own sake and for the profit which it will bring, but will do so selectively, step by step and with regard to the means available. In practice, he will seek to strengthen the influence and extend the interests of France where they are already implanted. This applies notably to ex-French West Africa and the French-speaking world generally. The bulk of French overseas aid—given in the past on a proportionately more generous scale than our own—will continue in the future to be directed to those areas. Attention will also be given to the United Nations, towards which there has been a change of tone in Paris, and where France enjoys a special position as a permanent member of the Security Council; and to the Middle East, where M. Pompidou may in time soften the asperities but will certainly maintain the profitable essentials of his predecessor's policies. Finally and nearer home, en effort will be made to develop a French Mediterranean policy.

9. All in all, one is reminded of the Churchillian concept of Britain as the centre of a system of concentric circles. This is certainly how General de Gaulle saw France. The difference with M. Pompidou is that the circles are both smaller and fewer in number. Not all of them are of the same importance; other than that which surrounds the

French frontiers themselves, the strongest and most emphatically traced chalk circle is, not Caucasian, but *Communautaire*.

10. The Mediterranean policy is worth a glance because it is very largely all M. Pompidou's work (even though he is often reaping where his predecessor has sown); and because it intermeshes with what Pompidou is trying to do in the world elsewhere. There is, typically, so far no cut and dried doctrine: merely the idea that, by all available means, France should assert a "presence". Being on her backdoor step, the Mediterranean is a region where French economic aid, political, cultural and linguistic influence and also military strength can conveniently be brought to bear to good effect. The policy can take its departure from the special position that France enjoys in the Maghreb and which she is in the process of acquiring in Libya and to some degree reacquiring in the Levant. It can draw strength from the alliances or affinities which exist between France and Italy, Greece and Spain. (We should remember, incidentally, that M. Pompidou is a Greek and Latin scholar and that his father was a teacher of Spanish; also that the Pompidous discovered St. Tropez long before Brigitte Bardot and still spend their holidays in the South). Apart from the advancement of trade, the Mediterranean policy can be exploited to serve a wide range of politico-strategic purposes—whether to obstruct discreetly further Soviet penetration by offering to the smaller countries an "alternative" to the "choice" between the US and the USSR; or to strengthen the French hand in the Four Power talks on the Middle East; or to counteract to some degree any Northward shift in the centre of gravity of an enlarged EEC by balancing Teutonic, Nordic and Anglo/Saxon influences against a measure of Latinity; or to help keep the Pax Gallica South of the Sahara; or simply to enhance French prestige and show that France is still capable of playing an independent role, Gaullist style, in the world game. In a

nutshell, the Mediterranean policy gives M. Pompidou lustre, influence and elbow room.

11. It is perhaps worth stressing, what I wrote at the beginning of this despatch, that M. Pompidou is still learning the ropes, as he himself would be the first to admit. This means that mistakes are likely to be made. Not every unexpected French move will be Machiavellian—no more than Albion has always been so perfidious as certain devious foreigners have been inclined to suspect. The major lesson for M. Pompidou so far has been his experience at The Hague Summit last November, at which he was able to see for himself and at first hand that the Five were not prepared to tolerate Gaullism without de Gaulle. The point was not lost: and he came away realising that France can no longer be sure always of calling the European tune. The second phase in his self-education is being enacted by Pompidou in the United States as I write this despatch. The third, which will be no less important, will be his visit to the Soviet Union in the autumn. The President has not yet fully addressed his mind—as we know he intends to do in due course—to the all-important field of defence, so closely related as it is to foreign policy and forming as it does the other part of the "private domain" of the President. His thinking about the future shape of Europe is also still somewhat fluid: and his attitude to the United Kingdom is rudimentary. His knowledge of us must be largely based on French history books, on what he learnt about us at the General's knee, and on his one and only visit to Britain in July 1966. He thus has a lot to learn—and unlearn—and this process can begin to crystallise only as negotiations for our Common Market entry proceed. He will be able to use these negotiations, and such further personal contacts as he may meanwhile have acquired with HMG, to judge us as clearly as he needs to and incidentally as clearly as we seek to judge him. Against this background, I do not, therefore, believe that M. Pompidou's foreign policy will acquire a precise content until well into next

year; and even then his sceptical pragmatism seems likely to exclude such a global and definitive vision as de Gaulle so clearly described in his memoirs.

12. In concluding this despatch, I would add how much I am struck, on this as on other aspects of the French scene, by the extent to which France under General de Gaulle seems somehow to have stood still. M. Pompidou inherited a foreign policy in which nothing had been learned or forgotten since the close of the Fourth Republic (some would say since Fashoda or even Sadowa). The General's powers as a magician protected the French from the realities of a changing world, as if Marianne were a Sleeping Beauty in a spell-wrought castle. Pompidou is the Beast who must awaken the Beauty if he is ever to become her Prince. If the task were not so considerable, it would be easy to mock the unreality and old-fashionedness which still informs so many of the prejudices and pretensions of the French Government. We should not forget, however, that M. Pompidou is now at grips with root problems of national diminishment to which we ourselves had begun to face up only ten years or so ago and to which we have still not fully found the solution. The French, for their part, certainly have a stony path to tread, and many more illusions to shed, before they will have found a satisfactory destiny in the world of tomorrow. Nevertheless, under M. Pompidou, they are at least now moving in a more realistic direction. As he said the other day to Time magazine, *Ma preoccupation principale est donc de faire de la France un pays moderne.* Like us, he seems at last to have realised that his best chance of achieving this lies in constructive partnership with others: and therein lies some hope for both our countries.

I have &c,

Christopher Soames

(Ambassador)

Confidential

Planning Staff, FCO
20 October, 1970

THE FRENCH ANALOGY

In the immediate post-war period, France was in eclipse. For most of the Sixties, however, French foreign policy often appeared more glamorous, and more successful, than our own. Much of the glamour and some of the success was superficial: General de Gaulle's personality was hypnotic. French policies themselves are moreover today on the change. But the question deserves to be asked—how do the French do it and what can we learn from their example? Is there a French analogy?

The Appearances of French Foreign Policy

2. The picture projected by French diplomacy in the Sixties was glossy and enviable. France appeared to have achieved a miracle. French politics had been a joke under the Fourth Republic and were now stable. Their currency had been notoriously weak and had now become strong. Their nostalgic and self-destructive involvement in Indo-China and Algeria was replaced by positive and forward-looking attitudes. The French seemed quite simply better at foreign policy than we were. They put France first. They were independent. They decided what the national interest required and did it. They did not allow themselves to be shoved around or deflected by international pressures. They sometimes got away with murder (for example, in their sale of arms to South Africa). Even their mistakes were carried through with a flourish and part concealed by panache. Above all, the affairs of the nation were directed by a charismatic national leader who, whatever his ultimate success with domestic issues, seemed capable of rallying a wide majority of Frenchmen behind his efforts to

assert the influence of France abroad. The French indeed made themselves felt, or at least talked about, in almost every corner of the globe.

The Realities

3. France has had some major "successes". These include:
- French domination of the E.E.C. and veto on U.K. entry;
- Their withdrawal from NATO;
- The mended fences with the Arab world;
- The subservience of ex-French Africa;
- Their disengagement from the Maghreb;
- Their increased trade with the Soviet Union;
- Their successful world-wide arms sales.

But appearances can be misleading. The French Government have had to pay a high moral or material price on each count (except the last two), whether in Government expenditure, domestic outrage or trouble for the future.

4. France was able to call the tune in the E.E.C. chiefly because, during the first ten years of the Market's existence, concern to build up the Community was much stronger on the part of the Five than of France. The geographical position of France at the heart of Europe played as large a part as French diplomatic skill. As regards NATO, France could safely withdraw only as long as everyone else stayed in and no threat materialised from the East. These conditions may not be valid in the Seventies. The good relations and modest but tangible degree of influence which France at present enjoys in the Middle East is almost entirely due to the determination of General de Gaulle to take a major political decision, extremely unpopular domestically, in what he conceived as the national interest. The June war gave him the

opportunity to de-emphasise the traditionally close links between France and Israel and frankly and openly to pay court to the Arab world, where the overwhelming French economic interest lay. But this relationship has not given France decisive influence with the Arabs and it is liable to erosion now that the General is no longer President. The Maghreb settlement was perhaps the General's greatest single achievement; but there have been periodic quarrels with Morocco, Algeria and Tunisia and the Evian Agreements have proved expensive and difficult to sustain. Stability in West Africa has absorbed a great deal of aid, some of which might have been better directed elsewhere. Gaullist policies have called for Gaullist methods—notably those of the Secretariat-General for African Affairs run from the *Elysée* by the notorious M. Foccart, and answerable virtually to none but the President. It is a strongly paternalistic organisation, enjoying the executive advantages of the centralised and authoritarian French Civil Service, but further strengthened by the ruthless use of strong-arm and espionage techniques. These methods have hitherto been very effective in maintaining powerful French influence in West Africa, although they may prove less so in future as the local African leaders develop confidence and sophistication.

5. Even the foregoing is by no means the whole story. While Gaullist achievements are well known, Gaullist failures are all too often overlooked. France has usually done well where she has operated from her central, naturally powerful European position. But the record is less good where she has gone beyond the limits of her resources. Thus the following diplomatic enterprises got almost nowhere, despite the ballyhoo at the time:

- The effort to encourage secession in Nigeria and Canada;
- The wooing of Latin America away from the U.S.;

- The ambition to preside over a Viet-Nam settlement;
- The endeavour, after belated recognition of Peking, to establish a high-level dialogue with China;
- The campaign to establish a special relationship with the U.S.S.R. which would cut across the relations between the super powers (killed by Glasboro, Prague, and Willi Brandt);
- The war against the U.S. Dollar;
- The military intervention in Chad.

The Factors in Favour of France

6. In considering whether we can take a leaf out of the French book, we need to be clear that the resources of the two countries are different. The following factors have helped the French in the conduct of their foreign policy, and to some degree hampered us in ours.

(a) Strength of the economy

In the Sixties, the French economy has enjoyed a consistently high rate of growth where ours has not. Until the last two years, French monetary reserves have been remarkably strong where Sterling has been weak (and French monetary recovery since the 1969 devaluation of the Franc has been good). Given her position of strength within the E.E.C., and her relatively self-sufficient trading pattern, France is significantly less vulnerable than the U.K. to world fluctuations. Her overseas investments are less extensive and less exposed than our own to foreign interference. Our currency and overseas trade are certainly assets; but they have also proved limitations upon independence in British foreign policy.

(b) Domestic political freedom

The French Government enjoys far greater freedom from domestic pressures in foreign policy matters than H.M.G. This is not because the man in the street is less interested in foreign policy (except that the case can be argued that the native chauvinism of the French tends to marshal a majority for almost any foreign policy which puts France on the map and the foreigner in his place). The explanation lies more in the political system itself. In France, Parliament, the press and the various political lobbies are much less powerful and there is a tendency to accept that foreign policy has a mystique which is the monopoly of the Administration.

(c) Commitments

Where ten years ago the reverse was true, today France has fewer overseas commitments than the U.K. and consequently greater freedom of manoeuvre. The French do not participate fully in NATO, belong to CENTO, or assert more than nominal membership of SEATO. Until recently, they have paid little or no real attention to the United Nations. Although they started late in the day, and suffered traumatic experiences, the French have disposed of their empire more completely than we. Their remaining imperial commitments are their small island overseas territories (firmly under the grip of Paris and regarded as extensions of France, not as entities destined for eventual independence) and the Francophone mini-States of Equatorial West Africa (controlled indirectly from Paris by neo-colonialist methods and with a relatively small capacity for trouble-making).

(d) Character of overseas aid

The French devote a higher percentage of their G.N.P. to aid than any other Western country. They get the maximum political advantage from this generosity by operating selectively and bilaterally. Selectively, because they do little or nothing in whole areas of the world which are not important to them or in which they feel that their resources do not enable then to operate seriously. Bilaterally, in ensuring that the strings of aid run wherever possible straight to Paris and that such aid is administered ultimately by political rather than development criteria.

(e) Continuity

Since the decision to grant independence to Algeria, France has benefited from continuity in foreign policy. In Britain, on the other hand, the alternation of Labour and Conservative policies, often involving substantial changes of objective and method, has sometimes left an uncertain impression overseas.

(f) Double standards

The Third World employs double standards in its dealings with the larger powers. In some respects this helps the French and hinders us. In their relations with the Third World, the French have moreover traditionally been less inclined than we to invoke moral standards. Less is therefore expected of them. (This and their tighter central control of the Francophone States are the main differences between the French "Commonwealth" and our own.)

(g) Responsibility of France's partners

France has to some extent lived on the sense of responsibility of her partners. While we have soldiered on, upholding the framework of security upon which the West depends, and practising the virtues of cooperation, France has been free to enjoy the advantages of independence. An alliance can afford one, but probably only one, maverick.

The Personal Equation

7. The benefit which France derived from the double standards at (f) above sprang from the powerful image which General de Gaulle projected and which widely commanded admiration and respect in the Third World. Thus he gave France the reputation of:

(i) anti-Americanism (where we were seen to be the closest ally of the United States);

(ii) toughness and inflexibility (no one thought they could change the General's mind once it was made up and consequently few men tried; he had cut off Guinea from all aid and never relented; he had quarrelled with the King of Morocco over the Ben Barka case and never patched things up. On the other hand, Britain was seen as being more democratic and reasonable and hence more open to argument).

(iii) non-racialism (we were lumbered with Rhodesia and our immigration policies; the French, with their emphasis on the universalism of French culture, the absence of a permanent colour problem at home, and their very generous aid to their own ex-colonies, appeared more reassuring).

Is French Policy good for France?

8. We have already seen that the French record is a mixture of failure and success, with some question-marks left over for the future (paragraphs 3-5 above). On the whole, the record is positive; but success has had to be paid for. It has cost :

(i) money (in aid and defence expenditure higher than our own);

(ii) friends (the French may wonder in the Seventies whether they were right in the Sixties to have been so hostile to the Americans, high-handed to the Germans and indifferent to ourselves);

(iii) illusions and disappointments (France has been larger than life. The devaluation of the Franc in 1969, the events of Prague, the growing strength of Germany and the development of the German *Ostpolitik* have each unmasked weaknesses in the capacities and assumptions of French foreign policy);

(iv) internal stability. (France enjoyed internal stability in the middle and late Sixties which she had not known for decades. She still enjoys it today. But the arrogance and disregard of domestic public opinion of General de Gaulle's foreign policy was part and parcel of the central authoritarianism of the Gaullist state and therefore played its part in provoking the upheaval of May 1968).

9. Looking to the future, France will have to recognise that she is subject to many of the same basic limitations as the other middle powers. Her independence of action is likely to become increasingly circumscribed. The contradictions and dangers of her role are becoming more apparent. The French must already be asking themselves what will happen if :

(a) U.S. troops are withdrawn from Europe in large numbers;

(b) an enlarged E.E.C. moves over to majority voting;

(c) Germany turns Eastward or even becomes Gaullist;

(d) their neo-colonial set-up in West Africa proves impermanent or less useful to them than it has in the recent past.

All these considerations are believed to have been weighed by M. Pompidou. This is probably why French policy on British entry into the Common Market has changed. Further policy changes are likely to become apparent over the next few years as General de Gaulle's shadow grows less and as France's willingness increases to cut its coat according to its cloth.

The Implications for British Policy

10. It will be evident from the above that French diplomacy cannot readily be imitated by the U.K. because:

(a) the material factors are different: the two countries are simply not in the same boat. Moreover, the traditional foreign policy methods of the U.K. cannot be changed overnight, because they are rooted in the national character and because they take account of conditions which are peculiar to us and foreign to France. The history of our Commonwealth has, for example, created expectations on the part of our partners which cannot be easily disregarded.

(b) the reality of French policy has been different from the surface appearance. This reality has more often been one of instant success than of enduring achievement. French policy is in any case changing under M. Pompidou, who is more realistic, cautious and pragmatic than his predecessor;

(c) future trends for the European middle powers will increasingly militate against the sort of foreign policy conducted by France in the 1960s. If these powers are to achieve anything, their future will lie in cooperation and self-restraint rather than in independence pursued for its own sake. Past French readiness to opt out when they considered it to their advantage to do so should then give ground, from the very nature of things, before the traditional British sense of responsibility for maintaining the structure of international arrangements.

11. To give too much admiration to the French is perhaps to surrender to secret vices—the covert admiration of the good citizen for the delinquent, or nostalgia for the age of the unfettered nation state. None of these moods will be appropriate to the world of the Seventies. This is not to say, however, that we have nothing to learn from the French. In style, we would no doubt do well to be more hard-headed and less emotional; to add a dash of peasant meanness to our not ungenerous mercantile character. On substance, we would do well if we could follow General de Gaulle's example of the early Sixties and ensure our future influence and success overseas by first putting our own house in order.

12. Our success in the Seventies will depend on securing a high rate of growth without unacceptable economic and social penalties; on finding a solution to the problem of Sterling; and on securing entry on the right terms into the E.E.C. No British foreign policy, of whatever description, will succeed unless our domestic and economic policies are sound. In this sense, and perhaps only in this sense, is there a French analogy.

<u>Letter to Percy Cradock, Head of Planning Staff, FCO, from Michael Palliser, Minister, British Embassy, Paris.</u>

7th January, 1971

Dear Percy,

THE FRENCH ANALOGY

1. Many thanks for your letter RS 13/3 (1970) of 21 December enclosing Leslie Fielding's paper. We have read

this with both entertainment and instruction and I should like to congratulate Leslie on a first class job.

2. We really have no comments to offer. I have often asked myself the question which is the subject of the paper only to come up with the same kind of answer. I think that, if anyone is tempted to disagree, a period of service at the Paris Embassy is probably the best antidote!

Yours Ever,

Michael

(A.M. Palliser)

6. DESPATCHES FROM TOKYO

FIRST IMPRESSIONS OF JAPAN

Mr. Fielding to Vice-President Haferkamp

SUMMARY

Three obvious but important paradoxes. Westernised Japan is oriental beneath the surface (paragraphs 3 and 4). While she looks strong from the outside, Japan faces serious economic problems and suffers from an infirm political decision-making process (paragraphs 5-7). The Japanese think they should not be expected to behave as others do, on the grounds that their country is a 'fragile barque tossed on a stormy sea' (paragraphs 8-9).

The current political mood is an odd one and there is uncertainty about which way Japan should point. There is a sense of frustration and sometimes of resentment towards the US and (more so) the European Community (paragraphs 10-16).

The Japanese are openly polite towards the Community as such, but are less impressed than they were. The Member States have quite close links with Japan but are not as important to Japan as we would wish (paragraphs 17-19).

The Community's bilateral trade deficit with Japan is serious and structural. It is not all our fault: our competitors experience similar difficulties in gaining access to the Japanese market. The Government cannot readily, or will not, do much to resolve the underlying structural problem, although they will offer other concessions at the margin. We are not going to get a better deal than the Americans, who are themselves not getting very far with Japan (paragraphs 22-25).

We need very cool heads to handle this situation, which is not all black and white, and where our own scope for action is also limited (paragraphs 26-28).

In conclusion, and without claim to originality, it is suggested that:

(a) on substance, we should continue to press our trade grievances, but in a catholic context of overall partnership (paragraphs 30-32);
(b) on form, we should be guided by certain "rules of the game" which pay off in Japan (paragraph 33).

The general picture is admitted to be a stark one (paragraph 34).

Confidential   EC Delegation
                                                                      Tokyo
                                                     9 February, 1979

1. After three months in Tokyo, I have the honour to submit my first impressions of Japan. While I have naturally compared notes with my collaborators, these are essentially my own personal observations. They are broad brush in character. I set them down in the hope that they may be of use as a general background to our current trade difficulties.

2. I will not attempt to describe this fascinating country in any depth. Hundreds of books have been written on the subject by people more expert than I and perhaps none of them does Japan full justice. But I should like to begin with

three paradoxes. They may seem cheap and obvious; but they have an important bearing on our work here.

First Paradox: East and West

3. The first is *Oriens in Occidente*. Post-war Japan is at present, and will probably remain, firmly a part of the western industrialised and democratic world. Yet it continues to be an oriental country, in that things are not as western as they seem on the surface. The labels seem familiar; but when you unwrap the parcels you see that personal relations, business methods and the way the economy is run are sometimes different (even if only subtly so) from what one would expect. This seems obvious enough, but never ceases in practice to surprise me. If I were in China, I would expect everything to be Chinese from top to bottom and would be ready to make, from the outset, the necessary psychological adjustments. In Tokyo, with its skyscrapers, multinational companies, New York-style bustle, and its English speaking *élites*, one has to make a special effort to penetrate beneath the surface and to conduct relationships sensitively and in the Japanese way.

4. In the daily work of this Delegation, for example, we find ourselves operating in a closed, prestige-conscious and hierarchical society, where it takes time and labour to come by the facts, and even more time to cultivate the large number of personal contacts which alone get results. The Japanese are a charming people and their way of life, despite the overcrowding, an agreeable and civilised one. But dealing with them is a labour-intensive process (hours of repeated calls, meetings, committees, etc.) and much complicated by questions of rank. In the process of these dealings, I have the uneasy impression (as I did years ago in Cambodia) of being discreetly watched, while the Establishment slowly makes up its mind whether or not I am to be accepted. And all the time, as in Cambodia, I ask

myself whether what they say is what they mean and whether they understand what I say to be what I mean!

Second Paradox: Strength and Weakness

5. My second paradox is that while the received image of Japan's economy current in the west is one of strength, prosperity and dynamism, there are also areas of weakness. The estimated economic growth rate (whether Prime Minister Ohira's 6.3% or the 5% favoured by private analysts) is remarkably high; the Yen is strong; and a powerful new international capital market is being created; the balance of trade and of payments is notoriously positive; the motor car industry highly efficient; technology often highly advanced; and the industrial workforce dedicated, well-paid and well-organised.

6. But there are serious short-term and even more serious longer-term structural problems. Thus, the bankruptcy rate amongst smaller enterprises is high; the lifetime employment system is undergoing strain; Japanese light industry is often not internationally competitive and needs present levels of protection to survive; important areas of heavy industrial activity (like shipbuilding, aluminium, petrochemicals, and synthetic fibres) are losing their competitiveness, and are now being placed in moth balls or dismantled on a scale exceeding anything we know in Europe. In the longer term, Japan faces the formidable task of returning an economy geared to exceptionally high growth, and with emphasis on heavy industries, to a future of lower growth, uncertainty of expectations, austerity of management and savings in material inputs. Most of us think that Japan will somehow achieve a major industrial restructuring which will permit the economy to make a further leap forward in the 1980s into areas of advanced technology where the country will enjoy continued comparative advantage and may even find itself a complete world beater. Yet the strain will be considerable and the

demands on discipline will be great; and the transformation will need to be accompanied by wider economic and social adjustments (including a politically very unpopular move towards heavier taxes, as well as long overdue improvements to infrastructure, distribution networks and social welfare) which are not going to come about overnight.

7. By the same token, the politics of Japan are both impressively stable and unexpectedly weak. Thus, the ruling Liberal Democratic Party (LDP) remains firmly in the saddle. The Communist Party is weak in the Diet, as is the Clean Living Party on the Right, even though both enjoy some popular support in the country, at grass roots level. The two socialist parties, which constitute the principal nexus of parliamentary opposition to the LDP, are ineffective and currently divided. As far as can be judged from early opinion polls, Mr. Ohira is popular in the country. Nevertheless, the LDP continues to be riddled by factions. Mr. Ohira personally, while undoubtedly very intelligent, is generally depicted by local political commentators as a philosopher rather than a man of action, inclined by nature to adopt an aloof and noncommittal posture. His Cabinet is of uneven and to some extent untested ability, because it reflects a difficult factional balance. And even if his Cabinet were to unite behind crisp and tough new policies, their ability to implement such policies would be closely circumscribed by the need to reconcile powerful lobbies and pressure groups, not only in the Party and in the Diet but also in big business; and by the need to rally the active cooperation of a powerful and self-esteeming civil service, with views of its own not always by any means in conformity with Ministers' wishes. It is a well-known common-place among sociologists that Japanese organisations tend to lack strong and dynamic individual leadership at the top. The qualities most highly valued in politics here are those of accommodation and consensus. This tends to make foreign

policy (including external economic policy) reactive and passive, and of course frustrating for the foreigner.

Third Paradox: Japan as seen by the Japanese

8. My third paradox shows up clearly in the view which the Japanese have of themselves and their country. The strength, moral as well as material, of modern Japan and her claim to be an economic super power goes hand in hand with self-doubt and quite profound apparent psychological anxieties. This is what I might call the "shoku" (i.e. "shock") mentality. They brood on the vulnerability of their country, a fragile barque tossed on a stormy sea. They dwell on their almost total dependence on external energy supplies, their high dependence on imported raw materials and 50% dependence on imported foodstuffs. The Japanese are keenly aware of the volatility of their regional environment. Their strategic military dependence on the United States sits uncomfortably with their awareness of American defeat in Viet-Nam and disengagement in Korea. They see the strength and influence of the USSR increasing—and Soviet military bases are now in the process of being built on Japan's disputed Northern islands. They coin the word "shoku" to describe unpleasant surprises—President Nixon's sudden move to recognise China, the Middle East oil crisis, the collapse of the dollar and the associated vertiginous upward movement of the yen.

9. This general attitude (to the effect that Japan is special, must nurse herself like an invalid, and must follow imperatives peculiar to herself) comes close to the root of the arguments sometimes heard here why Japan cannot be expected to do this or that thing (e.g. increase overseas aid or reduce overseas trade surpluses) in fulfilment of her important new international role or at the reasonable request of her close partners. However strong the balance of trade and of payments, Japan must still import a much

lower percentage than anyone else of manufactured goods. Or must apply environmental constraints or testing procedures different from anyone else. For example, because the tractor is said to be a new experience to some Japanese farmers, new designs and even little improvements have to be elaborately tested to avoid hazard, to the disadvantage of European exporters. Or because Japan is an island of great phyto-sanitary vulnerabilities, it cannot import tulip bulbs from unhealthy tropical places like Holland.

The current, unsettled, political mood in Japan

10. So much for my three paradoxes. I should now like to come a step closer to a discussion of Japan's relations with the Community, by speaking of the general political mood in Japan. This is passing through a curious and unsettled phase. In a word, it is a crisis of identity, made manifest inter alia in an attitude of uncertainty, and sometimes even of resentment, towards Japan's traditional Western partners. The halcyon years of high economic growth started off Japan's steady weaning from America. But now that the apron strings are loosened, and economic life is no longer so easy, which way should Japan look? Big Brother is no longer so big; who are the other brothers of the 1980s to be? We are looking at the end of one politico-economic process in Japan; and neither we nor the Japanese can yet see the successor process clearly.

11. The Japanese have more than the normal human share of myopic and insular characteristics, inducing an inability to see themselves as others see them—or to place themselves in other people's shoes. Thus, the failure of Japan to obtain a seat on the Security Council, and the election of Bangladesh in her place, came as a painful surprise to Japanese leaders who do not understand the ambiguity with which their country is still regarded, and the suspicion and dislike it can still attract in the Third

World. The general consequent chagrin in Tokyo was only intensified by the fact that Japan was not asked to join European leaders and the US President at the recent mini-summit at Guadeloupe. This 'snub' is privately ascribed to a mixture of western motives, from indifference to jealousy to doubts as to the quality of Mr. Ohira's English.

12. As if to express these pent up disappointments and loss of face, the recent normalisation of Tokyo's relations with Peking has touched off a "China-boom" in Japan. The newspapers are covering to a monotonous degree all events Chinese, the financial and industrial openings for Japan in China, the visit of Vice Chairman Deng in Tokyo and so forth. The correspondent of Le Monde has written of a *rendez-vous historique* between the two countries and of an associated *appétit d'identité* in Japan. Japanese political leaders have also been speaking about the need for Japan to reinforce her relations with other Asian neighbours. The Prime Minister has set up a task force of officials to re-examine that old Japanese dream, the possibility of a "Pacific Community", looser in character than the European Community, but which would associate Japan more closely both with South-east Asia and with the Pacific seaboard countries of the South American continent. In this way, Japan could hope to have the best of both worlds, i.e. both continued close relations with her principal partner, the US, but also an Asian and Pacific field of influence. One hears less talk these days of the "Triangle" (Japan/US/EC) so dear to Mr. Ohira's predecessor, Mr. Fukuda.

13. Towards the traditional Western partner, there is a mood of frustration, perhaps also of withdrawal and occasionally even also of truculence. Relations with the United States remain the cornerstone of Japan's foreign policy, for historical, economic and strategic reasons. But even the Americans, with all their political muscle and all the time, effort and manpower which they devote to their relations with Japan, have for example been unable so far

to extract any serious bilateral agricultural concessions from Japan (other than some marginal phased improvement in future access for beef and oranges);or more importantly to obtain any satisfactory unequivocal guarantee that America's colossal visible trade deficit with Japan (of the order of 12 billion dollars in 1978) will be substantially reduced by means of long term Japanese structural trade policy measures.

14. As to the European Community, there is equally little sign at present that the Japanese government are either able or willing to make similar structural adjustments.

15. I would not want to exaggerate this, or to suggest that Japan has no intention of going beyond mere window dressing. Ministers and senior people in Tokyo share much of the concern which we and the Americans feel at the trade surplus. But they are puzzled as to what to do about it and suspicious of or irritated by externally suggested remedies. They see us, as well as the Americans, as laying down requirements of a kind we would never allow others to lay on us.

16. We are still very far from the alarmist picture which Prime Minister Fraser of Australia painted when he visited the Commission in 1977, of a Japan whose frustrations and sense of encirclement in some ways recalled the politico-economic situation prevailing in the early 'thirties, on the eve of the resurgence of Japanese militarism and economic imperialism. These latter options would not recommend themselves to the leadership of modern Japan, even if they were technically viable, which they are not. Nevertheless, there is at least a potential readiness here to examine the advantages to Japan of a slightly different profile and external emphasis from that which has prevailed over the past twenty years.

Attitudes to the Community: polite rather than impressed

17. I should like now to say something about the European Community, where relations, although correct and even at the personal level reasonably cordial, cannot be said to be very close. There was a Community "mini-boom" in Japan in the early 1970s, when the Japanese fully discovered us. But the novelty of this has since worn off. Leaving aside for a moment the problem of trade imbalances, the fact is that, despite the *ouverture* shown by Prime Minister Fukuda during his visit to Brussels last year, the Japanese Establishment have still not yet fully come to terms with the existence of the Community, or rid themselves of their habit of thinking in terms only of their relations with individual Member States. In the big debate on external policy in the Diet two weeks ago, not one minister mentioned the Community as such, everyone preferring to speak of "Western Europe". This may be partly because, insofar as the Community impinges upon their lives, it takes the negative form of a trade bloc which is applying pressure to Japan. Partly also, the Japanese are less inclined than we are to be impressed by the Community's present achievements and more apt than the Commission is, to take full note of the Community's weaknesses and tot up the areas where the Community is encountering obstacles to its continued advance. The initial difficulties of the European Monetary System are a case in point.

18. But the underlying Japanese reserves go further than this. The Japanese government is very much aware of how Member State practice can differ from Community theory. This is evident to them, for example, from the way in which residual trade restrictions and administrative non-tariff barriers are operated by individual Member States in a way which renders the Community, for Japan, no longer a common market or a single export target. More than this, Japanese ministers note with bewilderment the extent to

which the Community dimension is sometimes absent from their dialogue with ministers and senior officials of our larger Member States and of the way in which individual Member States can take a different line, in their bilateral relations with Japan, from that collectively adopted in the various joint resolutions of the EC Council of Ministers. The tenor of the Japanese Foreign Minister's recent exchange in Bonn, at any rate as recounted to the press by Mr. Sonoda on his return, is the most recent case in point; but other Member States have been at least equally to blame.

The basic image: Europe a cultural museum?

19. In the last resort, the position here seems to me to be this. Senior officials and ministers in this country, while they are aware of, and some of them weigh very seriously, the claims of the Community as such to their attention, were for the most part educated in Europe before the Community grew up and are still inclined to think of themselves as German hands, French specialists, friends of Good Old England, etc. Beyond this inner circle, Japan as a whole remains quite strongly influenced by European culture and sensitive to historic links with individual Member States, of whom Germany, France, Britain and Italy are built into the Japanese education system. But (with the exception of Germany, whose post-war economic revival and current economic strength are much admired), the basic rock-bottom image of the European nations is probably recessional, lazy and in some cases (UK, Italy) even decadent. I may be wrong in all this, and I am having a professional opinion poll conducted to measure opinions more scientifically. But I sense that, for the broad majority of Japanese, the Europe of the past is a prestigious cultural museum; the Europe of the present, a good place to go on holiday, to shop and (if one cannot do so in the States) to study; the Europe of the future, not likely to do anything very earthshaking.

Bilateral trade problems

20. This brings me to our current troubles. My own first impression is that the trade gap with Japan is indeed of a long- term structural nature. It has been building up over the past ten years and more. Over the past four or five years, it has been widening steadily at the rate of about one billion dollars per annum. Part of the explanation of this may be found in our own lack of competitiveness and the absence of a sufficiently dynamic long-term approach to the Japanese market. But I am struck by the extent to which almost every other trading partner of Japan experiences the same deficit in manufactured goods, just as the Americans, Australians and others encounter the same general difficulties (soya beans apart) in developing their agricultural trade. Some of the foreigners can be uncompetitive and inefficient some of the time; but not all of them all the time. A large part of the explanation of trade imbalance is surely to be found within Japan.

21. Here it is partly the government but partly also the system and the nature of things which are to blame. The government for their part, whether on cool commercial policy grounds or because they are at the mercy of the bureaucracy and the pressure groups, have tolerated for too long a system of tariff and non-tariff barriers which is excessively import-impervious and autarkic. But it is not necessary to go in for conspiracy theory and to point the finger at a supposed "Japan Incorporated" as sole scapegoat for our woes. What we are faced with is also the Japanese way of life. Nearly one quarter of the working population is engaged in the mostly inefficient and antiquated domestic distribution sector. At the receiving end, the consumer, while increasingly these days open to foreign produce as the electorate becomes more sophisticated and more and more young people travel abroad and learn foreign languages, is still without an effective organisation or form of expression to assert his

interest in cheaper goods and a wider variety of choice. At the next step up, the average small merchant in Japan, who might be expected to import competitive foreign goods, depends for his survival in business on his relations with the leading Japanese manufacturers and the large merchant houses. The latter operate closely-knit production-distribution networks of a semi-feudal character—i.e. with a strong vertical power component into which foreign penetration is extremely difficult. The inclination of the average merchant is thus to play things safe, confining his operations in imported goods either to economic necessities or to luxury items which can be marketed in small quantity with high profit margin. Behind these men and their clannish networks is a world of red tape, powerful and meddlesome bureaucrats and conservative bankers whose interest is more often than not in the status quo.

The limited possibilities of early structural change

22. Against this background, it is not altogether too surprising that the Japanese government, while ready to engage in serious bargaining in the MTN in Geneva, and to make bilateral concessions at the margin to the Community, do not at present see their way to do very much more to balance the books.

23. European politicians can often make electoral mileage from the intimacy and range of their contacts among other European or world leaders. No general political constituency of that kind exists in this country, and very few Japanese political leaders seem to have close working relationships outside Japan. This absence of a natural international dimension has been exemplified by the decision of both the previous and the present Prime Minister of Japan each to appoint an a-political English speaking diplomat to supposed ministerial status, with theoretical responsibility for "Japan's external economic

relations" and the practical task of keeping the impertinent and exigent "Gaijin" (foreigners) off ministerial doorsteps. This is doubly a pity for the fact that Ministers in Japan are unusually uncritical towards, and dependent upon, the advice submitted to them in the general economic and external trade policy area by their civil servants. And the lower echelons of Japanese bureaucracy probably actually believe in (or are too ethnocentric to feel comfortable in questioning) their own trade propaganda. In this respect, as in certain others, the people who really run this country are not the politicians.

24. The Japanese are therefore not going to give us what they refuse to give to the Americans. And there is some room for doubt whether, given the basic paradoxes aired above, and in the present domestic economic climate, the Japanese Cabinet could agree upon and force through the necessary structural changes to satisfy the Community and the US. Probably only a new "shoku" in the form of e.g. the absolute certainty of concerted US/Community trade sanctions could achieve this purpose; and in the present mood of uncertainty in Japan no-one could be certain whether the effects of such a "shoku" would be in all respects beneficial to us.

25. The Japanese economy and its associated trade policy is, in other words, a ballistic vehicle without MIRVs; once launched, it tends to remain on course, cannot be much deflected by the authorities in Tokyo and has to be either intercepted or allowed to splash down comfortably.

The need for dispassionate appraisal

26. I would now like to draw some practical conclusions for our relations with Japan. Before I do so, however, I should like to put in a word for a cool and calculated approach. As a Community institution, the Commission is bound to be sensitive to what this or that hard pressed

European industry is experiencing; and it goes without saying that the conclusions of our Council of Ministers are crucial to us. But we must also hold to a balanced over-view of our own, which the Commission is uniquely placed to acquire. The Council of Ministers does not always bring enough depth to its discussion of Japan, so often brief and influenced by the anxieties of the moment. I noted with interest, in this connection, that most of the Member State Ambassadors here, at their regular meeting in January, were uneasy with the Council's decisions last December on Japan—this, despite the fact that the same Ambassadors agreed with the balance of the Commission's input to the Council debate.

27. Although it is exhilarating to play the hawk (and my first public speech in Japan last week was fairly hawkish), we need always to be clear in our own minds that we are not in a black and white situation. While the trade imbalance with Japan is painful, and Japanese trade policy irritating, we have in practice been able, by fair means or foul, to blunt the edge of the Japanese challenge in the key industrial sectors (cars, ships, steel, etc). The fact is moreover that the Community remains a multilateral and not a bilateral trader. Our deficit with Japan is matched by our surplus with Austria and Switzerland. Australia and New Zealand have *mutatis mutandis* similar difficulties with our market to those which we experience on the Japanese market. The Community, moreover, was in 1978 in a comfortable overall visible trade surplus. We should not dismiss out of hand the prospects of cooperation with Japan in other areas (e.g. development aid, international monetary affairs, technological and R&D cooperation, energy dialogue, industrial joint ventures where they make commercial sense). Nor neglect our basic political and military interest in the continued pro-western profile of Japan.

28. We also need to be clear that there is a limit to the Community's power to pressurise Japan. The GATT rules and our relations with other partners (including the US) impose obvious constraints. Aside from demanding continued or possibly intensified sectoral Japanese export restraints and short of a totally new world in which the MFN principle of the GATT would have been abandoned and in which protectionism all round would have to become the order of the day, the Community could not convincingly strike *machismo* postures. Japan has, moreover, a large and relatively self-contained domestic market (her exports account for only around 12% of GNP); is not dependent on us for energy, food or raw material imports; and sends only a modest portion (currently 10-11%) of her exports to Europe. Even if we were to cut off these exports, we would face painful retaliation against our own exports to Japan (over UCE 3.5 billion on visible trade alone in 1978) and we would, of course, intensify competition from Japan on third markets.

29. For what they are worth, I would draw the following conclusions from these first impressions of Japan, first as to substance and second as to form. There is nothing startling, or indeed original, in these conclusions: I do no more than endorse and re-state the policy which is already in practical effect.

First Conclusion: Substance

30. There is clearly every reason why we should be firm and persistent in our efforts to attain significant redress of trade grievances, in the defence of our own legitimate interests. But short of a major international crisis, we would do well to continue to use carrots as well as sticks, and to try to treat Japan fairly and squarely as the major partner she really is. This means essentially a two-tier policy, with a political as well as a commercial sense to it.

31. The first tier would be the continued effort to "strengthen the third side of the triangle". We will probably never enjoy the politically close relations which the Americans have with Japan. But it makes sense to try to place our dealings with Japan on a footing as near as can be to that on which our relations with the United States have been built up over the past ten years. This will require the steady pursuit of a semi-political dialogue with Japan parallel to, and in complement of, our commercial policy exchanges, and embracing such areas as monetary matters, industrial cooperation, our mutual interests in aid to development, etc. As noted above, this is not quite the spirit of the hour in Tokyo; and the "triangle" concept is in any case more of a catchphrase than a precise blueprint for action. Nevertheless, it is still to my mind the best policy open to us. The Japanese are emotionally insecure people who need friends and have an appetite for international recognition. We should build on this. Visits to Japan by Commissioners, if well prepared, have been and will continue to be a very important instrument of such a dialogue at the political level.

32. The second tier would be continued commercial pressure along existing lines designed first and foremost to keep before the eyes of Japanese leaders the necessity for structural reform (as much in the interests of Japan's relations with the United States as with her, lesser, relations with ourselves); and second to obtain concrete and technical adjustments sector by sector which would make it easier for our own manufactures and processed agricultural goods to reach the Japanese market in fair conditions, comparable to those which Japanese exports encounter in the Community. Comparative advantage and reciprocity are our best arguments in seeking to prize the oyster open. We are of course already doing this in our regular high level consultations, in the technical meetings on motor cars, chemicals, etc. which are now taking place, and in the steady grind of day to day diplomatic encounter

through this Delegation and through the Japanese Mission in Brussels. Once again, however, the dialogue must continue to be pursued at the political level also.

<u>Second Conclusion: "Modus Operandi"</u>

33. The ground rules for effective day-today operations in Japan look to me like these:

(i) Personal Relationships: These matter a good deal. The Japanese much prefer to deal with foreigners they know and trust. Acquiring these relationships takes time and patience but is worth it.

(ii) Common Politeness: However *fortiter in re*, it is essential to be *suave in modo*. The Japanese do not hold the Community so much in awe that they are ready to be bullied by it; and considerations of Japanese psychology make it desirable to avoid placing one's interlocutors in a position where they lose face with their own side.

(iii) Careful Presentation: To enter a genuine dialogue with a Japanese Minister, it is necessary to prepare him (and his advisers) well in advance. They are mostly not individualists as we are but mouthpieces of their own internal consensus. Brilliant new ideas on our side, presented at short notice or without warning, are not likely to evoke a helpful or even an immediate response. They need time to talk things over among themselves.

(iv) Common strategy: Internal consistency on the European side is vital, whether between our Directorates General, or the Members of our Commission, or the chancelleries of Member States. The Japanese tend to be baffled by our internal divergences; and are sometimes tempted to play us off against each other. The order of the day in this respect should be the following extract from the conclusions of the Community's Council of Ministers of 7 February 1978:

> "The Council is convinced that a common strategy of the Community is an essential pre-requisite to an effective dialogue with Japan. Only in this way will the Community institutions be able to speak with the necessary authority and precision. The Member States will also be guided by this approach in their contacts with Japan."

(v) Staffing: We will always be out-numbered by Japanese manpower resources and the constraints of the Commission's personnel policy are well known. But I wonder whether we do well to be so completely swamped. At present I understand that there is only one official in the Commission working full time on Japan. This Delegation's effective strength on the economic and commercial side is less than that of the financial section of the French Embassy.

Personal Postscript

34. I am aware that, while the above conclusions are orthodox enough, the general tenor of the preceding analysis is stark and in some ways depressing. Have I taken too negative and pessimistic a view?

35. Perhaps I have. These are only my first impressions of Japan and not my last. On the surface at least, our relations with Japan do not work too badly and our interlocutors can and do show charm, sympathy and insight towards us. At Geisha parties here, singing European drinking songs, recalling student days in the West, exchanging reminiscences of common professional

life, the culture gap seems to close up and one can find oneself metaphorically (on occasions perhaps literally also) on all fours with Japanese mandarins, bankers, businessmen, journalists and the rest. On the whole, they are a sincere people, and personally very friendly.

36. But one has to be strict with oneself in these matters. Everything in the garden is not beautiful and will probably never become so in my time. To change the metaphor, we have a long slog ahead of us.

Leslie Fielding

(Head of Delegation)

A HIGHER INTERNATIONAL PROFILE FOR JAPAN?

Mr. Fielding to Vice-President Haferkamp

SUMMARY

Japan now seems willing to assume a higher international profile. Iran, aid and maybe defence are straws in the wind. (Paragraphs 1-4.)

The explanation lies both in Japan's sense of growing economic and strategic vulnerability (paragraph 6) and in growing Japanese self-confidence (paragraph 7).

The change will be gradual. Certain factors (time needed to form a national consensus; lack of a bold leadership; inadequate budgetary resources; doubt about the economic future) will constrain the Government. (Paragraph 8.)

The new style will be pragmatic, the new substance fairly predictable (paragraphs 9-12). The dangers, if any, will be those of non-achievement and/or ineptitude (paragraph 13).

The implications for the Community. Not all is beautiful; but there have been some successes; and a foundation exists for a higher-profile response to Japan, if desired. (Paragraphs 14-23.)

A higher-profile Japan will be "nationally self-confident enough to insist on being an equal to be consulted, rather than a rich but simple-minded relative to be fleeced …. and she will have ideas and priorities of her own." (Paragraphs 24-25.)

Confidential   EC Delegation
                                                                        Tokyo
                                                                  9 May, 1980

1. A few months ago, the correspondence columns of the Japan Times carried a letter from a US reader who complained that "the Japanese people do little to offset the impression of a small people occupying a position internationally that is too large for them". While expressing familiar past frustrations, this harsh view does not do justice to Japan in 1980, where (in my view) at least a willingness to assume a higher international profile is now in evidence. A careful judgement is required. It is as important not to over-state the phenomenon as not to dismiss it with cynicism. The following are my purely personal impressions.

The Straws in the Wind

2. The move towards a higher international profile for Japan has been maturing quietly for some time, under the present Administration and its predecessor. But this year, there have been several important new straws in the wind.

3. The basic thinking emerged clearly in the National Diet debates last January. Prime Minister Ohira saw Japan as standing at a "crucial crossroads". Describing the 1980s as likely to prove a "very trying decade for global peace and economic development", he said that a more dynamic Japanese posture was called for and a shift in foreign affairs "from a passive to an active responsibility". Foreign Minister Okita said that "the world expects Japan to take a more positive political and economic role".

4. This kind of broad sentiment has been voiced before. But we have three pieces of evidence that something is indeed beginning to happen. First, despite the importance to her economy of Iranian oil, Japan has declared herself in principle willing to follow Community countries in

applying economic sanctions to Iran if significant progress is not made towards the release of the US hostages: a foreign policy move which, if finally carried out, will be without precedent in Japan's low-profile post-war history. Second, the commitment to double Japanese ODA in US dollar terms within 3 years, entered into by Prime Minister Fukuda at the Bonn Summit in 1978, is at last assuming tangible form, despite acute budgetary constraints and last year's collapse of the Yen. More significantly, some of the additional effort is being deployed in areas of the Middle East and Asia in which Japan has hitherto shown little aid interest, but where the US and Europe are attempting to counter growing Soviet involvement. Thus, significant additional aid has this year been decided for Turkey and Pakistan and the Government say they are ready in principle to do something for Oman, Somalia and Kenya. Third, there are plans for increasing annual defence spending within a 5 year period from 0.9% to 1% of GNP. This may not seem dramatic. But the percentages would be higher (1.3% to 1.5%) if the so-called "NATO method" of calculation were employed; and the size of the GNP being what it is, Japan, even today, has the 6th or 7th largest defence budget in the world.

The Reasons Why

5. Paradoxically, this new tendency stems from perceptions of both the weakness and the strength of Japan's position.

6. The motivation from weakness goes as follows. In the halcyon days of all-out economic growth in the 1950s and 1960s, Japan could pursue her own business interests under the total protection of the US and without any real responsibility for, or even much concern about, the outside world. This was the good news. Then came the bad. In the early 1970s, Japan found herself expelled from the Garden of Eden by the first oil shock and by international trade frictions, from which it became evident that exponential

economic growth and the thitherto boundless exploitation of foreign markets had hit the buffers. By 1980, Japan's sense of vulnerability had been further enhanced by the shift in the global balance of power between the US and the USSR. The Russians, for whom the Japanese have a thorough dislike tinged with a mixture of fear and contempt, are expanding their military influence in the Far East and South East Asia. Over a quarter of Soviet ground forces are now deployed in the Far East theatre, and over a third of Soviet naval strength, with air support to match. Soviet warships and reconnaissance aircraft are now being seen regularly round Japan's periphery. To be sure, much of this is a function of Sino-Soviet relations. But for the first time in twenty years, Soviet troops are back at division strength on the Northern islands claimed by Japan, where permanent base facilities now appear to be under construction. The Russians may be crude; but no one can say they do not appear self-confident. The US, on the other hand, defeated in Viet-Nam and uncertain in Korea, ineffective in the Middle East and of a contested superiority over the Soviet Union in the strategic nuclear balance, faces what may prove to be the pangs of a super-power in decline. But the US is by far and away the most important partner for Japan, the cornerstone of her foreign policy and an ally upon whom she has no alternative but to rely. The Prime Minister last week, in an improvised speech to a party rally in the provinces, said that the US was no longer a super-power and that the era had passed when Japan could depend on the US for everything. Characteristically, he made this point in justifying the need to strengthen ties with the US as a partner and protector who was now in need of support. But I doubt whether any Japanese leader has let slip such language in the post-war era. The undertow of anxiety is obvious.

7. This said, Japanese anxiety does not bespeak Japanese inadequacy. So next, the motivation from strength. A higher-profile Japan will be an expression of growing

national self-confidence. The psychology of subordination in Japan is different from that in Europe and too complicated to explain here; but it is broadly true to say that a gradual process of weaning from too passive a Japanese dependence on the US has been under way for many years and has probably now been largely achieved. The Japanese have been able to point to their twin post-war miracles: 30 years of unbroken economic prosperity and growth, accompanied by a smooth political transition from the xenophobic police state of the 1930s to a consensual and internationally well-informed democracy, dull and conservative in its politics, but unquestionably broadly rooted in the desires of the electorate. To this, one could add that while modernisation has brought sweeping changes to Japan, the tribal identity remains intact; this is not a society where the fabric is crumbling because traditional values have been washed away. The image which the Japanese have of themselves has in consequence improved by leaps and bounds. The opinion polls suggest that the Japanese now acknowledge inferiority to no other nation (not even the admired and emulated Federal Republic of Germany), and they believe themselves superior to most. Younger people in particular, while not at all chauvinistic, seem to have their full measure of this national self-confidence, which seems likely to emerge as an important internal conditioning element in Japanese foreign policy for the remainder of this century.

Some Qualifications and Constraints

8. It would, however, be wrong to leap to the conclusion that dramatic modifications are to be expected in Japan's international profile. Gradualism is more likely to prevail, given the existence of the following constraints and qualifications:

   (a) Nothing very significant can be achieved in Japan in any field in the absence of a national consensus, the building of which at the popular level always requires time, as well as subtle conducive efforts by the leadership. My own impression is that an informal public readiness to face new realities already exists of a kind which would permit a higher profile. But the key words and initial steps are only now beginning to be said and taken to actuate and exploit the consensus of the future.

(b) Boldly innovative leadership of the personalised kind is not currently the Japanese political mode. True, the present leadership, and the next generation of political leaders waiting in the wings, are shrewd and balanced men, closely in touch with international realities through Japan's first-class bureaucracy and through symbiosis with Japanese big business. True also, Mr. Ohira personally has learned much, and grown in international stature, since becoming Prime Minister. Nevertheless, the Government of this country still tends towards the gerontocratic, the reactive and the internationally ill-at-ease; while the dominant Liberal Democratic Party (LDP), prone to bitter factional rivalries and shot through by persistent scandals, seems to be a slowly declining force.

(c) A more specific constraint is the relative poverty of the Government in what is now a rich country. Because taxation has remained low while Government expenditure has inevitably grown, the point has now been reached in which 40% of the national budget is financed by Government borrowing. A higher international profile will cost money which can be raised only by fiscal reform. The necessity of such reform has been recognised in Japan since the early 1970s, when the first studies of a possible VAT were initiated. While taxation is no more popular in Japan than anywhere else, it is probably now only a matter of time before the necessary reforms are implemented. But the first step will be difficult. Prime Minister Ohira was obliged to withdraw his VAT proposals last year in the middle of a parliamentary election campaign in which the tide seemed to be turning against the LDP.

(d) Uncertainties about the further development of the Japanese economy over the next 10-15 years will also no doubt act as a brake. Most observers continue to believe, with this Delegation, that Japan will succeed in restructuring her industries, in securing (or somehow compensating for shifts in the supply of) raw material and energy supplies, and in obtaining reasonably increased growth and social prosperity, without too dangerous a level of trade friction, whether with Europe and the US or with the newly-industrialising countries of Asia. But this is not certain. A really major earthquake, of the kind which some experts now believe to be overdue, could set the country back. And much depends on the volatile Middle East situation. The Japanese are born worriers, who live on their nerves, but who are likely on that account to look twice before accepting any commitments likely to bind them for further ahead than they can see.

What Kind of Profile?

9. What shape, then, is a higher international profile likely to assume? In style and inspiration it is likely to be cautious and pragmatic, operating for the most part within limited time horizons. It will be based on domestic compromise and may for that reason occasionally seem maladroit from outside. Externally, it will look for a congruence of international interests—but a congruence which will tend from its very nature to shift from place to place and from time to time. The profile is thus liable to prove, on occasion, a little *perfide*, Anglo-Saxon style. It will not be logical in the Cartesian sense, nor closely grounded in immutable philosophical principle.

10. Major components in a higher international profile in the 1980s will be enhanced expenditure on aid and on defence. I would expect Japan by the mid-1980s to have gone beyond the present doubling of the aid budget. While civilised and decent enough, Japan is not very noticeably a country of bleeding hearts. The misfortunes of Asiatic boat people or the victims of famine and flood in the Indian and African continents are not the objects of spontaneous popular concern outside the Christian fringe. But aid is closely connected to trade and foreign policy, and Japanese politicians and bureaucrats are aware of the expectations placed upon them by other Western Governments. As regards defence, the popular reticence is slowly changing as memories of the war recede and the necessity for some degree of self-help becomes clearer, both for its own sake and as a prudentially increased membership fee in the American Club. The opposition parties in the Diet are less pacifist than they used to be, and the LDP, as well as the civil and military bureaucracies in Japan, are becoming increasingly defence-minded. Again, the business implications are not absent from their calculations, whether in terms of spin-off from military to civil industries or, in a remoter future, the prospect of arms exports (which under present policies are firmly

discouraged). The emphasis, as required by the Constitution, will be on defensive, not offensive, military operations. One can expect the up-grading of present equipment, and improved surveillance and defence capabilities in Japan's sea and air approaches (more and better reconnaissance and interceptor aircraft; more frigates and short-range submarines; better ASW weapons etc). Also, no doubt, increased support cost payments for US bases.

11. Beyond aid and defence, we can also expect a progressively more active foreign policy, still within the ambit of existing alliances and partnerships, but more identifiably "made in Japan". The major initial objective will be to use Japan's economic strength to provide a swifter and more substantial response to US requests for international support. But a more active attempt will also be made to win friends and influence people more widely in the world, with the main emphasis on countries which can supply energy and raw materials, or which constitute major export outlets, or which offer convenient political partnerships. Canada, Mexico, Australia, the Arab Gulf, China and Europe seem likely to qualify in one way or another. We shall certainly hear more of the presently embryonic concept of a Pacific Basin Community, so far very much the brain-child of MM Ohira and Okita, but in which other Pacific partners, including Prime Ministers Fraser of Australia and Trudeau of Canada, are beginning to show at least polite interest. It will also remain a long-term objective of national self-affirmation to secure at least a semi-permanent place for Japan on the UN Security Council.

Potential Dangers and Disappointments

12. I mention one theoretical danger in order to rule it out. There will be no revival of militarism in Japan. The susceptibility of the densely-packed Japanese Islands to total nuclear annihilation, and the still-present and

officially-tended recollections of the atomic bombings of Nagasaki and Hiroshima, are reason enough in themselves. Militarism was, moreover, possible in the Japan of the 1930s largely because of the totalitarianism of the State, the tight censorship it exerted, and the associated ignorance or misperception of the outside world among all but a tiny Japanese pre-war *élite*. Information, education and knowledge of foreign languages are now too widely disseminated in this country for such recidivism to be possible. The same considerations largely (although not completely) exclude the growth of xenophobic chauvinism of a non-military type. The LDP leadership for years to come will remain closely linked both with the bureaucracy and with industry, both of them in turn sophisticated in international affairs and fully aware of the value to Japan in economic terms, both of the US strategic umbrella, and of the position of partnership which their country has achieved in the industrialised world as a whole. It may be that the current Japanese sense of self-confidence referred to above is tinged with affectionate condescension and feelings of superiority towards some Western partners. And this is always something that can get out of hand. But it has not yet surfaced in any overt manifestation of arrogance towards us, and is unlikely to do so as long as Japan remains unready to go it alone in the world.

13. The likely twin disappointments to be faced are those of non-achievement and mis-management. On the first count, it is certain that Japan will move towards a higher profile only progressively, and at times perhaps even with timidity. Japan's partners may be tempted to dismiss the attempt as "all talk and no do", and withdraw their interest at a time when Japan would most benefit from it, and when she could otherwise the more readily be influenced by Europe and the West. On the second, we must be ready to put up with occasional doses of Japanese ineptitude and mis-judgement. We Europeans are of course still ourselves capable of both. But some patient allowance

will need to be made for the fact that Japan is unaccustomed to burden-sharing and inexperienced as a principal protagonist in the international game. She will inevitably on occasion act small. The risible initial Japanese offer of $2 million to newly-independent Zimbabwe is as much part of the pattern as this year's splendid contribution of $100 million to the OECD Turkey consortium. Sometimes you see it; sometimes you don't. Insensitivity to others, too obvious a lack of compassion, too limited an international vision and too open an espousal of national interests narrowly conceived will, no doubt, from time to time, goad us all to resentment.

The Implications for the Community

14. Some readers may find all this a rather disquieting prospect, and may ask themselves why Europe should be expected to do very much to assist Japan to further prominence of a kind which would change the international status quo and might arguably challenge our own interests. I personally believe that a higher-profile Japan will on balance prove beneficial to us. But this is beside the point. The fact is that the process has already started. Rather, Europe will need to live with the new situation and learn how to turn it to good effect.

15. As a diplomat myself, I like to think that Foreign Affairs Ministries in Europe can be counted on to use their opportunities. But what contribution can be made by the Community's own institutions? I shall walk a circular path to answer this question.

16. Not all is joy unbounded. I have described on a previous occasion the ambiguity which underlies Japan's polite diplomatic acceptance of the Community dimension in European affairs. A generation of Japanese politicians and senior civil servants still exists which is accustomed to thinking of Europe only in terms of bilateral relations with its constituent Member States. To such men, even though

they be well-disposed, the Community can too often look like an international grouping whose achievements do not always match its pretensions and whose principal significance for Japan is in any case merely that of an a-political, exigent and protectionist trade caucus.

17. The tactical situation is that in recent months we have see-sawed up and down. Thus Mr. Ohira's new Administration, admittedly less experienced in these matters than its predecessor, was inclined, until recently, to give less emphasis than Mr. Fukuda's to the importance of the Community connection. There was no initial ministerial rush to visit European capitals. Late last year, the new Foreign Minister declined an invitation, conveyed through our local European Presidency, to a working lunch with the Member State Ambassadors and myself. Notwithstanding its references to the development of Japan's relations with friendly European countries, Mr. Ohira's Diet speech this January (paragraph 3 above) did not at any point acknowledge the existence of the European Community as such. Today, on the other hand, it is roses, roses all the way. The Iran crisis, and Japan's need for international cover in any operations it might undertake in support of the US, have given a significant, if perhaps only short-lived, boost to Community prestige in Japan, for which we have to thank the achievements of European Political Cooperation. Prime Minister Ohira's latest speeches make prominent allusion to the European Community; and he is indeed having talks in Bonn as I write this despatch. The Foreign Minister last month flew to Luxembourg at the drop of a hat to concert with European Foreign Ministers; he accepted with alacrity the invitation to a Community working lunch in Tokyo; and he will probably be again back in Europe (in Paris, London and Bonn, if not in Brussels) in ten days' time.

18. We must hope that this precarious upswing can be further prolonged. Meanwhile, however, we should not

lose sight of certain other successes, less spectacular but harder won, and which go further back in time.

19. Thus, on the trade front, the Commission probably succeeded in the late 1970s, albeit somewhat brutally, in jolting the Japanese out of their complacency and into seeing that the sole serious requirement was no longer to keep the Americans sweet. This has not been either an easy or a grateful task; nor one in which our Council of Ministers, too often "blow hot, blow cold", could invariably be counted on for systematic and wise support. But the various measures which have been taken since the Haferkamp/Ushiba communique to open up the Japanese market, while modest as seen from Brussels, are without recent historical precedent in Japan's relations with Europe. The levelling off of the Community's bilateral deficit with Japan last year furthermore won both sides a certain respite, even if the rain clouds are now banking up again for 1981. The exploration of the prospects for industrial cooperation, while still in its early stages, has headed the relationship in a healthier and more constructive direction and consequently aroused great interest in government circles.

20. At a more mundane and modest level, the sheer persistence of the Commission's personal diplomacy has, I think, begun to pay some dividends. What do I mean by this? Not so many years ago, the Japanese contacts of the Berlaymont were confined more often than not to the no doubt intelligent but not always very luminous individuals who represent Japan diplomatically in Europe and at international organisations. Trying to get a real feel for Government thinking back in Tokyo through such indirect means was about as hopeless a task (to adapt the simile of my Troop Sergeant of 30 years ago, who employed it, however, in a more earthy context) as attempting to wash one's feet with one's socks on. Through the instrument of the twice-yearly High Level Consultations, through the

visits to Tokyo at frequent intervals of Commissioners and senior officials for the discussion ad hoc of a wide range of political and technical matters, and through parliamentary links between the Diet and the European Assembly, many new windows have been opened on both sides and an information picture set up conveying to the Commission much more depth of field than it enjoyed in the past. The modest physical presence of this Delegation in Tokyo since 1974 has also helped.

21. The foundations therefore exist on which a higher-profile Community response to a higher-profile Japan could be constructed, should we so desire. The question is, what can we realistically aspire to achieve as a Community that we cannot achieve as Nine (shortly Ten) separate European States?

22. The Commission's bilateral policy objectives in the late 1970s were admirable as far as they went, namely:

- to secure a further opening up of the Japanese market for European exports of manufactured goods, processed agricultural products and financial services;

- to require some degree of sectoral restraint in Japanese exports to the Community (while opposing thorough-going EC protectionism), so as to avoid market disruption and to furnish a breathing space where necessary for the restoration of European competitivity;
- to broaden out the EC/Japan dialogue to embrace exchanges of view on other topics (aid, energy, transport, environment *und so weiter und so fort*) both for their own sake and in recognition of the political necessity of a more rounded and comprehensive relationship.

23. While still absolutely necessary, this triple aim is to my mind, however, no longer entirely sufficient for the pursuit of a more balanced and harmonious relationship with Japan in the 1980s. As already noted, the Commission has done well recently to add at least a tentative and exploratory discussion of industrial cooperation and cross-investment. If a Community consensus on this develops, and if European industry, technology and capital carry it into effect, the economic relationship with Japan will be greatly strengthened and perhaps even transformed. But the process of *rapprochment* seems unlikely to be able to stop there. Other issues will also need to be addressed. Still within the ambit of the Common Commercial Policy, there is the question of residual Member State trade restrictions —difficult to tackle in present economic conditions, but in the long run both bad for the Community's internal cohesion, and objectionable (not so much in their trade impact as in their discriminatory aspect) to a higher-profile Japan. Then the 1980s may pose us institutional questions. Should we appoint Wise Men? Should there be an Economic Agreement, with a consultation or safeguards clause? Can the machinery of European Political Cooperation be adapted to assist the development of closer EC/Japan relations? Needless to say, these are all big questions, to which there are no immediate and easy answers, and the future resolution of which will put both Europe and Japan to a searching test.

Conclusion

24. I reported soon after my arrival in this country the first impression which I then derived of a sense of unease, of self-questioning and sometimes of externally-directed resentment behind the facade of a well-established and comfortable if uninspiring Japanese international policy profile. I still detect this process at work. It is perhaps a necessary accompaniment to the long march of Japan away from the comforting certainties of the immediately post-war period. What is arguably now clearer is that this process may have been slowly preparing Japan for a more conspicuous role in international affairs as a more constructive ally of the US and conceivably as a better potential partner of Europe.

25. A higher profile Japan will be a Japan more willing than in the past to concert with the Community in fields where the Community is active in the international front rank. Such a Japan will, however, be nationally self-confident enough to insist on being an equal to be consulted, rather than a rich but simple-minded relative to be fleeced when required. And she will have ideas and priorities of her own. In order to consolidate our gains, to cope better with tomorrow's new economic headaches and to profit actively rather than passively from the benefits of a higher Japanese profile in the 1980s, I believe that a more ambitious EC approach needs to be devised, not necessarily for tomorrow, but over the years immediately ahead.

Leslie Fielding

(Head of Delegation)

THE OTHER SIDE OF JAPAN

Mr. Fielding to Vice President Haferkamp

SUMMARY

1. Like the moon, the Japanese economy has two sides to it. The bright side is the one we all know about: the success story of high growth, technological sophistication, and human intelligence and hard work (paragraphs 1-6).

2. The reverse face is less impressive. This is the not notably competitive and slightly old-fashioned Japan of small enterprises, low productivity, underdeveloped infrastructure, and over-regulated domestic financial services (paragraphs 7-9). It embraces a volatile national currency and unreformed fiscal and budgetary practices (paragraphs 10-11).

3. There are also at least six "time-bombs". These are: deleterious demographic change; the potential erosion of social disciplines; the long-term unemployment outlook; the risk of a further energy crisis; the danger of technological isolation; and finally the threat of a major earthquake (paragraphs 12-19).

4. The dichotomy of this "shack and sky-scraper" economy accounts for a pervasive Japanese sense of insecurity and self-doubt, combined paradoxically with another behavioural mode of over-confidence and self-assertion. On balance, it makes Japanese external policy cautious and inclined to sit its fences (paragraphs 20-26).

5. We need consequently to be firm with Japan where our own interests are concerned, but patient and conciliatory too, since it will take Japan some time to learn

to strike a more robust and constructive balance (paragraphs 27-28).

Confidential   EC Delegation
                                                                   Tokyo
Sir,   21 July, 1982

1. Like the moon, Japan presents a shining face to earthly observers. But the country also has its reverse side, of which foreigners generally take much less account, but of which the Japanese themselves are naturally very well aware. In economic terms, this dichotomy goes some way to explain the current ambivalence of economic mood in Japan between on the one hand the current spasm of over-confidence and condescension towards others, and on the other hand the more habitual self-doubt and gnawing economic uncertainty. I therefore propose to examine each side of Japan in turn, and to draw out the implications of each for the other, and of both of them for ourselves.

The Bright Side of Japan

2. The shining surface of Japan is its economic success story, strikingly apparent to any foreign visitor to this country, all too well-known to international trade negotiators and entirely familiar in its broad outlines to all European citizens who read newspapers or buy Japanese goods.

3. This is the Japan which, over the past 20 years, has achieved mass production first on a national, then on a global demand basis; and in the process experienced vertiginous economic growth. In 1960, Japan's GNP was 7.8% that of the US; in 1970, 20%; in 1980, 40%. In the latter year, her GNP was well ahead of Germany's and nearly twice that of either France or the UK. This is the Japan which today claims to possess 70% of the world's industrial robots and the highest computer population per head.

Mistress of the micro-chip, able and willing to learn from others and to improve on what she has learnt, socially conditioned for good team work, Japan certainly seems well established in the very front rank of the technologically advanced democracies. On the basis of growth projections of a steady 4% per annum, Japan, which accounted for nearly 2% of world GNP in 1955, and which today has reached 10%, could well be a 12% country by the year 2000. Some sources even predict that, by 2000, Japan will have the highest per capita GNP in the world.

4. This striking story of success has owed much to an international economic system created and sustained by other countries, and by a fortunate concatenation of market circumstances. But it is also deeply rooted in the Japanese people themselves—the country's primary resource, as their own leaders frequently acknowledge.

5. The recently published evidence suggesting that the average Japanese performs better in IQ tests than does the average European or American does not come as a complete surprise to those of us who live in this country as foreign observers. Educational standards are also exceptionally high (94% of all Japanese remain at school until the age of 18; 37.5% thereafter proceed to universities and polytechnics). Numeracy is as highly prized as literacy and the acquisition of at least a passive knowledge of foreign languages. Engineers, technologists and applied scientists are trained in large numbers and are dominant in broad industrial management as well as in the technicalities of production and planning. The Japanese news media, serious and comprehensive in their coverage, keep their huge and attentive readership well informed on international affairs. Many millions of Japanese have now travelled abroad on business or pleasure. A recipient of other people's bright ideas and a copier of foreign techniques in the early stages of her post-war development, in more recent years a skilful adapter and

developer of imported technology, Japan today, while still far from strong in pure science, has developed a certain industrial inventiveness of her own—to the point that over the past 10 years, measured by licenses, Japan has exported more technology than she has imported. She now registers more new patents in the US than do France, Germany or the UK.

6. All this has been underpinned by a powerful and high-quality bureaucracy in close symbiosis with Japan's already impressive industrial establishment. (In 1980, 78% of retiring senior Japanese civil servants found ready re-employment in business). And on such a foundation, supported by consistently very low interest rates, a very high savings-to-income ratio (around 20%), an exceptionally high debt/equity ratio (85:15 is not unknown), by high investment rates, falling unit labour costs and steadily increasing productivity in the key industries, the transformation of Japan's economy from capital-intensive heavy industry to knowledge-intensive high technology is already far advanced.

The Darker Side of the Japanese Economy

7. So far, so good. What precedes is commonplace enough in Europe. Such is the bright surface which "Japan as No 1" presents to the outside world. The other side of Japan is one which reveals considerable areas of low labour productivity, poor techniques and consequent lack of international competitiveness; and where a number of time-bombs of different magnitudes and of unpredictable damage potential are quietly ticking away.

8. To change the metaphor, Japan is a country of shacks as well as sky-scrapers. Across the board (as opposed to in select areas of technological advancement), Japan's gross domestic production by employee is lower than that of the US and most West European countries. The primary,

secondary and tertiary sectors of the Japanese economy each have their flaws. Agriculture, while now much of it mechanised, remains notoriously costly and uncompetitive. It flourishes only by virtue of huge Government subsidies and a very high level of trade protection. Industry is varied in its performance. Processing and assembling industries (automobiles, machinery, electronics) are technically efficient and commercially successful; but the basic material industries (aluminium refining, petro-chemicals) have lately suffered a decline; while light industry has always tended to be internationally uncompetitive (some consumer goods, for example, can be unimpressive). Although Japan boasts industrial groupings the top six of which (Mitsubishi, Sumitomo, Mitsui et al) have the largest turnover in the world, it also contains a host of small enterprises existing at and beyond the margin of economic viability. Thus there are 830,000 small and medium manufacturing enterprises in Japan—rough one to every 140 people in the country; 99% of Japanese firms employ less than 300 workers each; three-quarters of the Japanese work force is organised in groups of less than 10 people. Many of these small enterprises fall into the tertiary sector and help to explain why the retail and distribution system in Japan (in which over 22% of Japanese workers are employed) is so complex and curious. In all these small firms, physical working conditions are frequently very tough and the terms of employment are often well below what would be acceptable in Europe (wages, social security, holidays etc).

9. Banking and insurance practices inside Japan are also somewhat old-fashioned and subject to a surprising degree of government regulation. Logistic infrastructure is inadequate—autoroutes are few, railways (despite the vaunted but untypical bullet train) are loss-makers. Housing is as cramped as ever. Social infrastructure and services could justly be described as generally behind the best in Europe and the US. Even in technologically

advanced sectors, Japan does not enjoy comparative advantage across the board. Bio-technology (while admittedly undergoing rapid and promising development) is still behind; the weakness in computer soft-ware (while also remediable in a longer time-frame) is even more marked; nuclear technology (while first class in itself) is still derivative, and advanced nuclear fuel cycle technologies are being developed later than in Europe and the US; there is as yet no significant aviation or aerospace industry (although this is an area where Japan intends to make progress).

10. In the monetary field, Japan suffers from the defects, as well as the advantages, of its currency. The exchange rate of the Yen against the dollar has in recent years gone up and down like a child's "yo-yo". It plunged to Y307 in December 1975; rose to Y176 in October 1978; fell again to Y260 in April 1980; and has oscillated between Y199 and Y255 over the last 18 months. The currency is currently grossly undervalued by reference to such fundamentals as Japan's relative economic performance as measured by growth, inflation, current account surplus, industrial productivity and long-term prospects. The causes of this are complex and controversial. The performance of the dollar, the psychological impact on international confidence in Japan of two oil crises, the large swings from black to red and back again of Japan's current account (insofar as this is a cause as well as an effect), the magnitude of high US interest rates, the recent loosening of Japanese controls on capital outflows, have each in turn contributed. Manipulation for nefarious commercial purposes by the Bank of Japan and the financial establishment seems ruled out, even if more could sometimes have been expected from Japan to contribute to international exchange rate stability. Certainly, volatility on this scale constitutes a potential weakness if it persists into the longer term. When the Yen soars, while raw material imports cheapen, export profit margins fall. And

there can be both export and import penalties when the currency is undervalued in terms of both enhanced trade friction and of higher industrial input costs. Instability of this kind is bad for international confidence in Japan.

11. To the foregoing could be added the problem of Japan's politico-economic self-management, in which a vicious as well as a virtuous circle can be detected. The virtuous circle accounts for some of the successes already noted above. The vicious circle, increasingly in evidence over the past 10 years, can be illustrated with reference to the budget problem. Government revenue falls so far short of Government expenditure that over 20% of the annual budget has to be funded by the floating of Government bonds. For some time, fiscal reform has been seen as necessary, and was half-heartedly attempted by the previous Prime Minister; but appears now to be politically beyond the reach of the present LDP Administration, as well as economically incompatible with the current efforts to stimulate demand. Interest rates, now absurdly low, cannot be raised significantly without provoking bankruptcies, dampening domestic demand, and increasing the cost of Government borrowing. This in turn helps to depress the international parity of the yen, increases the import bill for energy and vital raw materials, and risks the intensification of trade conflicts with Japan's other advanced partners through a reduction in demand for manufactured imports and through an enhanced incentive to export.

Six Possible "Time-Bombs"

12. And now I reach the time-bombs ticking away in Japan. They come in all sorts of shapes and sizes. I list them for what they may be worth, in no particular order of importance, since there is no possible common measure of their potential significance. They should not be overstated

—all countries have a problem or three in the cupboard. But these have their bearing on Japan's future.

13. First, deleterious demographic change. Japan, which has an almost stable population, now has the longest life expectancy in the world (by 1981, the median life span had reached 73.79 years for Japanese males, surpassing the hitherto highest world average of 73.7 years for Icelandic males). In consequence Japan, which already has on average the oldest work force in the world, will have to shoulder increased social burdens by the turn of the century. At present 9% of the population is over 65 years old. In just over 30 years' time, this will have risen to 21%. Today, around 450,000 Japanese are bed-ridden geriatrics; by the year 2000, there will be 1 million of them. In 35 years' time (unless the working life of the populace can be extended, and suitable employment found for all), there will be only 2.7 workers to support each geriatric where today there are 7.4. Recent estimates show that social security spending will have to increase by 10 percentage points over the next 35 years (i.e. from the present 9% of GNP to around 19%) simply to keep pace with the changing demographic pattern. This is one of the reasons why some Japanese experts estimate that economic growth will have to be sustained at above 3% per annum if Japanese living standards are not to fall.

14. Second, possible relaxation of traditional social disciplines. This bomb does not tick loudly and may well never detonate; but it nevertheless exists. Japanese society is more homogenous and group-oriented than that of any other Western country. The work ethic, sense of collective responsibility, willing acceptance of hierarchy and discipline; the readiness of many Japanese to tolerate what we would consider crowded and stressful work conditions and a generally impaired quality of life; the common honesty of the people and the safety of their homes, streets and places of amusement—all these combine to confer

exceptional advantages upon the national economy. Labour/management relations usually are smooth and effective; politics are stable. It is unlikely that such a tightly knit social fabric will unravel significantly in the foreseeable future. But, equally, one wonders whether it can be sustained indefinitely in its present pattern. The pressures of modern living and the relative openness of Japan to Western influences of every kind are beginning to have some measurable effect.

15. In post-war Japan, an ostensibly egalitarian society without marked divisions of class, rewards have been fairly evenly distributed across the social scale, and great wealth, while it has always existed, has remained modestly concealed. In consequence, 9 out of 10 Japanese have come to feel themselves as broadly middle class. But the latest polls suggest that this massive majority self-perception may be shrinking at the margin. This could be due to the downward pressure on living standards created by recent more sluggish growth; but other factors could also be at work. On a different plane, there is an intangible but real change in the role of women, traditionally subdued and confined to household tasks, but now well-educated, better informed and with more appetite for emancipation and involvement. What is clearer is the beginning of change in the orientation of the young. In the schools, there is evidence of indiscipline, and occasionally of violence, where previously they were all but unknown. While it is true everywhere in the world that the younger the age group, the greater the individualism and the hedonism, nevertheless opinion polls seem to show up a qualitative difference in mentality between those above and below the age of 25 in Japan. The present younger age group is nicknamed the "my generation", because of their preoccupation with personal rather than collective goals. It may be, as historical parallels elsewhere in the world would suggest, that what the young people absorb in their mothers' arms and learned in their infancy, to that they

will revert in their final adult state. But one questions how long will Japan be able to remain culturally insulated and to resist forces that in other industrialised democracies have already changed paternalistic patterns into more egalitarian ones? It all needs to be watched: a sea change may now slowly be in the making.

16. Third, unemployment. This has not in recent years been a problem, but it could become so with the advance of robots, word processors and means of instant communication, and as a consequence of the inroads slowly being made into the grossly over-staffed retail sectors by the controversial but popular new supermarket chains. The systems of lifetime employment and continuous on-the-job training operated by the larger Japanese companies are unique. But smaller companies can and do shed staff and go bankrupt. Unemployment (officially 2.2%, but in reality closer to 4%) is now rising slightly. Looking ahead, can Japan hope to re-tool and re-deploy all the technicians, blue-collar workers, clerks, typists and shop assistants likely to become redundant in the rapid conversion of their country to a post-industrial state? Yet significant unemployment, if finally registered, would be all the more de-stabilising for being unfamiliar. All in all, the social consequences of Japan's current technological revolution seem likely to be as far-reaching as those which followed the Meiji Restoration or Japanese defeat in World War Two.

17. Fourth, the danger of a renewed international energy crisis. Japan's external sources of supply of basic raw materials for industry are sufficiently secure or diversified not to create a weakness greater than that of any other Western economy. Even as regards energy, Japanese vulnerability is not different in type, but only in extent, from that of Western Europe as a whole. Nevertheless, 84% of Japan's energy is currently imported. All but a fraction of Japan's oil comes from abroad, over 70% of it from the Middle East. There is a limit to the pace

and scope of possible diversification. Japan would be harder hit than any other single country by a Middle East oil embargo, or by a significant price increase. A future such increase could not be handled in the same way as it was during the oil shocks of the seventies (i.e. by engineering an export boom and a sharp cut-back in the volume of imports); Japan's trade relations with the other Western partners are now too fragile to bear it, without incurring the penalty of anti-Japanese protectionism.

18. Fifth, the danger of falling behind in the technological race. As the achievements of Japanese industrial innovation succeed each other, one has to remember that Japan's originality and sheer inventiveness are unfortunately far from absolute. The group ethic, so useful in other respects, may yet prove a lasting handicap in pure science. It is at least conceivable that Japan could be left behind when the next generation of new ideas is introduced by other Western researchers; in the race to develop a 5th generation computer (or any other advanced concept), she might for example simply back the wrong horse. Nor can Japan be sure of acquiring other people's technology as readily and as cheaply over the next 20 years as she has been permitted to do over the past 20. With the growing involvement of many Western governments in industrial research and development—outside as well as inside the field of defence—any new cards are more likely than in the past to be hugged to the partner's chest rather than to be carelessly or boastfully displayed for Japan's benefit. Meanwhile, the effect of the latest industrial espionage scandal involving Japanese companies in Silicon Valley will undoubtedly be to close doors in the US which were previously wide open.

19. Finally, the risk of a major earthquake. There are nine active volcanoes in Japan, the islands of which are of geologically recent formation, strung out along a major fault line in the earth's crust. Minor but perceptible earth

tremors are a regular feature of life in Japan; but over a period of centuries, really major earthquakes have tended to occur at intervals of 60-70 years. The last such event, in 1923, caused widespread destruction of flimsy traditional buildings. Modern Japanese cities would be much more damage-resistant; but no one really knows just how disruptive the next big quake could prove to industry and to society at large. Fear of a catastrophic earthquake is an important aspect of the Japanese psyche and explains in part the emphasis often put on the fragility of any success Japan may achieve.

The Policy Consequences of Economic Dichotomy

20. Let me now attempt to draw one or two conclusions, since the dichotomy between the two sides of the Japanese economy, and the likely persistence of an associated national sense of insecurity, seem to me to condition a certain Japanese frame of mind in international affairs.

21. For a long time after the close of the Second World War, Japan had little confidence in her international position. The self-perception was of a geographically isolated, materially and economically weak country in which the Japanese were left with no other option but to work hard and hope for the best in the worst of situations.

22. Gradually this sense of weakness was overcome, as high economic growth yielded its results. Confidence in the country's economic strength grew further as the Japanese found themselves surviving the two oil shocks of the last decade faster and more comfortably than any other of their industrial partners. Acceptance of the need for a more positive international profile has grown, albeit reluctantly; but Japanese self-assertion has grown with it. As noted at the outset of this despatch, the Japanese can sometimes now appear both over-confident in their abilities and achievements and just a little condescending towards—perhaps even disdainful of—other Western countries.

23. Yet the predominant mood in Japan remains more one of caution and self-doubt than of condescension or disdain. Japan still sees herself as the "fragile barque tossed on a stormy sea". Despite changes in their perceptions of the world, many Japanese still tend to see the international system as something created by others. In this optic, the challenge to Japan, as they see it, remains basically how to survive within the system with maximum attainable benefit and with minimum unrequited contribution to the system's continued viability and well-being.

24. This prudential attitude is one which combines a firm Western anchorage with the desire to sail in many and varied waters. Japan must have as many friends and as few enemies as possible. The GATT, the OECD, the IMF, the Western Economic Summits are vital, and must feature prominently in Japanese external policy. But attention must also be paid to North-South manifestations (Cancun), the UN Security Council, an active interest in South East Asia, and relations with the state trading countries which neatly balance the countervailing claims of Beijing and Moscow. Tentatively and without taking any lead of a nature which might revive unpleasant past memories of economic hegemony, Japan also feels prompted to explore the possibilities of a loosely-knit "Pacific Basin Community", for its long-term possibilities in terms of security of supply, market access and political partnerships.

25. Reinsurance policies of this kind are perfectly natural; and we Europeans also perch ourselves prudently on certain international fences. Where the difference between us and the Japanese begins to show is over what we term 'burden sharing'. The present Japanese instinct is that the cost to the national exchequer and to the economy at large of Japan's inevitably expanding international role should be kept within very strict limits. Japan still spends approximately only 1% of her GNP on defence—and this,

for hard financial, as well as for historical and domestic political, reasons. Japan's ODA spending, while tending to increase, barely exceeds the rise in the country's GNP; and in 1981, it even actually fell. Far from aiming to achieve the OECD DAC target in terms of percentage of GNP, Japan is likely to be content with the lesser outlay which would bring her to "overtake Germany" —i.e. to take second place in absolute volume terms after the US.

26. In international trade, there will continue, as in the past, to be certain limits to what it is politically possible for the Japanese Government to do in breaking down traditionally autarkic commercial patterns and in throwing open its internal markets to competitive foreign manufactures. Agriculture in particular will continue to be lavishly protected, on the basis of politically plausible, if economically spurious, strategic arguments in favour of national self-sufficiency. More generally, the instinct will remain to export as much and to import as little as is consistent with the avoidance of protectionism in North America and Europe, and of comparable penalties in trade relations with her Asian and Far Eastern neighbours. Cautious conservatism also seems likely to hamper any serious effort to achieve the early liberalisation of the Japanese capital market, and to defer the eventual stabilisation and internationalisation of Japan's volatile national currency. Finally, while overseas manufacturing investment, and a genuine two-way traffic in scientific research and development, will interest Japan increasingly in the 1980s, the extent and enthusiasm of the Japanese commitment to them may fall short of what her principal partners desire.

Conclusion

27. This is not in the least intended to be either a pessimistic or an unfriendly assessment. Nor one which necessarily implies continuing tension and mistrust in our

relations with Japan—there are positive as well as negative forces at play. Rather, this despatch argues for a higher degree of subtlety and understanding in our approach to partnership with Japan.

28. In my opinion, the Japanese, whether or not they consciously intend it, will in practice inevitably find themselves continuing a precarious balancing act throughout the 1980s, both domestically (in adjusting to internal structural changes) and also internationally (in seeking a posture of equilibrium amid the conflicting pressures exerted upon them). It is reasonable that we should assist our Japanese friends with their balance, by showing the right mixture of firmness and understanding and by making some attempt to be fair. To be sure, it needs to be more widely accepted in Japan that the country is not alone in having weaknesses and flaws. Other nations, too, are exposed to time-bombs. Japan's countervailing economic strengths mean that she really has no excuse not to remedy certain deficiencies in her international posture. Therefore, she fully deserves to be kept up to the mark by her partners. But on our side it needs to be equally widely accepted that the necessary Japanese transformations will take time and will lay legitimate claim on our patience. Japan is a resilient country, and a great one, and thus a partner for whom it can sometimes be worthwhile to wait awhile.

Leslie Fielding

(Head of Delegation)

A FAREWELL TO JAPAN

Mr. Fielding to Vice-President Haferkamp

SUMMARY

As regards the immediate issues in EC-Japan relations, serious trade tensions continue to exist, despite superficial improvements. The unstable Yen does not help. But bilateral trade is not the whole story. Industrial and scientific cooperation, financial dialogue and appropriate inward investment should continue to be encouraged. So too (but without illusions) should political and ODA cooperation (paragraphs 2-8).

Japan does not really understand the Community, or very much like the Commission. This is due partly to her greater preoccupation with other parts of the world; but also in part to trade friction. Japan does not yet see herself as rich, nor does she yet fully grasp the extent of other countries' economic difficulties (paragraphs 9-12).

The Japanese are factually well informed about the world, but do not feel an integrated part of it. They can be parochial and passive in political outlook; their decision-making process on external issues is inadequate (paragraphs 13-16).

The Europeans are handicapped by their own mistaken mythologies about Japan. We should de-mythologise, fast (paragraphs 17, 18).

History proves the Japanese to be a great, if potentially volatile, people. Their post-war achievement—political as well as economic—is without parallel. But they have their weaknesses and anxieties; and nothing is forever (paragraphs 19-24).

The 'bottom line' for us, in our dealings with them, is obviously lucidity and firmness; but also friendship and a determination to learn from them and work with them (paragraphs 25, 26).

Japan has been fun, my staff first class. Thank you for having sent me here (paragraphs 27-30).

	EC Delegation
Confidential	Tokyo
Sir,	29 July 1982

1. It is traditional for diplomatic envoys, on finally leaving post, to set out their valedictory reflections on the country where they have been serving. Today, on my fiftieth birthday, and the eve of transfer back to Brussels to become the next Director-General, I have very much the honour, but not in every respect the pleasure, to write a farewell despatch, from Japan. Not fully the pleasure, because my farewell thoughts are as conflicting, and as difficult to express, as the first impressions of this country which I submitted to you on my arrival. The kind of European who seems to know most about Japan is all too often the top banker or businessman on his first visit, who will start to offer you his confident and clear-cut analysis almost as soon as he has presented his passport for inspection. Certainly, the longer you stay here, the less you have to say; generalisations lose their validity and particular insights become too deep and diverse for facile expression, with the passage of years.

The Immediate Issues in EC-Japan Relations

2. Where things stand at present in EC-Japan relations will be familiar from our detailed day-to-day reports and I shall content myself with a brief personal overview.

3. Last summer, the London 'Financial Times', describing Japan's trade relations with Europe and America, wrote of "what are almost certainly the worst tensions in existence at present between any advanced industrial country and its trading partners". Notwithstanding the heat of current EC-US controversy, this description still broadly fits Japan's relations with the Community, despite the considerable efforts which the Commission have deployed by way of economic dialogue and remonstrance with Japan, and despite the undoubted, if modest, efforts which Japan has made in response.

4. The autarkic corporate structure of Japan, its incompatibilities with the spirit and practice of the GATT, and the associated abnormal trade imbalances, have been comprehensively treated in the Commission's GATT Article XXIII representations this spring and summer and need not detain us here. Despite a degree of export restraint in sensitive sectors, and some slightly less than awful recent monthly statistics, the twin trade problems remain. First, the imperviousness of the Japanese market to competitive foreign manufactures; and second, the potential or actual threat posed by sectorally concentrated high-quality Japanese exports not only to industries which already exist in Europe, but also to those as yet undeveloped which, thanks to Japan, may never see the light of day. And both problems are exacerbated by the current undervaluation of the Yen—or what one qualified observer has recently termed "the tendency of the Yen to live in a world of its own". The Japanese Government have been brought, for the first time, to a point of genuine political awareness of the dangers of this situation and of the need to take appropriate action. Unfortunately, however, even though time is not in the least on Japan's side, the two recent Japanese packages of trade measures have gone only a shortish way in the right direction. There is still a substantial gap between what we expect of Japan and what the Japanese are able and willing to do for us. Nor is there

any immediate prospect of restoring a more rational Yen parity. Consequently, the risk of politicisation of economic problems, and thereafter of damaging confrontation, remains.

5. Today's visible trade balances are naturally not the whole story. They illustrate only yesterday's decisions, not tomorrow's opportunities. The Commission have been right to develop further with the Japanese our ideas for industrial, technological and scientific cooperation between the Community and Japan. This cooperation will be slow to materialise and will assume complex and possibly confusing forms at a variety of levels (Community, Member State, private enterprise groupings and companies); and the Japanese leadership, beyond the lip-service which they pay to such concepts for obvious tactical reasons, do not yet appear actively committed to the achievement of early results. But the Commission should clearly persist. The innovative and purposeful language-training scheme for European businessmen (the Commission's "Executive Training Programme") is complementary to our cooperation efforts, and may need to be further expanded.

6. There are also other expedients which can help to compensate for trade imbalance. Hence our dialogue with Japan on financial services. Notwithstanding our traditional surplus with Japan on invisibles, European banks and insurance companies have much more difficulty in this country than Japanese financial services generally experience in developing their European operations. Nor should we lose sight of inward investment. Overseas Japanese investment is already modest enough, whether world-wide ($36 billion) or by region (10.6% in the Community); and barely a quarter is directly related to manufacturing activity. Nevertheless, once precautions are taken against Trojan Horses, I believe that the benefits of enhanced Japanese manufacturing investment in the Community can out-weigh the disadvantages.

7. Finally, a word about more political matters. Foreign policy cooperation with Japan, still in its infancy, deserves to be progressively built up by the Ten, as the international role of Japan finds increasing political expression. But such cooperation is not at present a means of significant persuasion; nor are the immediate benefits to us very great. Co-operation over Iran, Afghanistan and to some extent Poland has been worthwhile; over the Falklands, however, and any future such issue where there is nothing in it for the national interests of Japan, there have been and will be disappointments for the Europeans.

8. The same will be broadly true, at least initially, of the practical cooperation which the Commission quite rightly seek to establish with Japan in regard to official development assistance.

The Japanese View of the Community

9. The Community as such is not greatly understood, nor the Commission very much liked, in Japan. But, over the four years of which I have had the direct experience of living in Tokyo, Japan's knowledge of the Community has increased somewhat, and her acceptance of the Commission become slightly less reluctant. It has not escaped Japanese notice that, on most international economic issues of importance (and on many foreign policy issues also), the Ten are consistently in the international headlines. Regular personal contact with the Japanese has helped to win the Commission wider recognition—from the annual rendez-vous at the Western Economic Summit, through our twice-yearly High level Consultations, down to the local operations of this Mission and its visibly close working relationship with the Embassies of our Member States. The European Parliament's links with the National Diet, under Sir Fred Warner's leadership, have been built up in a constructive and business-like way.

10. Nevertheless, difficulties remain which seem to go deeper than the mere novelty of the Community in international relations, than our geographical distance from Japan, and than the inevitably much larger place occupied in Japan's world picture by the US, and by Japan's Asian and Far Eastern neighbours. An opinion survey conducted last year by the Prime Minister's office showed, in a multiple-choice question, only 13% interested in Western Europe (the latter coming after the US, Asia, the Middle East and Eastern Europe). In a single choice question, only 2% thought that Japan should strengthen relations with Western Europe (the same percentage as that achieved by the USSR; the US scored highest with 38%, followed by China with 16%).

11. Part of the explanation of this lies in the image of the Community in Japan as, above all else, something to do with trade friction and European protectionism. Trade friction touches not only the pockets of Japanese exporters, but also the hearts of a sensitive and proud people. The same opinion survey showed the Japanese man in the street to be divided fifty-fifty between conciliatory and chauvinistic sentiments on trade friction with Europe and America.

12. We need to remember at this point that the Japanese as a nation are still unaccustomed to the idea that their country has suddenly become rich. Despite significant advances in material well-being, the individual is not overwhelmingly under the impression that he has "never had it so good". Housing, travel and working conditions in this country are in striking contrast with what leaps to the eye in Europe. Japanese visitors to the Community mostly do not see the dole queues and the depressed industrial centres; instead they observe the yachts, the luxury motorcars and the spacious residences of the gainfully employed European bourgeoisie. The fact that we have

genuine economic difficulties of our own has therefore yet to be fully grasped by the thinking Japanese public.

The Japanese View of the World

13. The Community is not, however, the only one to be misunderstood or overlooked by Japan. The Japanese international outlook as a whole, while guided by comprehensive media report and a great deal of shrewd business intelligence, is liable on occasion to be insensitive and myopic. There is, for example, no real sympathy for the developing world. Nor is there any great sense, outside *élite* circles, of the nation's interdependence with other people; rather, the popular feeling is one of Japanese uniqueness—of being different from (and mostly superior to) the inhabitants of the outside world. Thus self-absorption and parochialism can sometimes go hand-in-hand with the sensitive national pride already touched on above.

14. True, in political and bureaucratic circles, there is today an appetite for more active responsibilities in world affairs, and a willingness to pay some sort of price for them. But the tacit assumption is elsewhere still widely made that the Western world in which the Japanese enjoy partnership was created by others to the incidental but happy benefit of Japan; and that, for the maintenance of this system, no strenuous Japanese exertion, no major sharing of burdens, need consequently be volunteered. This, despite the rising quotient of irritation with Japan which is being registered in so many quarters—particularly this year in the US—and of which the Japanese are uneasily aware.

15. Indeed, despite their remarkable ability to learn, adjust and expand in the industrial field, the Japanese can still prove over-cautious—or even plain inept—in their political and economic dealings with outsiders. Japanese

domestic politics do not help: while admirably stable and for the most part fulfilling what the electorate appears to expect, they are also dullish and devoid of distinction. The national decision-making process is unlike anything we know in Europe. On external issues, it is not merely laboriously slow and unimaginative; it is even infirm—as if outside realities, other than those which are brought to Japan's attention in forceful fashion, have no inside writ or validity. Whaling practices are a minor but eloquent illustration of this seeming inability of the Japanese to abandon remunerative bad habits when not absolutely compelled to do so.

16. In particular, Japanese official diplomacy tends to be short-term and public-relations-oriented, rather than long-sighted and substantive. Individual senior officials are always hard-working, usually well-intentioned, and not infrequently of brilliant personal calibre; but inter-ministerial rivalries, amazingly unconfined, cripple the consensus which the Foreign Ministry and others are called upon to articulate. Half-hearted efforts are made to dispose of problems *seriatim* as they arise. Concessions, sliced thin like salami, are invariably addressed to symptoms rather than to causes, without any apparent consideration of the possible necessity for adjustment to this country's basic habits or policies. While the bargaining process is taking place, considerable efforts will be deployed to enlist the "understanding" of the partner: a euphemism for explaining why little or nothing can be done. If the bargaining fails, there follow bitter Japanese complaints that it is all the other person's fault; that the latter is ill-informed, insincere or of evil intent (i.e. the "Japan-as-scapegoat" syndrome). The debate is shrouded in a smoke screen of what I have elsewhere termed "Black Propaganda"—a false naive or slanted argumentation designed to obfuscate the issue or to score mere debating points.

Our View of Japan: A Clash of Mythologies

17. To be fair, Europe too has its weaknesses, and makes its own idiosyncratic errors, in approaching modern Japan. Japanese ethnocentric and myopic tendencies can be matched by European myth-making and ignorance. Speaking here not of the skilled Japan-watchers, but of the common run of Europeans, we not only love generalising about Japan (which is of course inevitable—I have had to make some hair-raising simplifications in writing this despatch); we also quite often then draw the wrong conclusions (which is dangerous as well as avoidable).

18. Broadly speaking, there seem to be three mistaken European ways of seeing Japan: the first (too hostile), one of impatience, mistrust and aggressivity; the second (overgenerous), of sentimentalism, idealisation and misplaced advocacy; the third (over-negative), of defeatism and neglect. Thus, we sometimes think of "Japan Incorporated" and adhere to the comfortable pre-conception that, since the Japanese market is closed and the Japanese way of doing business incompatible with our own, we need not fatigue ourselves with the stressful acceptance of challenge: protectionism is the better course. Alternatively, we seek to use the Japanese, as Tacitus used the ancient German tribes, as a mythically virtuous people, efficient and competitive, to be held up as a reproach to ourselves, and as a paradigm to those desirous of rejuvenating Europe's industries and reforming its economic mores. In between these two schools of thought, here are those of us who follow a neglectful and fatalistic "business as usual" approach to Japan, ready to take a little investment here, to export a little there, yet with no real commitment to a better partnership or belief in the prospects of success. In all three mythologies, there is little evident confidence in the possibility of a relationship with Japan based on a common position of the Ten; indeed the Europeans sometimes find themselves sniping at each

other, and at the Commission, in full view of the Japanese—
only to confirm the latter in their doubts as to the
Community's seriousness of purpose towards them.

A More Balanced, Historical, Perspective

19. A more balanced *and* realistic basic view of Japan
would need, in my view, to take some account of the
following reflections. Setting aside all day-to-day matters
and technical preoccupations, one does well to see from
the outset that the Japanese are a great people who deserve
our respect and, in a number of ways, also our admiration.
Like any other nation, they are not without their
shortcomings—a certain racism and lack of compassion, for
example, are very much apparent. But their diligence,
group-consciousness, effectiveness and intelligence are
exceptional.

20. If the domestic political situation of feudal Japan had
been slightly different at the arrival of the Portuguese,
Spanish and Dutch, and if the Japanese had not then finally
expelled all foreigners and withdrawn into isolation, the
Japanese industrial revolution would have come a century
or two earlier; much of South East Asia could have been
first colonised by Japan rather than by Western Europe;
and Australia and New Zealand might even have become
the extension of a Japanese, instead of a British, mother-
country.

21. As it was, events were to follow a different course.
After hundreds of years of self-imposed isolation, Japan
was to be opened up against her will by American, Russian
and British sea-power in the 1850s. Miraculously, Japan
adapted in short order. Under the aegis of a revived
monarchy, a small ruling group exercising draconian
powers set out to modernise full tilt — and to catch up and,
if possible, overtake the West. The aim was "rich country,
strong army". Relations with near neighbours quickly
became tense; wars were fought with Korea, China and

Russia in an attempt at regional hegemony. After the brief appearance of a more broadly based and democratic system of government in the 1920s, there followed the "dark valley" of 1931-1945. First came the growth of militarism, the renewal of war on China, the development of an authoritarian police state; next the opening of the Pacific War and the promotion of the "Greater East AsiaCo-Prosperity Sphere"; finally, attrition, nuclear bombardment, abject defeat, and alien occupation. In 1945, all was in ruins.

22. Yet, thereafter, Japan was to make greater economic progress, in less time, than any country in modern history. And the post-war Japanese political miracle, despite the absence of a historically secure democratic tradition, was to prove hardly less remarkable than the economic. So it is that in 1982, in her own idiosyncratic but harmonious fashion, Japan finds herself rich, modern, and open to outside ideas and influence, with a stable parliamentary democracy and a vigilant press and judiciary, and without militarism or apparent belligerence. From a violent and struggling past, she has moved to a more balanced and pacific present: in place of poverty and impotence, Japan now has prosperity and a power to do things in the world. It is a remarkable story and, in its current phase, one to be proud of.

23. But nothing is for ever. Japan may change. There is the "other side" to the Japanese economy which is the subject of my separate despatch. Self-confident and full of aggressive energy, and very well able to adapt to change, the Japanese are paradoxically also an insecure people, haunted with doubts and anxieties. To be sure, the future economic prosperity of Japan is on balance at least as assured as, and arguably more promising than, that of the European Community. There remain, however, areas of industrial and technological weakness, vulnerability to

natural disaster and man-made embargo, as well as potentially disquieting domestic social shifts.

24. More than this, Japan is also potentially a volatile country. As noted above, she has known periods of instability and of rapid change in her recent history. While this country needs friends and allies, and dislikes overt confrontation, it is also capable of assuming, in the process of sustained economic success, a self-assertive and even arrogant international posture. One sees no sign of a potential re-run of the political and military scenario of the 1920s and 30s. Nevertheless, as pointed out in an earlier despatch on Japan's coming higher international profile, we must expect a subtle change of mood in the leadership of Japan as the existing cautious and low-profile gerontocrats pass away. To be sure, the next wave of "young Turks" (i.e. those in their 60s!) seem cautious enough and likely to assure continuity. But their eventual successors are liable to want to walk taller and to be more assertive on the international scene than those who are now in or near power. And if the world economy were to surrender to the centrifugal forces which are now beginning to tug towards regionalism, and if Japan were to slide back into a more isolationist attitude, then the consequences in Japan could conceivably prove frustrating and unpleasant for all of us.

The "Bottom Line" in EC-Japan Relations

25. It follows, therefore, that our admiration and our respect need to be active rather than passive. Seriousness about Japan, a determination to become closely involved with her, and a willingness to learn from her where appropriate, are much more our need than any short-term defensive view or protectionist expedient. Naturally, we must be firm in the protection of our own interests. (Indeed, in being thus firm, I myself can claim to have run some risks for my own personal acceptability in this

country at various points over the past four years.) But Europe requires positive policies also. We need to take Japan more fully into account in what we do upon the world scene, and in some of the things we do at home. And this will mean operating with Japan whenever possible as the Ten together, on an agreed Community basis. The Japanese respect strength in a partner and will not think the more of us for our disunities.

26. My US colleague, the former Senator Mike Mansfield, is fond of saying, as he wrote in newspaper articles as recently as the Fourth of July this year, that "the relationship between the US and Japan is without question the most important single bilateral relationship in the world". This odd *obiter dictum* has the merits as well as the defects of the diplomatic slogan which it no doubt is. Europe cannot hope to enjoy in contemporary Japan the prestige and influence which—for obvious strategic, political and economic reasons—the US still commands. Nor are Europe's immediate direct interests in Japan as great as those of the Americans. But the impact which is now being exerted on our world by Japan is great and increasing. It is not merely that we cannot afford to neglect her (no more than she can afford to neglect us). It is that a cooperative relationship with Japan, despite some effort to achieve it, is going to be better for us than a confrontational relationship of the kind into which we might otherwise progressively drift.

Life in Japan and in the Tokyo Delegation

27. I will conclude this despatch on a more personal, and less sombre, note. Japan and the Japanese can be seductive, and I personally have become fond of both. Tokyo is, in its fashion, a comfortable diplomatic post. Everything works splendidly, from Palace Protocol to domestic plumbing. Service is efficient and ungrudging. Although congested and far removed from any green open spaces, the city

centre is clean, secure and well-equipped for urban relaxation. People seem generally satisfied with their lot; the crowds at the wrestling tournaments and on the evening streets are happy enough and the many midnight drunks touchingly *bon enfant* as they weave their way home to bed. A feature of the group consciousness of the Japanese is the importance they attach to person-to-person relations. To this Delegation, as to most foreigners, the Japanese are unfailingly correct—and frequently cordial. Social entertaining flourishes in a country where it has been estimated that expense account spending in the private sector aggregates between US$30 and US$40 million per day. Cultural pursuits are wide open to the imaginative. The spectacle of Japan is one of great fascination and intellectual challenge. For my own part, I regret nothing in the time I have spent here.

28. But Japan is also a country of certain inner emotions and tensions, some of which can be caught by the sensitive foreign resident. For the most part, these feelings are concealed and kept under control. The serene unfolding of the Tea Ceremony, the unruffled contemplation of a miniature garden, or the pleasure taken in the play of moonlight through a paper screen, help the Japanese to set at a distance, for a space, their cluttered and anxious daily lives and the jangling discordances of city existence. But the tension remains, particularly where the individual cannot retain a satisfactory relationship with his group. Suicides are daily reported, not merely of bankrupt businessmen, but even of school children who can find no other escape from unloving parents or over-severe teachers. It was a Japanese pilot on a domestic flight who deliberately crash-landed his DC 8 airliner at Haneda Airport in February of this year, killing and injuring scores of passengers.

29. Against this background, and the total picture painted in the present despatch, the European Community

requires of its servants in Tokyo steady nerves, a cheerful extrovert disposition and an assured level of professional competence. I take pride in reporting that my collaborators in this Delegation, whether as individuals, or as the tightly knit team which they constitute, have fulfilled these desiderata to my full satisfaction. My successor in Tokyo will find a staff which is second to none in the Commission's external service. I am thankful for the pleasure of having worked with them, and for the privilege of their personal loyalty and friendship, over the past four years.

30. Finally, I am grateful to you too, Sir, for having first appointed me to this post of honour; and to your Directorate-General and yourself, for having thereafter given me, at so great a distance, such careful audience and generous support.

Leslie Fielding

(Head of Delegation)

IN RETROSPECT : A EUROCRAT IN JAPAN

Lecture by Sir Leslie Fielding to The Japan Society, London, 14 November, 1995

The European Community—or Union, as we now call it— is a living organism. It changes shape as it develops and enlarges. In the historical perspective, it is still young. To work for the EU in its Brussels nerve centre, the European Commission, or in EC offices around the world, is therefore to assist in a growing process.

In a modest way, the trend is illustrated by the Commission presence in Japan. Today, the EU has a Delegation in Tokyo headed by a senior Japanese-speaking Eurocrat, on his third period of residence in Japan. He is accredited to the Japanese government, after what is technically known as *agrément*, by the presentation to the Emperor of formal *lettres de créance* issued jointly by the President of the European Commission and the President of the EU Council of Ministers. The EU Ambassador's team includes 11 diplomats with expertise embracing not only commercial policy, economics and finance, but also science and technology, energy, industrial affairs, export promotion, and press and information activities. There are also over 30 Japanese nationals on the staff—many in senior and responsible administrative and executive positions. The Delegation is housed in compact but well laid out diplomatic premises, enjoys daily contact with its Brussels headquarters, and works closely at all levels with the national embassies of the 15 EU Member States in Tokyo. In short, today's EU Delegation is an established and fully professional feature of the Tokyo scene and of the foreign diplomatic corps in Japan.

When I assumed charge of the Delegation in Tokyo 17 years ago, it was a much more modest affair. It had been opened only three years previously; and consisted, beyond its Head, of a diplomatic staff of two. Staff of all grades numbered less than twenty. Its main expertise was confined to trade matters. While the Head of the Delegation counted as a Head of Diplomatic Mission under the terms of the Vienna Convention, no formal agrément had been gone through with the Japanese government; accreditation was by means of an informal letter from the Vice-President of the European Commission to the Japanese Foreign Minister. The Delegation was housed on the ground floor of temporary premises. Liaison with the embassies of the Member States was regular, but not intense, at the Ambassadorial level; barely adequate, at the level of the Commercial Counsellors; and virtually non-existent in other areas. Instructions from the Commission to the Delegation were intermittent; and the reporting from Tokyo to Brussels, episodic and ad hoc. Within the Delegation, still in its first phase of existence, there was inevitably an air of improvisation. To outsiders, the Delegation's purposes were sometimes little understood.

First, some autobiography. I joined the UK Diplomatic Service in 1956, serving in the Middle East, South-East Asia and Western Europe, in small, medium and large scale diplomatic missions. For three years, in the 1960s, I ran a small Embassy of my own, as Chargé d'Affaires in Cambodia. In the Foreign Office in London, in the early 1960s, I sat on the NATO and WEU desk. In the early 1970's, I succeeded Christopher Everett (now Director-General of the Daiwa Foundation) as the number two in the Planning Staff—the FO 'think tank', where my first boss was Percy Cradock (later Ambassador in Beijing, and foreign affairs advisor at No. 10 Downing Street), and my colleagues included Roger Tomkys (later High Commissioner in Kenya and now Master of Pembroke College, Cambridge) and Charles Powell (later a Private Secretary to Prime Minister Margaret Thatcher).

In 1973, on Britain's entry into the European Community, I was seconded to the European Commission in Brussels, as one of the Directors (in Whitehall terms, 'Under Secretaries') responsible for External Relations. Most of the time I was grappling with agricultural trade policy and with bilateral trade relations with the United States, Canada, Australia and New Zealand. In addition, however, I was assigned supervision of the EC Protocol Service, and of a small new unit set up to rationalise Commission policy on external representation. It was in this latter context that I first had EC dealings with Japan.

Next, a word about the transition in 1973 from a Foreign Office career of 17 years to what was to prove a 15 year career as a Eurocrat of the Commission.

The initial 'culture shock' on arrival in Brussels was pretty massive, even for a seasoned professional. Language alone was a problem: to draft documents much of the time in French, and to speak, most of the time, French all day, demanded a level of effort greater even than that which I had been called upon to make during four years in the British Embassy in Paris. The French language demands facial and labial exertions different from those required when one mutters away in English; the throat, cheek and lips used to rebel after eight or nine hours non-stop; and I regularly suffered from 'French face-ache' in the first week or two back in Brussels after a spell of leave. A greater difficulty was the shortage of Brussels staff, compared with the ready availability in Whitehall. In consequence, the work load was absurdly high. Another kind of handicap was imposed by the bureaucratic tradition of the Commission: Old timers used to joke that it was an amalgam of the worst practices of each of the civil services of France, Germany, Italy and the Benelux—the six founding members of the European Community. There seemed little or no career planning or in-house training. I looked in vain for the kind of teamwork and the co-ordinating structures familiar to me both within the Foreign Office and between government departments in Whitehall. I had to watch out, initially at least, for banana skins from the ill-intentioned. To start with, I greatly missed the Diplomatic Service and longed for the day when I could 'come in from the cold'.

The foregoing may seem condescending and negative. Indeed, from time to time during my early years with the Commission, I felt rather as a fastidious and slightly narcissistic Guards Officer might have felt who had suddenly found himself an outcast, on transfer to a line regiment stationed in a remote outpost of some insalubrious equatorial colony. But these personal feelings were mistaken, and anyway faded with time.

I came to realise that I found myself in a set-up which had more in common with a London merchant bank, or the upper layers of a multinational company, than with an imperial bureaucracy. There were not a few precocious prima donnas, and a good working relationship with colleagues had to be earned, rather than expected as of right. Average ability, in the Brussels bureaucracy, seemed to fall slightly below that habitual in top Whitehall departments like the Foreign Office and the Treasury. But the key officials—at least in DGI, the External Relations Directorate General in which I served—were people of most marked ability. Among many, I was impressed by the polished and astute Jean-Pierre Leng (subsequently a Head of the Tokyo Delegation); the wily Trân Van Thinh (our Ambassador to the GATT throughout the Uruguay Round); the tough-minded Paul Luyten (later one of my Deputy Directors General). These, and other Euro-colleagues, possessed international negotiating skills, developed over long years doing the same sort of job, that were unsurpassed—perhaps even unmatched—anywhere in the world. I had much to learn from them: initially, they were probably less convinced that they had much to learn from me.

Nevertheless, one of the things which I could offer to the European Commission in the 1970's was a more professional notion of how the Community's External Representation might be organised and expanded.

The overseas offices for which I assumed responsibility in 1973 were very few, of recent creation and operating on an improvised, even hand-to-mouth, basis. There was nothing whatsoever in Asia or the Far East. Confidentiality and discretion was less than what I had been accustomed to. The Washington Delegation was rumoured to possess an ancient cipher machine, but did not know how to use it, and left it locked up in a safe. There was no diplomatic bag service. Indeed, the Commission took pride in being a 'House of Glass'. Asked by a Foreign Office friend how I was finding things, a few weeks after my first arrival in Brussels, I recall replying that while in London you locked away official papers on leaving the office at night, in Brussels you left your files on your desk, but locked up the telephone, so that office cleaners did not spend their evenings making long international calls to distant relatives. Internal organisation, too, was deficient. Thus, I recall the Washington Delegation once reporting the same US Government policy announcement twice to Brussels, by two separate telexes, drafted by two different officials who had not consulted each other or their boss. In another overseas office, its head sometimes assigned the same piece of work simultaneously to two separate officials, to see which one did a better job of it—a procedure absurdly described by its practitioner as using a 'two-headed eagle'.

One glaring omission in the network was the absence of EC representation in Tokyo, given the increasing weight of Japan in the international economic system, to say nothing of the trade difficulties which were already much in evidence by the mid-1970s. Soon after becoming Vice-President in Brussels in 1973, Sir Christopher Soames therefore approved my recommendation that a Delegation should be opened in Tokyo.

To our surprise, the Japanese authorities were initially far from enthusiastic. It was indicated that, while the Commission could set up an Information Office in Tokyo, a full Delegation was not necessarily a good idea. Explanations of this less than warm welcome were several, and not mutually exclusive. The Japanese Foreign Ministry, punctilious in matters of protocol, was unsure of the legal character of a Community representation; of the extent to which it would amount to being an Embassy requiring reciprocal exchange of privileges and immunities; and of how the phenomenon could be squared with the bilateral representation in Tokyo of the European Community's Member States in the form of their own national Embassies. The MITI probably felt that a full Delegation, with negotiating competence under the Common Commercial Policy, would increase their exposure to European complaints about trade problems, whereas a glorified documentalist in an Information Office would present less of a problem. One or two Member State Ambassadors in Tokyo, questioned by Gaimusho, and themselves with only hazy notions of the then still embryonic European Community, or fearing that they would be up-staged and ordered about by a fearsome EC *'Gauleiter'* from Brussels, apparently reinforced Japanese official scepticism about the desirability of the whole exercise.

But Cabinet Ministers and senior officials back in Europe who dealt directly with Community matters, and were driven by Community-wide policy concerns, backed the Commission, which persisted with the request for full diplomatic representation in Tokyo. Finally this was conceded. I flew out to finalise the agreement with the Japanese Government. The administrative departments in Brussels then got busy; temporary premises were found; and a senior trade policy official from DGI sent out as 'Founding Father' of the Delegation. Although without previous overseas diplomatic experience, Wolfgang Ernst embraced his duties with enthusiasm and proved popular all round, receiving, before leaving, the Order of the Sacred Treasure, First Class, from the Emperor of Japan.

Meanwhile, and back in Brussels, I got on with my main responsibilities. Serious trade problems with the US required attention; and I was also required to plunge into the negotiation of an Economic and Commercial Co-operation Agreement between the EC and Canada. It was not until three years later that thoughts of Japan returned to me, on the approaching retirement of Wolfgang Ernst at the age 65. It so happened that I had been fascinated by Japanese culture since an undergraduate at Cambridge; and I had always hoped, once in the Diplomatic, to be posted to Tokyo. Indeed, in 1956, as a new recruit to the FO, I had actually applied to become a Japanese language student. But John Whitehead, my friend and contemporary, had put his name down before I had; and so I was sent off to learn Persian, instead. I nevertheless duly satisfied my ambition to travel around Japan, while on leave from Phnom Penh in the 1960s. Later on, in London, I had taken part in our annual meetings with the planning staff of the Gaimusho. But this had only whetted my appetite. I therefore decided to apply for the EC Tokyo Delegation, asking, before that, for some months leave of absence at Saint Antony's College, Oxford, to read up about Japan and acquire some notions of the language. The Commission approved the plan of action; and in September 1978, I was in Tokyo, still a Eurocrat, but also joyously once more a diplomat and, indeed, Head of Mission.

From the beginning, I set myself five objectives: to re-build the Delegation's 'zareba'; to establish a closer working relationship within the wider European 'family' in Tokyo; to educate the Brussels bureaucracy in the Japanese phenomenon; to tackle resolutely the problems arising in EC/Japan trade—including the (non-tariff, and sometimes hidden) barriers to our exports to the Japanese market; but, finally and most important, to get the EC understood and accepted in Japan as something more than an instrument of trade friction—clearly, the basis of EC/Japan relations needed to be broadened and strengthened.

A major defect of the Delegation 'zareba' was the Chancery premises, where the Head of Delegation's office, and indeed everything else, was located on the ground floor. It was an in-house fantasy that well-informed and kindly Japanese passers-by on the pavement outside, having inspected the desk of the Head of Delegation through the window, as he was preparing a report to Brussels, were sorely tempted to draw attention to mistaken statistics or defects in the economic argument. So, we re-organised, by taking offices on the first floor and leaving only our press and information section to the attention of passers-by. I tried, and failed, to get Brussels to purchase a suitable site, and construct there a purpose-built Delegation and residence modelled on that recently inaugurated by the Danish government in Tokyo. I could never get Brussels to understand the difference between land values in Etterbeek and Ichibancho. In one vitriolic telegram to headquarters, I pointed out that the budget which they were ready to assign to me for this purpose would purchase no more than either a smart front door, with nothing behind it, in central Tokyo, or a farmhouse on the further slope of Mount Fuji. So we continued to be tenants rather than owner-occupiers in Tokyo.

The establishment of minimum viable staff structure was the next priority. Business was becoming too brisk for us to continue much longer to operate only with a Mission Chief and two First Secretaries, admirable although the latter were—Endymion Wilkinson, a distinguished sinologue, Japanese speaker and author, today the EU Ambassador in Beijing; and Jörn Keck, a simply first rate German Japanologist and economist, today back in Tokyo as the Head of the Delegation. Eventually, I was to add a Dutch Minister Counsellor, a French Press and Information Counsellor, and an Irish Financial Attaché. I also recruited additional high-grade Japanese staff, thereby maintaining the European Commission's sound practice of offering careers of responsibility and trust to local employees, who always form the large majority of the staff in any of our overseas missions. In the annual group photographs of the Tokyo team which hang proudly on the walls of the Chancery (a practice which I initiated and which has continued ever since), there are more Japanese than European faces.

As regards links with the European 'family' in Tokyo, more clearly needed to be done to build a tighter working relationship between the Delegation and the national Embassies. Naturally, as an EC official, I had to be entirely helpful to the Embassies, but to be impartial between them, and to take orders from none. The Commission, under the Treaties, had to take the lead in anything concerning the Community's Common Commercial Policy. In this area, while there could and should be local consultation, my instructions had to come from the Commission and the Council of Ministers in Brussels; and it was to Brussels, and ultimately also to the European Parliament, that I was accountable. Before taking post, I therefore paid calls on senior officials dealing with Japan in all the capitals of the EC Member States; and I made it my business to stay in touch with as many as I could, when back for consultations in Europe. Once on the spot, in Tokyo, I found to my relief that there was little or no problem at the level of the local Ambassadors. Life-long friends in the British Embassy were, naturally, very supportive. Among the other Embassies, it helped to be considered a member of the 'Club', as a diplomatic professional on loan to the Commission, rather than as a 'Eurocrat' born and bred. I furthermore made it my practice to send copies to each European Member State Ambassador records of my conversations with Japanese Ministers and senior officials, and of my major reports to Brussels. This limited application of the 'house of glass' principle paid off handsomely. Seeing to it that the 'family' knew what I was doing seemed to rule out suspicion and misunderstanding before it arose. It also opened the door for useful feedback.

I come next to the tutoring of the Commission in Brussels. The latter possessed valuable experience of Japanese diplomacy and negotiating tactics in international for a such as the GATT, but enjoyed at that time no collective in-depth expertise on the Tokyo scene and inner Japanese realities. Taking my cue from professional diplomatic practice, I sent off to Brussels some in-depth 'think pieces', on the model of a British Ambassador's despatch'. I did not do this often or at any great length. The Brussels establishment, over-worked, under-staffed and immersed in the nitty-gritty, had neither time nor inclination for frequent in-depth meditation on far-away countries, even of the first rank. But I gave them as much as they could handle.

There is nothing more tedious than an envoy who is over-indulgent towards the locals and who ends up—like Ambassador Mike Mansfield—with the reputation of painting most things in the country to which he is accredited with white-wash. But one despatch, entitled 'The Other Side of Japan', described the country which lay—like the other side of the moon—out of sight. The Japan of anxiety, insecurity and inadequacy—a land whose weaknesses had to be allowed for, as much as its very evident strengths. This was in part a plea for patience and understanding. In various other 'think pieces', I argued— somewhat against the tide then flowing—that a more balanced and realistic view needed to take account of the talents, achievements and world rank of this great nation and people, the impact of whom on us Europeans was already great and becoming greater; and with whom we had so many international interests in common. A genuine partnership, however elusive, was going to be better than a cool, uncomprehending, and awkward relationship. In the Europe/US/Japan triangle, we could not allow the Europe/Japan side to remain so weak.

And now to the 'sharp end'. There was, in the late 70s and early 80s, serious trade friction, with equally political implications, and a down-side risk of real damage to the world trading system. As a result, my professional life was to be very far from a bed of roses.

The problems were essentially two: first, Japan's so-called 'laser beam' exports, narrowly focused and intense, which threatened to eliminate production of competing goods in Europe in a short space of time. Binoculars, cameras and motor-bikes went in the first wave. Consumer electronics and passenger cars seemed to be among the next targets. Second, the difficulty which all outsiders—not just the Europeans—seemed to face in exporting manufactured goods to Japan which competed with local products. In European and American eyes, Japan, although rich and getting richer, was then widely seen as still in the grip of an outmoded import-substitution and 'export-or-die' mentality, left over from the early years of post-war reconstruction. This, and the associated burgeoning external trade surpluses being accumulated by Japan, in turn gave rise to the accusation that Japan was not respecting the spirit of international trading rules; that she was a 'free-rider' in the GATT, deriving massive benefits from trade liberalisation without in practice contributing adequately to it.

The foreigners' case against Japan—let me say at once—was not, in my view, then or since, totally well founded. Japanese exports of certain products soared, because of their technical superiority and reliability; Japan's imports were low, in part because European or American exporters had neglected to follow a long-term approach to the market, preferring to pursue short-term gains in easier conditions elsewhere in the world; while Japanese consumers were in any case, for cultural as well as other reasons, accustomed to—and in some instances maybe preferred—local products.

Nevertheless the Japanese Government's defence was weak, and even counter-productive in the resentment it aroused among their major trading partners. The average Japanese industrial tariff was lower than that in force in many other countries. But clear evidence was emerging of complex non-tariff barriers, often stubbornly maintained by powerful petty bureaucrats, conservative by nature, and with a will of their own. In Scotch whisky, French cosmetics, German pharmaceuticals, British chemical products, and much else, the commercial 'comparative advantage' lay with Europe, but was curbed to protect indigenous Japanese industries. Strange reasons were adduced, to do with the alleged uniqueness of conditions and circumstances in Japan, as to why foreign products were ill-suited or undesirable. Where Europeans were concerned, not only were Japanese skins super-sensitive, but even Japanese snow had sui generis qualities; while decent US baseball bats were judged incompatible with Japanese safety standards.

Japanese official credibility accordingly grew thinner and thinner. At a GATT Ministerial meeting in Geneva, at which I was present, the unfortunate Japanese Cabinet Minister, faithfully reading from a script written by a bureaucratic amanuensis, proclaimed that Japan had the most open market in the world. This provoked a collective gasp, and a wave of murmurs among the hundred or so governmental Delegations seated in the amphitheatre. In 1979, the Financial Times, describing Japan's trade relations with America and Europe, spoke of 'what are almost certainly the worst tensions in existence at present between any advanced industrial country and its trading partners'.

EC/Japan tensions, in particular, began to run high. Japanese journalists at my press conferences or speeches seemed to enjoy the hype. The first question was always: 'When will trade war begin?' They were soon to have a field day. The new Director-General for External Relations in Brussels, Sir Roy Denman, had written a confidential memorandum, internal to the European Commission, which unhappily fell into the hands of the Brussels press and flew around the world to Japan. It likened the Japanese—for whom, in context, the author of the Memo clearly had a great deal of respect—to 'a nation of workaholics living in rabbit hutches'; and described the Japanese domestic market as having as much import propensity for manufactured goods as there was to be found party-giving spirit in Glasgow on a wet Sunday afternoon.

For those of us serving in the Delegation in Tokyo, this leak required careful handling. An essential first step was to take the unintended sting out of the memorandum, which had begun to arouse xenophobic reactions in nationalist circles, and which was being played up by certain Japanese officials as an example of 'scapegoat-ism'. Humour was the spanner with which to defuse the bomb. A photograph of me, arm in arm with a respected Japanese Keidanren figure, appeared in the national press, he wearing a sort of rabbit hat with floppy ears and I carrying a very large bottle, labelled 'workahol'. I also tried to get the conflict into accurate factual perspective in Tokyo, and better understood by the Japanese themselves. We prepared well-researched and fair-minded fact sheets; and circulated them to selected opinion moulders, including serious members of the Japanese and international press corps. A visiting French industrialist, having read one of them, reportedly told the French Ambassador that 'only an Englishman could be so even-handed'. (I still do not know whether this was a compliment or a criticism.)

More important than public relations shenanigans was the business of securing better access to the market. The Commission, the Member State experts and the European business community in Tokyo all did their homework together, sector by sector. Key obstacles were identified which Europe could realistically hope to overcome.

Immensely labour-intensive, stamina-dependent, long-term negotiations were then engaged, some of which were to go on for year after year, and a few of which have apparently still continued to this day. As Sir John Whitehead said, in his talk to The Japan Society as recently as February this year: 'It is odd that it should take so much .... pressure to make the progress that has been made'. Certainly, in my day, results came initially in salami slices. Sir Roy Denman, on returning to Brussels with meagre results from one particular set of negotiations, warned journalists to 'get out your microscopes'. But things at least began to move in the right direction in the early 1980s.

At the same time, anti-dumping procedures had to be tightened, and a degree of commercial defence had to be negotiated, mostly through informal 'voluntary restraint arrangements' of a temporary and digressive nature. These 'VRA's' were an obvious economic expedient, to give European industries a breathing space to adapt to Japanese competition on the European market. We could not allow whole industrial sectors to be taken out overnight. But there was also a political imperative: the Commission had to hold the Community together. The threat of national protectionist measures in this or that EC Member State, without regard to the others, and in breach of Community law, was from time to time a real cause of concern—as we saw, for example, in the disgraceful and unwarranted administrative delays imposed on French imports of Japanese video tape recorders in the so-called 'Poitiers Affair'.

But few of us Eurocrats really liked export restraints. The European industries concerned rarely took the necessary draconian measures of adjustment within the prescribed breathing space; Japanese manufacturers earned windfall profits from over-pricing their products in Europe in return for limited volume growth; the consequent trade deflection of Japanese goods to third markets was not always in the European interest.

There therefore had to be a better EC way with Japan than to rely on commercial defence alone. More needed to be done to learn how to operate on the sui generis Japanese market, through better market research, shrewder partnership and joint ventures, and better trained business personnel. In that latter connection, my colleagues and I initiated a training programme for European middle-managers, which still runs to this day, and which takes bright executives in their late 20s and early 30s out to Japan, puts them through a crash 12 month language course, seconds them for six months to Japanese companies, and then returns them to their parent enterprise for a business career with a Japanese orientation. Rather later, we set up a Centre for Industrial Cooperation in Tokyo.

Happily, and with time, the Japanese Government itself began to move from indifferentism and tokenism to the step-by-step opening up ('internationalising' they came to call it) of the Japanese economy. Initially, there was cynicism and even derision in Europe and America. First, the world was being assured by the Tokyo bureaucracy that the Japanese market was open; that there were no barriers; that it was simply up to foreign exporters to try harder. Then, the Japanese Government was announcing a package of definitive and exhaustive market opening measures to remove obstacles to imports. This package would then be succeeded by another, and another—a belated admission of the scale of the problem. 'Wise Men's' reports came and went, and measures to stimulate domestic demand rather than export-led growth; but progress was painfully slow. The impact often appeared, to the outside world, as 'too little, too late'. It was not, in fact, until April 1988, ten years after my first arrival in the Tokyo Delegation, that the EU's Council of Ministers in Brussels was to acknowledge the seriousness and scope—if not then yet the full practical effect—of structural reform in Japan.

By 1988, we had, however, come a long way from the situation when, in November 1976, the Heads of State and of Government of the European Community had first hoisted a storm warning to the mast—the European Council meeting in the Hague that month issued a communique expressing concern about 'Japanese import and export practices', in what was seen as a 'rapid deterioration in the trade situation'. A trade war had seemed to threaten for over a year until March 1978, when the Japanese negotiator, Mr. Nobuhiko Ushiba, negotiated temporary stand-offs with both the EC and the US. Less than four years later still, the Community was to initiate nullification and impairment proceedings against Japan under Article XXIII of the GATT Treaty, alleging that 'the benefits of successive GATT negotiations with Japan have not been realised, owing to a series of factors particular to the Japanese economy'. Had the Community thereafter actually started to withdraw past trade concessions made to Japan, and if (as would, I think, have been quite likely) the US, given its even greater trade difficulties with Japan, had followed suit, then the post-war structure of world trade would have been severely shaken.

The scene today is different. The Yen is over-valued, when then it was substantially under-valued. Measurable progress has been made to open up—and even to 'hollow out'. Japanese manufacturing investment has followed the trade flag to Europe, led by enlightened enterprises like Panasonic, Toshiba, Nissan and the rest. Even the conservative-minded have come to have second thoughts. Thus, in the 1970s, Toyota's boast was that their business was to make the best motor cars at the lowest possible cost within Japan, and to export them to the world. Today, Toyota plan to manufacture just under half their vehicles overseas by the year 2000. Deregulation and administrative reform are part of Japan's own internal agenda. Structural adjustment is being made. Monetary cooperation between our central banks and the Bank of Japan is close, and the Japanese presence in European financial centres, and particularly in the City of London, visible and beneficial. Industrial joint ventures have multiplied. A responsible foreign policy dialogue with Europe exists. A new partnership with Japan, proposed this spring by Commission Vice-President Sir Leon Brittan, has been endorsed by the EU Member States and the European Parliament.

Let me now leave these solemn matters and conclude with a few valedictory *obiter dicta* of a throw-away personal and private nature.

My first *obiter dictum* concerns the EC Member States as a whole, during both my four years' service in Tokyo and the five subsequent years in which I was back in Brussels as Director-General. The Commission, under Presidents Ortoli, Jenkins, Thorn and Delors, while always fulfilling its duty under the Treaties, generally saw little merit in 'blow-hot-blow-cold' attitudes and preferred to follow a consistent (firm but constructive) approach. But, while frustration with Japan was widespread, the Member States did not themselves always see eye-to-eye on what line to take. Swayed by the latest trade figures, or public outcry, or political pressure group, the Council would call for firmer EC policies; but (although the Brits and the Germans were usually a realistic and steadying influence) without achieving a genuine consensus on what might be done. The Commission was accordingly urged onward, only to be reined in, or vice versa; and was invariably left with little support when things got tough. Sir Roy Denman was publicly rebuked by one small Member State (Denmark) for his confidential memorandum, only to be asked by the same government five minutes later to do something about their blocked exports. The EC's Common Commercial Policy sometimes seemed to be regarded as a sort of 'fire-and-forget' missile, which the Council of Ministers could launch and then dismiss from its mind, while national governments concentrated on the pleasures of uncontroversial bilateral intercourse with Japan, in fields outside community competence. My immediate successors as Head of the Delegation in Tokyo—respectively an ex-Foreign Minister and an ex-Prime Minister of the Netherlands—I believed suffered from this as much as I had. If the Japanese were not always very impressed, we had only our own intra-European divisions and distractions to blame.

My second retrospective impression concerns the quality of the senior Japanese personalities with whom I dealt, and the satisfaction of personal relations with them. Even in the political class—more introverted and absorbed in clannish domestic intrigue than politicians normally are in the West—there was cooperation, goodwill and friendship to be found in men such as MITI Minister Esaki, Foreign Minister Kuranari, Prime Minister Hata and many others who worked for better relations with Europe. As to the bureaucracy, at its apex it was highly educated, linguistically well-endowed and of considerable international sophistication. In its stimulus and insight, an evening with Ambassadors Kiyo Kikuchi or Kazuo Chiba—both equally brilliant in conversation—*valait le détour*, to employ guide book terminology. Men such as the then Vice-Minister of the MITI, Naohiro Amaya, or Deputy Minister Reishi Teshima of the Gaimusho gave proof of both character and courage. With all this went much personal kindness. The Protocol Service of the Gaimusho, unfailingly helpful, included me in all the activities and excursions they organised for bilateral Heads of Mission. A polo-playing Oxford don, my wife was warmly welcomed to Keio and 'Todai' Universities; and given the privilege by the Imperial Household of exercising the Emperor's horses. Our little blonde, blue-eyed daughter, wheeled in her pram along the side-walks of Nibancho, was greeted with ecstatic cries of 'kawai-ne!' from Japanese ladies. If professional life as the EC Ambassador was tough, the personal living in Tokyo was surely very sweet.

My final thought is of a quite different nature: it is one of regret. In four years in Japan, I had very little time to travel for the pleasure of travelling. Most of the time, I was tied to Tokyo, saddled with difficult duties which I discharged, for the most part, with a haunting sense of personal inadequacy. Journeys outside the metropolis, tightly scheduled, and confined in duration, had to be directed towards factories, Chambers of Commerce, TV interviews and substantive public speaking commitments. 'Time out' was seized only fleetingly, with slight guilt, at the Sapporo Snow Festival, or on the palmy beaches of Okinawa, or in a few secluded cities and spaces in between. But such brief excursions from the official ambit of duty were a joy, the purer for their relative rarity. Summoned back to Brussels, at short notice, to become the Director-General in succession to Sir Roy Denman, I remember finally kicking over the traces, cancelling my Delegation commitments in Tokyo for a day or two, and taking myself off to walk among the Imperial Shrines at Ise, mid-week, in the rain, with almost no one about, like Matsuo Basho, the 17th Century poet and pilgrim. I will not now attempt to describe in words the thoughts that were mine then. But, for that one intense private experience—which can never, in the nature of things, be repeated—I shall always be especially grateful.

So, there I shall end this lecture. The times I have been reminiscing about, in the Tokyo Delegation and then in Brussels as Director-General, were the most demanding of my entire professional career. But my mission as a Eurocrat in Japan enabled me to realise the ambition of a lifetime. I recall it with pleasure, and with a sense of privilege at having been present, in a small way, at the outset of something new and worthwhile in the history of the post-war partnership between Europe and Japan.

7. NEWSLETTERS FROM BRUSSELS

THE DIRECTOR-GENERAL'S INTRODUCTORY PRIVATE MONTHLY LETTER

Director-General for External Relations
Brussels
Confidential   7 October, 1982

Dear Friends and Colleagues,

This letter (and I shall write once a month) resumes under my signature the admirable occasional letters which my predecessor sent to Heads of External Delegation. I myself, when in Tokyo, found them extremely useful for the background "feel" which they gave me to Berlaymont developments; and I hope you will all find them equally of value in the future. Please remember the background rules—treat these letters as not only confidential but personal. This means that you may at your discretion show them to one or two of your closest Delegation colleagues; but no wider. I should be grateful if you would keep the letters safely under lock and key, and preferably shred them once they have been read and digested. They are not official and are not entered into the archives, here in Brussels.

Let me begin by saying what a privilege it is to find myself back with this dynamic and highly competent Directorate General, and what a pleasure to renew relations with you all in my new capacity. Thanks for your various messages of goodwill; in times like these, one needs all the good wishes going. In my turn I wish good luck to Jan Van Rij, our Chargé d'Affaires in Tokyo, and his team, who are doing an excellent job in a remote yet demanding post.

I took over from Roy Denman in mid-September, on his departure to Washington. The Commission intend that Roy should have a free hand at his new post in coping with perhaps the most difficult period in EC/US relations that we have ever known. We have reinforced his Delegation; and, with such modest additional help for Raymond Phan Van Phi's Directorate at this end as we will be able to find, we shall as a matter of priority be flat out trying to give the Delegation in the US the support it needs. Roy has kindly agreed to see the GATT Ministerial meeting, with which he was intimately concerned from the beginning, through to its end in November; and will therefore have, in addition to his many bilateral concerns, the task of operating almost simultaneously in Washington, Geneva and Brussels until the end of November. We wish him every success, and (we hope, but do not bank on) calmer waters in 1983. Meanwhile, Roland de Kergolay is back with us in Brussels as *conseiller hors classe* to Willi Haferkamp until the end of this year and he is already hard at work with Raymond Phan van Phi on a special study of current and possible future problems in EC/US relations.

I myself am inevitably much concerned, at the outset of my new duties here, with personnel and administration matters as well as with the dossiers of substance. With the Vice President's agreement, I shall undertake only the minimal unavoidable overseas travel in my first 12 months. This will therefore mean that it may be some time before I can visit all of you at your overseas posts. But let me put down the marker that the next meeting of Heads of Delegation in Brussels is tentatively scheduled for the week 30 January-5 February. Details will follow later. One novel feature of the meeting will be that, with the cooperation of the other Commissioners concerned, Willi Haferkamp is arranging for an overlap with the meetings of the Heads of

DGVIII and DGX external offices, which will be taking place in Brussels at approximately the same time. The idea is not to have a completely joint meeting, which would be administratively unmanageable and operationally inappropriate; but there will be an opportunity for you to meet your colleagues outside the DGI network and possibly for one or two enlarged sessions on topics of interest to everyone. Incidentally, you will also be able to meet the new Heads of Delegation in Brazil, New Delhi and Tokyo, who will be selected by the Commission in the next few weeks.

As I write this letter, Adrian Fortescue's report on conditions of external service is almost complete. Jean-Claude Morel, with whom I have discussed it in advance, has promised Adrian's ideas a sympathetic hearing by DGIX.

Obviously, they will take time to digest; nevertheless, I am hopeful that some improvements can be agreed and implemented over the next few months. We shall be helped if we can find a few compensatory savings in other areas of the Commission's external spending; budgetary constraints are naturally very tight. But we will certainly give things a hard shove, inside the house.

In this first letter, I will limit myself to a few brief paragraphs on the all-important substance of our external relations. I have already been able to judge how busy the DGI Divisions are (I am visiting each of them in turn, so as to get to know the troops). And how actively engaged you all are in the field.

Inevitably, a principal concern of the Commission at the moment is the EC/US relationship in all its ramifications. These include the arrangement for limiting Community steel exports to the US, which (as I write) still hangs in the balance, but which has a sporting chance to be implemented by the middle of this month. A successful conclusion on steel would be a major political signal of our ability to improve relations with the US; failure would seriously compromise our efforts to get the relationship on a more even keel. The second major issue is the gas pipeline dispute, where opinions seem as divided in the US administration as they are in our Council of Ministers. Sooner rather than later, the Community as such needs to get actively involved in the search for a solution which could enable the US President to change his policy without too much loss of face, but without too much violence on the European side to our various policies and practices towards the Soviet Union. The other main volet of EC/US relations is of course agriculture, where there are undoubtedly sins on both sides, but where it should be possible, given good will, to reach an accommodation by mutual concession.

But these vital matters and the forthcoming GATT Ministerial meeting (of which more in my next letter) are not the only external preoccupations of the thirteenth floor. Thus our relations with Japan are once again tense, as we approach the decision on whether to proceed in the GATT to a Working Party on nullification and impairment under Article XXIII paragraph 2. On Central America, we are still trying in the Council to put together an aid package which it is hoped will contribute to the stability of this region, although there are difficulties in bringing all the Member States along with us on this, particularly as regards the number of countries to be covered. Meanwhile, in South America the return of Bolivia to democracy has revived hopes of a renewal of negotiations with the Andean Pact. Commissioner Burke will be visiting La Paz shortly.

More generally, on developing countries, you will by now have seen details of Mr. Pisani's memorandum on Community development policy. He has invested a considerable amount of personal capital in this and, after some retouches in the course of discussion in the Commission to ensure an appropriate balance between the ACP and other LDC's, it now represents an important statement of Community intentions. It received a reasonably cordial welcome from COREPER, and will be examined by both the Development and Foreign Affairs Councils between now and the end of the year.

Also in the coming weeks, we shall have to take a position on our relations with China. The present Cooperation Agreement expires early next year, and we have to decide whether to go for an extension of the agreement in roughly its present form or whether to push for (or accept demands for) something more far-reaching.

On the agricultural side the political hot potato of butter exports to the USSR has yet again bounced back to the fore. While, in terms of agricultural market management, there are undoubted attractions in the idea, the general feeling here in the Commission is that, quite apart from the risk of an outcry from public opinion and from the Parliament, it is precisely the sort of move which could upset the applecart in our present delicate pass with the US. My guess is that the subject will continue to be talked about; but that no resumption of butter exports to the USSR will take place for the moment.

Finally, commercial defence. The Council Working Group studying the French Government's proposals for more muscular community instruments will report this autumn and probably the Commission will then feel obliged to make at least a small move in the direction of M. Chandernagor.

I shall have more to say *tous azimuts* next time.

Yours sincerely

Leslie Fielding

A SELECTION OF SUBSEQUENT MONTHLY LETTERS

Confidential

Brussels
20 July, 1983

UN MINISTERIAL MEETING et al

I am off to the South of France for three weeks to share my holidays there with my wife, daughter, and 50 million devises-less French citizens, so I will try to make this letter as short as I can. But there is much to recount.

Stuttgart

A word first about the European Council meeting at Stuttgart, which on the whole did not go too badly. As usual, the European media interpreted the Council with their customary ribald scepticism. But expert observers detected what could prove to be the beginnings of a changing tide—or what Emile Noel privately described to me as *un début de démarrage* after the appalling *"marécages"* through which, largely thanks to the economic recession, the Community has been struggling in recent years. Nobody in their right senses would expect a very complete success at the next meeting of the European Council in Athens in the autumn. But if the work which the Commission has currently frenetically in hand on the budget and agriculture is well done and shrewdly presented, and if at least some genuine progress can be registered at Athens, then 1984 might well prove quite a good year for us. It goes without saying how much we need this if we are to make a success of further European enlargement, and if the Community is to play the decisive role in international affairs which will be required of us as and when (or if) international economic recovery finally gets under way.

UNCTAD VI

I promised, *slivović* permitting, to tell you something about UNCTAD VI Ministerial Meeting in Belgrade, of which I attended the last 4 days. I was glad that I did so, because the international trade volet proved to be extremely tough, and indeed the key to the success or failure of the whole Conference. The Group of 77 continued to press, almost until the very last moment, a rigid and largely unacceptable series of demands based on their Buenos Aires platform. The developed countries were being told that all was black and white. There was no protectionism, economic mismanagement or any other sin of omission or commission in the developing world. What was required was immediate, unrequited and long-overdue capitulation by the West (who were assumed to be universally in the wrong, and totally without economic problems of their own). Thus we were being told to drop immediately all forms of protectionism, or even subsidies, which could affect the interests of the developing countries; we were to cease operating anti-dumping and countervailing disciplines; we were to accept the re-structuring of our industries, and the consequent transfer of industrial activity from North to South, according to an agreed and mandatory time- bound programme. One felt like asking whether we could nevertheless retain our shirts and trousers, at least for the time being. The East European countries in Group D, together with Cuba, both of them in unholy alliance with the Latin American debtor countries, were urging an "all or nothing" stand, with a strong expressed preference by Cuba for a failed UNCTAD, a mass G77 walk out, and unspecific but radical subsequent policy realignments in the South. The normally subtle and moderate Ambassador Das of India, leading as trade spokesman for the G77, found himself stuck with this line almost to the very end, to the expressed embarrassment of Indian Ministers. The Chairman of the Trade Committee, a young and extremely able Bulgarian with a US education, very soon gave up all pretence of objectivity and ran his show along what seemed to some as Moscow-directed lines. The UNCTAD secretariat was useless; passive on the sidelines, they made no attempt to promote compromises and were of only minimal assistance to the Conference President.

The Group B countries for their part found themselves, at the outset of the final phase of the Conference, in a situation of tactical disadvantage, since they had left it until only 8 days before the close of the Conference themselves to table any sort of compromise; and thus came under criticism in several quarters (including from within their own ranks) for not having made it clear much earlier on (and preferably before UNCTAD VI had even started) that the Buenos Aires platform was totally un-negotiable. (There is indeed some substance in this last accusation: even at the Western Economic Summit at Williamsburg, as I mentioned last time, the Western leaders had been welcoming the "openness to dialogue" shown at Buenos Aires, without, however, choosing to set down any very clear markers on substance.)

Finally, however, Group B, with the Commission to the fore (Community coordination had started to operate very effectively at Belgrade from the moment that Roddy Abbott had hit town), moved over to the offensive. First a reasonable Group B counter proposal was put forward as an alternative to the G77 draft Resolution on trade. Next, further compromise wording was tabled in the consequent negotiations. This brought flexibility into the act and took the running away from the G77. With growing success, a diplomacy of persuasion was addressed to the moderates within the G77 (including our ASEAN partners, and the ACP countries). Then came a passionate appeal, at a plenary session of the Conference, from the Chairman of UNCTAD VI, Foreign Minister Mojsov of Yugoslavia. He (quite rightly) denounced the then prevailing composite draft, smothered from top to bottom in square brackets and unreconcilable opposed positions, as the worst international working document which he had ever come across anywhere in the course of a lengthy career.

As a result, a very restricted drafting group on trade was established at my suggestion, under the chairmanship of the dodgy "Vulgar Bulgar", with the object of breaking the deadlock. This group was popularly known in Group B circles as the "Death Squad" (or the *Escadron de La Mort*) on the grounds that its members were told to negotiate night and day until they either dropped dead or produced an acceptable result. This group was paralleled by a sub-group dealing with the minor points of disagreement, which was simply called the *"Groupe des Crochets"*. Group B were represented in the Death Squad by a competent American from the OECD, Brungart, and by Roddy Abbott. We were similarly represented in the "Brackets Group". I must pause here to say that Roddy Abbott's performance in the Death Squad was in the highest traditions of DGI. He worked almost entirely without sleep for 4 days and 3½ nights. Roddy inserted himself into the act, got it moving, and in the process helped to ensure that on trade matters the Commission (and not the Council Presidency) should be the sole spokesman. At a later stage, we thought it tactful to introduce a Japanese into the Group B team in the Death Squad; but the crucial role was played throughout by Brungart and Abbott.

Commissioner Pisani and I played a discreet, highly political back-up role in the various Community co-ordinations and Group B meetings (where I spoke for the Community on trade). Our role was to maintain contact round the clock not only with delegation leaders within Group B, but with the Yugoslav President and various other UNCTAD worthies. This kept me, too, awake for three nights running. There was no lack of moments of drama, including various nocturnal sessions with Mojsov (who summoned us at intervals to announce that the whole

Conference was within a few hours of total break-up). We "influenced" (by which I modestly indicate that I privily drafted for him—it helped that I speak some colloquial Serbo-Croat) the final compromise formulae which Mojsov tabled in his personal capacity on the penultimate day, when the Death Squad had reached complete deadlock and needed a fresh impetus from outside.

So much for the fun and games. The result was a final UNCTAD VI Resolution on trade which represented a victory for Group B. The G77 finally broke up and gave way. Group B were not completely successful—we could not secure any reference to the role of the GATT in the passage of the final Resolution dealing with services; we had to give a few millimetres more ground than we would have wished to the so-called "monitoring" role of the UNCTAD Trade and Development Board; and we were obliged slightly to water down the Williamsburg formula on roll back. (For the aficionados, the developed countries at UNCTAD agreed to "work systematically towards reducing and eliminating .... restrictions"; recognition of the fact that this process of roll back "may be accelerated by favourable economic conditions in individual developed countries"—i.e. acknowledgement of the Williamsburg words "as recovery proceeds"—had to be relegated to a separate, immediately following, paragraph.) But, by UNCTAD standards, and given that UNCTAD declarations do not have the same precise weight as GATT texts, the final outcome was not too bad. And various interpretative statements by the developed countries were tacked on to the main Resolution in the course of the final plenary sessions.

Quadrilateral Meeting

Vice President Willi Haferkamp met Brock, Reagan and Uno (the new MITI Minister) for a further informal meeting of the so-called Quadrilateral in London last weekend. The simplest thing for me would be to refer everyone who has not yet seen it to my reporting telegram, which is in the annex to this letter. As these meetings go (which is not necessarily saying very much), this one went not too badly. Not surprisingly, there was, however, a persistent pessimistic note. The Japanese, who are in an awkward position (see below) had nothing specific to offer except good advice and the expression of good intentions. The Canadians were, as usual, somewhat on the margin and on this occasion largely bereft of new ideas. The Community side had to point out that there was not much that we could do about rolling back protectionism until we were out of a situation in which, while inflation was falling, unemployment was expected to rise in Europe continuously for the next 18 months, and economic growth in the Community this year estimated at one half of one per cent. The Americans, being in a much better position, growth-wise, but suffering from enormous deficits and mounting protectionist pressures, were also in a fix. However, there was one fitful gleam of light (or was it the illusory glimmer of Will o' the Wisp over a benighted marsh land?). Possibly having a bad conscience about their latest specialty steel restrictions, and in any case very anxious to bring some movement back into a situation in which, at present, the protectionists in the US have all the best tunes, Bill Brock launched the idea that, without waiting for the kind of trade liberalisation round envisaged at Williamsburg for the latter part of this decade, a start could be made in the short term with the abolition of at least a restricted number of trade barriers. Brock made it clear that what he had in mind was steps which the US could take on Presidential authority, without going to the Congress. His problem was that it would be difficult for the Americans to move far without some movement from their principal partners. In London we held out little hope of this, saying it was for "them as 'as growth" to move first (i.e. US and Japan). But back in Brussels we shall, without any illusions, given our almost non-existent scope for manoeuvre, be mulling this over. (Please keep this very much to yourselves; even Brock was most anxious that there should be no leak of his intentions to the US media.)

Japan

We had our High Levels with Japan two weeks ago. All of you who are interested will already have seen the telegrams. The problem for the Japanese is that they now expect to have a global trade surplus this year of over $30 billion. This stands in stark contrast with the latest estimates for the US ($70 billion) and Community ($35-$40 billion) deficits. The EC/Japan imbalance is now starting to mount again as their exports increase and their imports from us decline. They are understandably at their wits end what to do, following the three packages of market opening measures which have emerged from Tokyo over the last 18 months. We nevertheless urged the Japanese:

(a) to announce limited but concrete further measures as soon as possible this autumn, if only as a confidence-building exercise; and

(b) to press ahead in the medium term with achieving what they have professed to have set out to do—i.e. to create the conditions in Japan for a structural permanent increase in imports and for a measurable consequent reduction in their external surpluses.

In a restricted side meeting, we also explained that the Community's GATT Article XXIII:2 initiative (calling for the creation of an open-ended GATT Working Party to look at the structural problems of Japan's trade with other Contracting Parties) continued to remain, as agreed in Geneva in April, "in the fridge, but not in the freezer", or "on the [Geneva] table, not under it". If, however, Japanese market opening measures proved inadequate and we ran into serious trade tensions again with Japan before the end of this year, it might be that our initiative would have to be reactivated. (No decision of any kind has, in fact, yet been taken on this and we in the Commission will continue to keep our options open until we see how Member State opinion firms up in the Council this autumn.)

Meanwhile, we continue to plug for all we are worth the development of wider cooperative links with Japan (including in the science and technology field, where we hope soon to obtain a directive from the Member States for the negotiation of a framework agreement). It remains essential for us to try to avoid the Community/Japan relationship being totally dominated by intractable trade wrangles. We are not getting as much help as we would like on this from the Member States or, for that matter, from the Japanese.

US Specialty Steel

This week's Foreign Affairs Council confirmed our view that we should take a tough line in response to the import relief measures announced by the US the week before last. We see no point in rushing into an 'Orderly Marketing Agreement' (OMA), although certain elements in the US Administration are spreading rumours (which we think unfounded) that others are sounding out the possibilities. In the first instance, we have a good case against the Americans in the GATT, where we have asked for consultations and shall be pushing for compensation. We shall also be mounting an attack in the OECD, as we already have done in the Quadrilateral (see above), to create a healthy degree of embarrassment for the US Administration, after the gung-ho free trade position it adopted in the OECD Ministerial and at the Western Economic Summit, Williamsburg, and to exploit the fairly obvious disarray on the US side about the justification of their measures. A second argument against an OMA at this stage is that there is no certainty—indeed there seems at present little likelihood—that the anti-dumping and countervailing actions will be withdrawn. Without this, an OMA would be of little use to many of the Community's steel exporters.

Export Credits

Had the Community deliberately set out to put itself in the most uncomfortable position possible, it could hardly have improved on last week's actual performance. The Community is basically *demandeur*—it is we who, for the most part, need lower interest rates, while most of our partners in the OECD Consensus would be quite happy to continue at the present level. Our position at the start of the negotiations was therefore not a strong one. Nevertheless, thanks to some rehearsed and nimbly executed footwork by Jos Loeff and his team, the Paris discussions were moving towards a broadly satisfactory compromise. Unfortunately, the Commission was unable, in last week's Ecofin Council, to overcome the opposition of 2 major Member States. As a result, we are now faced with a choice between death by hanging and death by drowning. On the one hand we could press for yet a further extension of the present Consensus. But our partners in the Consensus will probably insist on this being for not less than six months, in a situation where any delay in agreeing serves merely to weaken the Community's position. On the other hand, we could simply let the Consensus collapse. But this would probably lead to an export credits "war", which would not only be expensive, but would also expose us to attack under the GATT Subsidies Code, which renders countervailable all export credits not specifically legalised by the Consensus.

Australia

In line with the "new approach" in EC/Australia relations which I referred to in my last letter, Jim Scully, the top official in the Australian Department of Trade, led a Delegation to Brussels last week to prepare the ground for this autumn's High Level Consultations in Canberra. I had a long *tête-a-tête* discussion with Scully during which the mood was frank, constructive and relaxed. Scully confirmed to me his own personal conviction that the strident attitude to the Community pursued by the previous Administration had been misguided and counter-productive. We had of course already heard this from the mouths of Australian Ministers, but it was good to know that there is a genuine commitment to this at official level too. (Unfortunately Scully is retiring in the autumn and we do not yet know who his successor will be.) The ensuing plenary session, chaired on our side by Jos Loeff, also went extremely well. The mood was good, and we were able to identify a number of issues as being ripe for a constructive discussion during the High Levels. So far, so good.

New Commercial Policy Instrument

Our original proposal has been exhaustively discussed in the Council. Everything now depends, on the one hand, on progress towards the reinforcement of the internal market and, on the other, on whether an acceptable compromise can be found regarding the decision-making mechanism. Assuming that the momentum is maintained on the internal market dossier, our plan is for the Commission to put forward some suggestions after the holidays for possible amendments to the proposed decision-making mechanism. In this way, we may be able to move things forward and keep the initiative with the Commission. It will be a difficult balancing act. We could live fairly easily with certain changes (e.g. extension of the various time limits proposed); but if the mechanism is watered down too far it voids the new instrument of its purpose, which is to provide a quick and effective means of reacting to unfair trading practices by others.

Finland

Last month I spent a few days in Helsinki as part of my programme of bilateral visits to the capitals of our EFTA partners. I formed a similar impression to that which I had had the previous month in Sweden. Within obvious political limits, the Finns are useful partners. They also happen to be rather splendid people, unhandicapped by the over-juridical approach or general tendency to whinge which one sometimes encounters elsewhere in EFTA.

Greek Presidency

As you all know, we are into the Greek Presidency. On my way back from Belgrade I popped into Athens to meet the Presidential team dealing with trade matters. I found them a touch apprehensive, both in face of the wide-ranging yet often very technical matters which are on the Community agenda, and because of a certain unease about the relationship between Community Presidency and Greek National Interest. But I also found them intelligent, flexible and unquestionably ambitious for a good, small-country-style Presidency, on the model of the first Danish and Irish Presidencies of 10 years back. Their personal relationships with us in DGI look like developing satisfactorily. We promised to help them, particularly those totally new to the Community, such as their new delegate on the 113 Titulaire Committee in Brussels (who was until recently a professor of economics in the US), to the utmost of our ability.

Caracas and Belgrade

There are one or two personnel changes. Luigi Boselli has just been nominated to replace Manfredo Macioti as Head of our Regional Delegation in Caracas. There is no move yet to nominate anyone to the proposed new Delegation in Brasilia, because the Brazilians (for reasons which we do not fully understand) seem to be moving on a rather slow track, and the basic agreement on diplomatic privileges and immunities, while almost ready, has not yet actually been signed. Meanwhile (without wishing to jump any procedural guns) I expect the Commission shortly to designate Albert Maes, currently head of the North American Division in DGI, to replace Herman de Lange in Belgrade. Herman will be returning to DGI.

<u>Watch It</u>

To conclude, a brief word about Member State susceptibilities. Some of you may have read recent articles in Le Monde about the current state of morale in the *Quai d'Orsay* and the cheese-paring financial constraints which are being applied to our French friends and colleagues. I see that the UK Foreign Office is having its travel budget slashed in the current financial year. For some time now, Belgian Embassies have been told not to use the telex for reporting purposes other than in extremely important or urgent cases.

I know how well the national Ambassadors still tend to do themselves, often with imposing staffs in support. But the above should serve to remind us how important it is not to draw too much attention, in Member State Embassy circles, to certain advantages which (balanced off, I admit, by certain disadvantages) our external network currently still enjoys. One of these is largely unrestricted use of international telephone and telex services. Another is a reasonably liberal attitude in regard both to annual fare-paid leave and to travel *en mission*. Heads of Delegation should not expect to be able to come back too frequently from distant posts for consultations. Consultations with us should where possible be combined either with leave in Europe or with attendance (preferably at someone else's expense) at international conferences. You can always rely on me to authorise anything which is a genuine operational necessity. But please do not give your Ambassadorial colleagues the impression that you are all constantly whizzing round the world in first-class cabins at the expense of the European tax payer. By the same token, airy references to lengthy telephone conversations with Brussels, or the massive transaction of business by telex, should be avoided. I should make it clear that I have no particular instance of embarrassment or difficulty in mind. But we in Brussels have just endured a lamentably ignorant and critical, at times even hostile, session with the Member

State budgetary experts on the Commission's external budget for 1984. So bad, that I had to summon Strasser and Morel to a conference of war last week. So please all of you have an eye to our budgetary image.

It only remains for me now to say, as my first year as Director-General draws to its close, how splendidly the external network has performed in its different ways and manifestations. I feel sufficiently in touch with all of you to write this with complete conviction. It has been a rough year but, from the professional point of view, a good and satisfying one. I wish you all full relaxation and enjoyment on your own holidays. I can only hope you will suffer less harassment and disturbance from the Berlaymont than I expect to have to put up with in the South of France.

Leslie Fielding

11 October, 1983

Confidential

WIDER HORIZONS

The rentrée, as is often the case, has proved extremely animated and time-consuming. Regrets, therefore, that I could not send you a September letter.

Wider Horizons

Let me begin this epistle not, as usual, with multilateral diplomacy, or matters affecting the EC/US Japan triangle, but with some wider considerations.

Senior members of DGI had a stimulating brain-storming with Willi Haferkamp at the end of last month, to review the prospects for business between now and the end of the life of the present Commission. The Directors did most of the talking, and we deliberately kept off our triangular and multilateral obsessions. We concluded as follows.

In *Latin America*, prospects for a constructive resumption of dialogue with SELA now look extremely good. (By the way, the President of Colombia told Gaston Thorn here last week that, while Latin American solidarity with Argentina over the Falkland Islands was eternal and indestructible, the sub-continent wished to set the Falkland episode behind them. It was now ancient history—he said "Pharaonic".) The way has been unblocked to the fairly rapid conclusion of a cooperation agreement between the Andean Pact and the European Community, now likely to be signed a the beginning of next year (the Colombians were asking for the impossible in seeking signature in Bogota in December). Eduardo Volpi and his team have a number of modest but useful improvements of a more specific nature which they could bring to the EC-Latin American relationship over the months ahead. We shall also be opening a diplomatic mission I Brasilia to bring the Brazilian half of the sub-continent into closer bilateral focus. Although the timing of the opening in Brasilia continues to slip, it looks as though we shall be able to raise our (metaphorical) flag there by early 1984.

Elsewhere, our relations with the *Indian sub-continent* were expected to improve further. Here, Manfredo Macioti has matters well in hand and our permanent presence in Delhi is expected to pay off handsomely in the years ahead.

Another area of the world where we were feeling towards closer relations, but where we had not yet developed our thoughts as fully as we have for Latin America, was the *the Gulf*. This has of course always been an area for strategic economic importance for Western Europe, and in the last few years a growing market. The recent fall in oil prices has tended to concentrate both the oil and financial powers of OPEC in the Gulf States.

Jos Loeff was in the region in March of this year and had some useful and friendly talks with the senior people in the Gulf Cooperation Council (GCC), and it was agreed to pursue technical cooperation in certain areas of mutual interest (statistics, customs procedures, energy). While things have not moved ahead since then as fast as we would have like, this appears to be the result of a lack of organisation, rather than lack of enthusiasm, on the Arab side. Indeed at the political level the message has been that we are not doing enough. The view here in DGI is that we should envisage some kind of contractual arrangement on the lines of the ASEAN Cooperation Agreement.

Also as a result of Jos Loeff's visit to the Gulf, we are now exploring the possibility of a Cooperation Agreement with *North Yemen* (at their request).This project is further advanced than our plans for the GCC, and we hope to launch a proposal for draft negotiating directives in the very near future. Again, the sort of relationship we envisage would be akin to, but rather looser than, the ASEAN Agreement,

Meanwhile, the *Euro-Arab Dialogue* continues, as for several months now, to be on the verge of being re-launched. However, we are so used to this that I think we will only believe it when we see it.

There is a gleam in our eye in regard to China also. Here, we are beginning to think beyond the political High Level Consultations now slated to be inaugurated in Beijing by Willi Haferkamp next February, towards the replacement of the present Trade Agreement with China by a much more comprehensive framework Cooperation Agreement. The first reaction at working level of Member States to the latter idea has not been overwhelmingly enthusiastic. But we are not in any hurry, and at least we have a clear idea of the direction in which we would like the Community to move in its dealings with China.

Continuing the tour d'horizon, we thought that relations with ASEAN and with *Canada/Australia/New Zealand* were not doing too badly, apart from the usual hiccoughs, and a particularly messy problems with Canada over seals and fishing rights (of which I could measure the stickiness when I was over in Ottawa last month). We all agreed that we should continue to build on the excellent relationship with EFTA countries (see incidentally the paragraph on Norway below). On the Eastern front in Europe, where things were generally quiet, there was the particular conundrum of what, if anything, the Community could or should do to respond to recent overtures from Hungary (see separate paragraph below). Finally we all thought that there was still much to play for with the proposed new Commercial Policy instrument (see also in further detail below).

Hungary
Over the past few months, we have engaged in lengthy reflections, both internally and with the Member States, concerning the response which the community should make to the Hungarian request for closer economic ties (see May's monthly letter). A lot of detailed work has now been done here in the Berlaymont to try and identify the sort of concessions which we might be able to make on our side, and what we should ask for in return. This has been followed up by a series of visits by Horst Krenzler and Bob Kawan to the various community capitals to sound out thoroughly the position of the different Member States. Unfortunately, these have tended to confirm what we have feared for some time; namely that, while there is considerable interest among Foreign Ministries for closer ties with Hungary, as an element in our overall East-West strategy, there is considerable scepticism, among the

Economic Ministers, who are frankly reluctant to agree t the sort of concessions which would be necessary to get the idea off the ground. We shall now have to do some pretty smart footwork to force the Member States to get their act together, or else we in the Commission risk being sent out to do battle with the Hungarians with neither bullets nor flak jackets.

Meanwhile, we remain perplexed about the real motives of the Hungarians. In particular, is this just a purely national initiative to achieve certain economic advantages, or is it part of some wider strategy by the COMECON? (We have, for example, now received somewhat similar overtures from the Czechoslovakians). It is also unclear to what extent the USSR is involved in these moves. On balance, I suspect that it is a shrewd Hungarian move to grab markets and thereby maintain growth, with the possibility of avoiding any significant economic counter-concession. But, if so, should the Foreign Ministries of the Ten not temper their ardour?

Norway

The week before last, I was in Oslo, continuing my round of visits to EFTA capitals. It is clear that Norwegian accession to the community is not on the agenda for the foreseeable future. However, the Norwegians want to have the closest possible economic and political links with the Community short of membership. I was impressed by the similarity of our views on, and approach to, most key issues, and by the way the Norwegians seek (with the help of their informal links with the EPC mechanism) to line up with the community wherever possible on international questions. In bilateral relations there are very few points of difference, and even on these (e.g. fish) there is close and friendly contact between our officials and theirs.

New Commercial Policy Instrument

As foreseen in my July letter, we have now floated various possible minor modifications in the council with a view to keeping the momentum up, and in order to be ready when the moment is ripe for a comprehensive package. It is clear that we will only achieve agreement on the Instrument as part of some such package. Previously, the most likely candidate as a bed partner for the instrument was the Internal Market initiative for which the Germans were pressing strongly. For the moment, however, it is not clear whether this will see the light of day this year or not. Meanwhile, there is now the possibility of some package being stitched together involving Community initiatives in the area of roll-back of protectionism (see below). Certainly the French still seem keen to have the Instrument, as is witnessed by their comments in the recent Memorandum which they have contributed to the preparation of the Athens European Council. If we do not get agreement on the Instrument as part of some deal in the fairly near future, however, there is now a growing risk that it could fall victim to horse trading between the Member States on other trade policy dossiers in the course of the next year to the commission's disadvantage. So it is probably now or never.

The US and Japan

I will be brief on these eternally preoccupying relationships. On the US/EC front, the storm-clouds are amassing the horizon. The issues have been well advertised in Gaston Thorn's excellent speech in New York. On 26 September entitled "Turbulence over the Atlantic" as well as in Roy Denman's latest pithy general despatch from Washington. Our long-standing agricultural wrangle with the Americans is threatening to get out of hand as they react to the various ideas now current in the community for penalising imports as part of a deal to limit over-production in the Community dairy sector. The specialty steel problem, as the steel sector generally, is fraught with difficulty. But, more than this, powerful protectionist pressures are asserting themselves on President Reagan, some of which are naturally to do with next year's Presidential election, but others of which, accentuated by the commercial effects of an over-valued dollar, are more deeply rooted in the sectoral inconveniences which America experiences in finding herself a bigger importer than ever before in her history. I welcome the decision of Berlaymont between Secretary Schultz and a team of US cabinet rankers with key Members of the commission. But I expect some tough talking on both sides. As for Japan, which the Council of Ministers will be discussing in Luxemburg later this month, here also we are faced with old and new problems. The difficulty is that, while we in the Commission tend to take a steady, long-term view of Japan, the council tends to be swayed by the political mood of the moment, and this tends not to get the community anywhere. I will revert to this subject next month.

Roll-Back

The Commission has taken its courage in its hands in proposing, without any very extensive prior consultation with the Member States, a modest (but, if successful, undoubtedly politically significant) initiative on roll-back. By this I mean a move to give credibility to the undertakings at the OECD and Williamsburg restrictions as economic recovery proceeds.

What in essence we are proposing is that countries should undertake to accelerate Tokyo Round tariff cuts wherever their economic growth exceeds 2%; and that something should be done to improve access for the exports of LLDCs to the markets of the developed world. In addition, the developed countries should undertake to maintain and if possible improve, their generalised schemes of preference (I attach a copy of the Commission's very brief and highly "political" paper to the council to this effect).

The Commission's proposals are essentially short-term and symbolical, designed to have an immediate political impact, and to give the Community comfortable room for manoeuvre in the various discussions which will be taking place this autumn in Paris, Geneva, Lausanne and Zurich, some of them formal meetings of the GATT or the OECD and others informal ad hoc gatherings of Ministers or top officials. There is nothing at present the EC can do by way of *major* liberalisation, whether in sectors such as agriculture, steel or textiles, or in relaxing "grey zone" autolimitation restrictions on people like the Japanese. But, in the Commission's judgement, the community could readily accept the *modest* sacrifice now envisaged—not least because our other partners, including Japan and the US, would have to make bigger sacrifices than we. Their GSPs and treatment of LLDCs are less generous than ours; on advance tariff cuts, they would have to move before the Community, since Community-wide economic growth this year is 0.5% and may not reach 2% next year. Indeed, given the US need to go to congress to get approval for advance tariff cuts, and the apparent total inability of the Japanese to make any move on agriculture or to accept an unqualified commitment to the LLDCs, it may well be that a community initiative on these lines would fail for lack of wider support. If so, *tant pis*—we would at least have called the bluff of those say that the EC is the block.

I have no idea what chance we really have to get some sort of endorsement from the Council. Reactions among the 113 Titulaires, over coffee and (large) brandies last Friday, were disconcertingly favourable, almost without exception—even though some Member States would have preferred a more generous Commission proposal and others would have preferred that the Commission propose nothing at all. The key, to my mind, will lie at Ministerial level in Paris. In the present state of the French economy with negative growth, still rising unemployment and general austerity, it will not be all that easy for Mme Cresson and Mr. Chandernagor to explain to French public opinion why the Community should be making gestures of liberalisation, however much more symbolic than substantive.

Ottawa Quadrilateral Meeting

Willi Haferkamp met USTR Brock, MITI Minister Uno and Canadian trade minister Reagan in a comfortable hunting lodge overlooking a lake in the mountains near Ottawa at the end of last month. Never very keen on these so-called "Quadrilateral" meetings, for fear that they might become institutionalised and another high level nuisance, we went to Ottawa without enthusiasm, and solely because the Canadians had been complaining that they had never had the opportunity to act as host on Canadian soil. In the event, not only was the salmon and the reindeer meat excellent, and the wine EC in origin, but also the discussion turned out to be unexpectedly worthwhile. This, not only because of the bilateral contacts *en marge*, but for the discussion roll-back. Willi Haferkamp floated the ideas which the Commission has subsequently put to the Council. In doing so, he effectively dominated discussion, since none of the other three participants had any solid ideas of their own to put forward. It made a welcome change for the Community side to be the shakers.

Atmosphere for Athens

Since I last wrote about the run-up to the European Council meeting planned for Athens in December (my Private Monthly Letter of July) things have begun to get thoroughly bogged down, whether on the budget (despite some ingenuity on the part of the Danes and the British), on the reform of the CAP (despite some basically sensible proposals from the commission, if hair-raising at the edges, e.g. in regard to external trade) or on new policies (no identity of view, except that the other fellow has to pay for them). When I saw Emile Noel last week, his prognosis was fairly gloomy, although he seemed to think that the approaching deadline might precipitate some hasty last-minute trade-offs and bargains. A further shadow over community affairs is the serious question-mark now raised over Spanish and Portuguese accession. According to certain rumours, a formal veto by one Member State cannot now be totally ruled out in 1984. Well-informed sources say that there is in any case at least a serious prospect that enlargement might be further delayed to 1 January 1987. If you add to this the fact that, according to today's radio, we have now completely run out of money for the CAP and cannot pay our bills until we get the expected additional cash from the European Parliament, you may judge that, domestically, we are currently in something of a mess.

But, notwithstanding these difficulties, the morale of the other departments does not seem too bad. The feeling s that, somehow, the Community will certainly muddle through. Meanwhile, we have the consolation of DGI and the External Delegations that, whatever our own problems and difficulties may be, we operate what is still the most successful and smooth-running part of the European Community. Everything, after all, is relative!

Personnel Changes
As I write Luigi Boselli has just packed his bags and left for his new post as Head of the Caracas Delegation. Meanwhile, Albert Maes is busy mastering the intricacies of Serbo-Croat in preparation for his move to Belgrade, for which we expect shortly to obtain *agrément*. Albert has been succeeded as Head of the North American Division by Klaus Ewig, who in turn is succeeded Head of the EFTA Division by Herman De Lange. Other changes, too, are in the offing in the upper hierarchy of DGI. Thus Horst Krenzler is expected to leave us in December to succeed Michael Jenkins (returning to the Foreign and Commonwealth Office in London) as Deputy Secretary

General. The long-empty post of Umberto Toffano as Deputy Director-General is shortly to be filled. But more of this next time!

Leslie Fielding

Brussels
Confidential   14 June, 1984

CHINA; THE G7 SUMMIT IN LONDON et al.

Going back on what I said in my letter of 28 May, I thought I would write straight away about the Chinese Prime Minister's visit and the London Summit.

Visit of Chinese Prime Minister
   At the beginning of June, Mr. Zhao Zi-yang, the Chinese Prime Minister, came to see us in the Commission—the first visit at Premier level since China entered into diplomatic relations with the EEC 9 years ago. As so often on such occasions, the importance of the visit lay more in the fact that it took place than in exactly what was said: symbolism was more important than substance. Nevertheless it was an interesting occasion, on which the Chinese, friendly to the Community as always, spoke out in a relaxed and spontaneous fashion. Smart western clothes, jargon-free language and idiosyncratic self-expression marked the style on the Chinese side.

We got the impression that their chief objective was to mark the importance of Chinese bilateral relations with the Community, for three reasons: for their intrinsic value to date; for the purpose of giving new impetus to those relations in the future (especially in the hope of technology transfer); and for the satisfaction of demonstrating to other partners—particularly the USSR but also the US—the balanced and independent international posture to which China is attached. (On this last point, the Chinese Prime Minister stressed in private with President Thorn that, contrary to American claims, Chinese relations with the US had still not yet reached "the phase of maturity"; and that, contrary to what the Russians were suggesting, China's relations with the USSR fell far short of "normalisation".) A second major objective on the Chinese side seemed to be to press home the message that the modernisation of China now taking place was "irreversible". The "gates of China" to the outside world had opened, and would open yet wider in the years to come.

With this, went the customary specific Chinese endorsement of a strong and united European Community.

The Prime Minister brushed aside current Community difficulties, which he felt sure would be overcome by the "wisdom and tenacity" of the European people. In a lengthy exposé by the Prime Minister himself of the economic modernisation and adjustment process in China, he urged that European capital and technology should participate. While he described trade relations between us as good, he believed that two-way trade could be very considerably expanded; and implied that the Chinese did not wish to see the US and Japan collar too much of the expanding Chinese domestic market for foreign goods. The Prime Minister spoke disapprovingly of COCOM; warned everyone to avoid entering into official relations with Taiwan; and expressed himself in favour of a halt to further missile deployments in Europe, to be followed by a resumption of arms talks in Geneva.

The round table meeting broke up with lavish words of praise from the Chinese side for the pioneer role of the Commission in developing EC/China relations over the past nine years (including even a flower for the Commission textile negotiators!). There followed a remarkably easy-going, free-talking official luncheon at Val Duchesse, in which the Chinese came back to the theme of technological cooperation. They welcomed the prospect of early negotiations with the Community for the conclusion of a cooperation agreement, and asked many questions about the prospects for science and technology developments in the EC, and the chances for China to acquire European high technology.

The Commission have in fact now tabled proposals, and a draft negotiating directive, with the Council for a Trade and Economic Cooperation Agreement with China, to replace the more limited and anyway now expiring EC/China agreement of 1978. Our next fixture with the Chinese is in Beijing at the end of September, when Vice-President Haferkamp will inaugurate a new series of annual high level consultations; and when—if all goes well —we hope to be in a position to initial (although not, by then, actually to sign) the cooperation agreement.

London Economic Summit

This went off fairly smoothly. The protocol arrangements were impeccable. For protocol buffs, the Commission flag was flown everywhere; Mrs Thatcher's arrival reception for President Thorn included a redcoat band playing Beethoven's setting of Schiller's Ode to Joy— and even a Coldstream Guards Guard Commander speaking French.

The general tone of the Summit was, if far from detached from the world's problems, nevertheless somewhat serene in its attitude to them. There were no sudden surprises, as there had been at Williamsburg. Discussion, while at times distinctly animated (as, for example, over high US interest rates and budget deficit), was more consensual than conflictual, each party ready to take the other's political interests into account. Discussion was focussed more on the substance of debate than on the texts of the various Statements issued at the end of the Summit—thanks to firm chairmanship by Mrs Thatcher, as well as to successful "debureaucratising" tactics by the UK "Sherpa" over the preceding preparatory months.

While the main thrust of the Summit was economic, agreement was reached on a series of declarations on democratic values (an idea of Mrs Thatcher's), international terrorism (with the Libyans principally in most people's minds), East/West relations and arms control (with an appeal to the Russians to come back to the conference table) and on the Iraq/Iran conflict (deploring the loss of life but expressing confidence in the continued stability of oil supply and/or in arrangements to cope with any interruption).

The principal document, however, was the so-called "London Economic Declaration". This confirmed that economic recovery was now established, while calling for "unremitting efforts" to sustain it and spread its benefits to the unemployed. It was agreed that "continuously high or even further growing levels of international interest rates" could put the recovery at risk and exacerbate the problems of debtor countries. There was nothing very new said about the problem of debt itself, beyond the need to continue present strategies "flexibly, case by case", including the rescheduling of commercial debt where debtor countries were themselves "making successful efforts to improve their position". (The general feeling was that one should avoid institutionalising debtor/creditor relations: each country was different, and any aggregation would simply encourage debtors to think that a miraculous general solution to particular problems was somehow on offer.)

The Finance Ministers were told to carry on with their current work on ways of improving the international monetary system. There was nothing very novel said about North-South relations either, although the participants declared themselves "mindful" of LDC concerns and difficulties, and ready to maintain and if possible increase flows of resources. There was a special mention of poverty and drought in Africa. And the Japanese spoke vaguely (and no doubt for the record) on the need for "dialogue" with the LDCs.

The aspect of the London discussions which most directly touched the Community was, as on previous Summits, that of trade policy. There was little difficulty in reaching agreement to urge everyone to resist protectionist pressures, reduce barriers to trade and accelerate the completion of current liberalisation programmes (mainly in the GATT, but also in the OECD). Where difficulties arose was over Japanese advocacy of a stand by the Summit in favour of a new multilateral negotiating round, to be launched according to a specific timetable.

Here, despite President Thorn's own frank talks with Prime Minister Nakasone in Tokyo to which I referred in my last monthly letter, and despite the clear set-back which Japan experienced at the OECD Ministerial meeting in May, the Japanese were still arguing at the Summit for adoption of a precise calendar, in the form of a preparatory phase in 1985 and the formal launching of negotiations, if not at the end of 1985, at least in 1986. American attitudes were less extreme (thanks to a direct intervention by President Thorn with Secretary Schultz in advance of the Summit, and vigorous lobbying by Sir Roy Denman and his team in Washington). Nevertheless, the Americans, too, would have liked more precise agreement on timing, and they and the Japanese finally presented the other Summit participants, on the last morning, with communiqué language calling for consultation with GATT partners "with a view to decisions during the course of 1985".

Both President Mitterrand and Prime Minister Craxi had stated their view on the previous day that, while they were able to agree that preparations for a possible new round might begin in 1985, they could not agree to any particular date for decisions, which could in any case only be taken once the LDCs had been fully consulted and brought on board. President Thorn also argued this thesis, basing himself squarely in this respect on what the Community's Council of Ministers decided on 14 May. Both the German Delegation (mainly Count Lambsdorff) and also the British (although with greater discretion and subtlety, given their presidency role at London) would have liked something more positive. But President Thorn presented his arguments with great skill, avoiding giving the impression of a negative attitude on the basic issue; finally, both his persistence and his manifest sincerity won the day. On the suggestion of Mrs Thatcher, the final compromise (with which President Thorn was well satisfied) was wording to the effect that the Summit participants "building on the 1982 GATT Work Programme", agreed to "consult partners in the GATT with a view to decisions *at an early date* on the possible objectives, arrangements and timing for a new negotiating round". President Reagan gave way reluctantly but definitively. ("OK. You win. But you owe me one!")

Freed from the constraints of an artificial timetable, but with the advantage that all the Member States represented at the London Summit are today more or less committed to the idea of a new round, provided it is adequately prepared, we in the Commission can now organise ourselves for the future on rational lines. The first priority will clearly be to complete as much as we can of the GATT Work Programme by the end of this year, while at the same time working out our own longer-term ideas. There should then be a pause for reflection, followed by extensive consultations with all concerned in the GATT through diplomatic channels in the early part of 1985, possibly culminating, in the second half of that year, in an ad hoc GATT meeting at senior official level. This would take place theoretically with no strings attached, but in the hope that, at such a meeting, there would be at least the beginnings of a clear and broadly based consensus on the objectives, participation and timing for a new round. The new round itself might however not be launched officially until the second half of 1986, or even early in 1987, the interval being used to complete the preparations so as to ensure that there would be no crash on take-off. The new round itself might well not be concluded until around 1990 (a final burst of negotiating activity being assumed to follow the US Presidential election in 1988). A realistic scenario, I think—but only if *ceteris* remain *paribus*. A renewed slump, or a wizard oil crisis, could well stop the whole thing in its tracks.

Leslie Fielding

Brussels
29 January, 1985

Confidential

THE NEW COMMISSION

As you can all guess, January has been pretty frenetic here in DGI. In this letter, I will concentrate on the home scene, leaving the external substance (where a great deal is coming up, bilaterally, regionally and multilaterally) to next month.

The Mysteries of the Organism
The main news is that, while the Director-General of External Relations is to remain one administrative unit, with me at its head, there are now to be two Commissioners for external relations (Vice President Willi De Clercq and Commissioner Claude Cheysson) instead of the customary one!

The Commission has yet to approve the revised DGI organigramme, which will, as I indicated last month, require a certain number of changes. The Commission (with Mr. Cheysson present, he having been absent from Royaumont) have now confirmed the division of competences decided at Royaumont. Any suggestion of splitting up DGI into two separate departments is accordingly firmly ruled out. Excellent!

As I write, we are still working out which DDGs will coordinate which Directorates. At the level of Directors, there will be only the minimum changes. On Mr. Cheysson's side, Mr. Volpi's Directorate 'C' will remain as it is; but with the addition of Mr. Fossati's Division. We want to create a new North/South Directorate to embrace Messrs. Renner and Weingaertner and some kind of think-tank on North/South problems; but this may have to wait a little if (as at present) we remain without an A2 post for this Directorate. A new Mediterranean Directorate is planned, to be assembled from the collective competences of Messrs. Schwed, Bistolfi and Caporale; and a Director will be assigned to it very shortly. On the De Clercq side, I anticipate no changes, other than the probably grouping of the EFTA Division and the East/West people into something like a greater Europe Directorate. There will be equally minimal consequential changes at the level of Heads of Division.

Personal relations between our two principal Commissioners and (in regard to Enlargement) Mr. Natali, are good. Once the organigramme is out of the way, we should be able to settle down to our work, although it is obvious to everyone that the situation is still inherently unstable. I have asked all senior staff to work very closely together during the transitional period.

As regards the External Delegations, the rule of thumb is that Mr. De Clercq, as the Commissioner for External Relations, has a general interest in all of them; and Messrs. De Clercq and Cheysson have a particular interest in some of them, in accordance with the geographical and functional répartition between the two. Hence the fact that you will all have received an initial message of greeting from Mr. De Clercq and some of you will have received a parallel but additional message from Mr. Cheysson. The status of the Commission's delegates in the Maghreb and Mashrak is still undetermined; for the present, they continue to be administered by DGVIII, but report on general policy matters to Mr. Cheysson. My hope is that it will be possible for our Maghreb and Mashrak colleagues to participate in the Heads of Delegation meeting in Brussels which is planned for the coming Spring (details not yet fixed—we will let you know for your individual planning purposes as soon as we can).

Briefing for Commissioners

This has proceeded a pace. I enclose copies of the general briefing note (additional to that for the College as a whole) which we put up to Messrs. De Clercq and Cheysson earlier this month. Since then, a host of more detailed material has been submitted and digested, with which I will not bother you.

Orientations of the New Commission

You will all have received copies of President Delors' policy statement on behalf of the Commission to the European Parliament on 14 January, and an account of the subsequent debate. The *"Discours Programme"* is still being drafted. The principal priority, quite rightly, is with internal affairs—internal market, technology, monetary cooperation, economic convergence etc.; with everyone's eye on unemployment and growth. The reform of the CAP will continue (we are currently working out a price package, including measures to cope with over-production in the cereal sector). I do not expect any very significant policy shifts in external relations or in ACP/EC affairs. But please see below. Institutionally, the Delors Commission is determined to recover lost ground, and to seek not only fully to apply the Treaties but where necessary to go beyond them.

President Delors devoted four hours earlier this month to an exchange of view with his Directors General. He is an impressive man: quiet-mannered and candid, shrewd and tough. He inspired confidence and a certain measure of awe. He can at times be disarmingly direct and down to earth. Much was said on all sides. But I retain foremost from the President the following:

(a) *Gestion de l'acquis*: He expects us to be not only financially and administratively impeccable, but also proactive. *"Bien gérer, c'est renforcer l'acquis de la Communauté"*;

(b) *La marche en avant*: Obviously, yes. But the Commission will have to be concrete and to stick to what is realisable. (He had been struck in his tour of Member State capitals how extremely diverse everyone's ideas are on where the Community should go next);

(c) *Méthode de travail*: Necessity for "horizontalism". A modern administration requires not merely interservice cooperation but also an integrated multi-disciplinary approach. Information must flow freely and rapidly, set out in a simple and clear fashion. (The President said that, in Europe, only one Member State—not France—had fully succeeded in achieving this; he meant, of course, the UK!) The President was particularly critical of the quality of the papers served up both inside the Commission, and from the Commission to the Council. They would have to be subsequently shortened and shorn of unnecessary technical mystification. Simplicity and transparency were of the essence;

(d) Institutional: Not so simple. Does the Commission get up, leave and bang the door; or continue, with endless patience, to persuade the Member States? At what point should the Commission refuse to accept something which risked down-grading its function to that of a Council Secretariat?

Delors believed that we had to try to stick to the role foreseen for the Commission in the Treaty, even where the Treaty of Rome might no longer be fully appropriate. He had no clear-cut views, except that it was necessary constantly to struggle against "*le pouvoir paralysant*" of Member States' bureaucracies. There will be no Commission miracle; "*declarations tonitruantes*" would not help. What we had to find was the right "tone", and see to it that the Commission's proposals could "*passer la rampe*". But at the end of the day, after having done our best to separate the good grain from the bad, we had to be ready to say no. The Commission could not be expected to put up with just anything.

Turning to Mr. De Clercq, you will find in him a senior and very experienced Ministerial figure. Although still new to many aspects of the work of DGI, he is working with very Flemish discipline and determination, reading carefully and quickly, and absorbing, a wide range of briefs. He has submitted himself to teach-ins from all his deputies and directors, and will within the next week have completed a tour of all parts of DGI. On policy matters, his instincts and orientations are liberal and internationalist, as were those of Haferkamp and Soames. Like the President, he is very "ministerial" in his approach to briefs: he has repeatedly insisted that they should be not only comprehensive but clear. For meetings with outsiders, he expects the bureaucracy to take their courage and set out clearly: the objects which they recommend he should set out to attain; the objects of the interlocutor; active and defensive talking points; with all details relegated to background notes (the latter to be clearly marshalled so as to separate out what it was essential to know at a glance from what he could skip or keep to one side as deep background for occasional reference). There is nothing new about all this; I myself have been preaching it in the Berlaymont service since I first came here. But I recommend if you want to be read by the Commissioner, that you bear it all very much in mind.

Mr. Cheysson comes to us with the invaluable resources not only of his previous experience as the Development Commissioner but also of five years at the *Quai d'Orsay*. (I have known him personally since he was Ambassador in Indonesia in the 1960s, and I was the British Head of Mission in Cambodia). After a short holiday break in Egypt, he has returned with undiminished energy and fecundity. After brainstorming with our own experts and with his Cabinet, he is now defining his position, dossier by dossier, as he goes along. But from my conversations with him, it is clear that his major objectives this year concern the Mediterranean and the North/South Dialogue.

On the former, there will be a need for *"relance"* after Community Enlargement has been settled and parallel agreement reached in the Community on the Integrated Mediterranean Programmes. Taking that *acquis* as a starting point, we shall need to see case by case how cooperation with our non-Community Mediterranean partners, including all the Arab countries, can be improved. A thought that Cheysson and I share on this is that there may be scope for our EFTA partners (who have a similar aid and cooperation philosophy, and also largely similar strategic interests, to our own) to do more with us for stability in the Southern and Eastern Mediterranean, Yugoslavia etc.

As regards the North/South, thoughts are still in a very early stage only. Mr. Cheysson's instinct (which I think we would all share) is that, in present and foreseeable circumstances, talk of a "New International Economic Order" is no more than hot air; UNCTAD, while important, is a routine preoccupation rather than a major pole of gravity; the very term "North/South Dialogue" is a misnomer, since the "South" is not more than the theoretical sum of its in practice very different component parts. The Community's major real preoccupation in this context has to be what more can be contrived to stimulate an economic up-turn in the South, particularly on the part of the heavily indebted countries; not only are these our markets, but also they have the power to destabilise the international financial system. It is equally obvious that the US part in this upturn is crucial (not only in regard to interest rates and the dollar but also as to continued flows of capital). Mr. Cheysson's first instinct is that, should any Community initiative be proved possible, it would have to be very carefully explored and could scarcely be contemplated before the autumn of this year. Clearly, we are at the beginning of quite a considerable process of reflection here in the Commission.

Both Mr. De Clercq and Mr. Cheysson will be travelling a fair amount this year. Apart from certain obvious fixed points (Quadrilateral, OECD Ministers, Bonn Summit etc.), we are still in the process of working out coherent travel plans, which are unlikely to leave many of you unvisited in the course of 1985.

Admin

I know you are all hopping mad over 'provisional twelfths', freezes on recruitment, and the rest. The position here in Brussels is bloody awful. I argued your cases as cogently as I could at a small meeting chaired by Jean Claude Morel today. He will try to beat down the Financial Controller; but there is no way we can fully shield you from the budgetary crisis at home—this problem is "bigger than both of us".

Meanwhile, you will have seen that, to add to your "inside information", my Assistant has started a separate monthly letter on nuts and bolts. Let me know, after a bit (or when you are here in the Spring) whether it helps. You can give it a wider distribution than my own private monthly letters, which remains *for your eyes only* and those (at your personal discretion and on your personal responsibility) of your nearest and dearest collaborators.

Leslie Fielding

Brussels
14 October, 1986

Confidential

THE LAUNCH OF THE 'URUGUAY ROUND'

In the end, Punta del Este worked out all right; it was a success for the Commission, and a fair reward for the efforts of the moderates generally.

The misgivings announced in my letter of 10 September proved, however, to be all too well-founded. The Chairmanship of the Uruguayan Foreign Minister (tipped nevertheless as a possible successor to M'Bow in UNESCO, and even, in due course, to Perez de Cuéllar at the UN) was uninspiring. The Conference came close to failure on at least two occasions (over services and the other new questions; and over agriculture).

Señor Iglesias did not adequately command the basic substance; he turned out to be an indecisive Chairman of admittedly difficult meetings (if he had been a Eurocrat, he would not have survived his first tough COREPER or 113 Titulaires Committee); and, as we moved into the last night's session of negotiation, he seemed to me to be almost reconciled to failure (being too tired or too demoralised even to be able to speak out clearly) But he got effective support from us and the Americans; and the GATT Director-General, Arthur Dunkel played a deft and constructive role behind the Chair. So, by midday on Saturday 20 September (*after* the appointed hour at which 'Air Force Three' had been announced to be taking off for Washington with the three US negotiators), it was all roses and speeches of congratulations for Iglesias, and hearty back-slapping all round.

On services, intellectual property and investment, the Community got exactly what it had thought realistic to aim for, almost exactly as we had predicted it could be secured, but only at the very last hour (4 a.m. on the Saturday to be precise). All three subjects are now "in the New Round"; but there was a face-saving expedient for the Indians and Brazilians (for which we were warmly thanked by both their Delegations). Negotiations on these three subjects will take place in Geneva under the aegis of GATT, serviced by the GATT Secretariat, and constituting an integral part of the Round. But a decision will be taken only at the end of the Round as to whether the results are to be implemented by the GATT—i.e. as to whether the GATT is to be acknowledged competent in the new areas.

The Commission trick was for the decision at Punta to launch negotiations in these new areas to be taken by Ministers as Ministers, and not as representing GATT Contracting Parties (i.e. the fall-back position we had floated in July as part of our "Common Working Platform" —and so bitterly criticised by the US at the Sintra Quad last month). To this, the Americans added the astuce that all decisions at Punta del Este, even for the launching of negotiations on "classical " trade issues which are clearly of GATT competence, be decided not by Contracting Parties but by Ministers. This, to reduce the appearance of "two tracks". Nevertheless, there is a distinction in the Punta

Ministerial Declaration between "Part I: Negotiations on Trade in Goods", and "Part II: Negotiations on Trade in Services", so as to meet the worst fears of the "hardline" developing countries about trade-offs between goods and services. Two "Groups" will be set up to handle goods and services respectively in the Round, both groups coming under a single 'Trade Negotiating Committee'. And in addition, the US had to agree (as we ourselves had been ready to concede last July) that the liberalisation of trade in services should respect "national policy objectives".

All in all, not a bad deal. In a private letter to Willy De Clercq last week, the US Trade Representative, Clayton Yeutter, grudgingly admitted that "all worked out well in the end". Paul Trân and our team in Geneva must be smiling.

On agriculture, we were in semi-perpetual negotiation for the most part with the Cairns group of countries (led firmly, but with unexpected moderation and realism, by John Dawkins of Australia) and with the US (Dick Lyng and Dan Amstutz—the latter very tight-lipped and aggressive, the former dreaming of a paradise of his own, in which all export subsidies would disappear, together with Original Sin), sometimes separately and sometimes together. We succeeded, after two of the toughest EC/US Ministerial slogging matches in which I have taken part, in finding language which did not pick on the Community's export refunds in isolation as a candidate for phased reduction. Instead, the Punta del Este Declaration speaks of increasing discipline on "all direct and indirect subsidies and other measures affecting directly or indirectly agricultural trade". As a final concession to the Americans and the Cairnsites, we added the words "including the phased reduction of their negative effects and dealing with their causes". (The passage underlined was the crucial compromise, which the Americans accepted only grudgingly, but which seemed to please the Cairns people;

in practice, it gave nothing much away from the Community view point, being no more than a reflection of the conclusions of the last OECD Ministerial meeting, and of the Tokyo Western Economic Summit). (French Ministers MM Guillaume and Noir) at Punta del Este, with whom De Clercq and I were in constant contact behind the scenes, found this acceptable in the circumstances. While they claimed to have received instructions to invoke the 'Luxembourg Compromise' if the EC Council in special session at Punta were to try to out-vote them, it was clear to the French Delegation—as naturally to everyone else also—that the European Community could not allow itself to be saddled with responsibility for a failure to launch the New Round, merely over one rather than another version of gobbledygook language of no lasting importance beyond Punta. The essential was to begin the negotiations; to include agriculture; but not to spell out too clearly the shape of the wished for final outcome of the New Round.

One small footnote. The existence of the Cairns group (who were not monolithic—we were in touch behind the scenes with several of its important Ministerial components) was not necessarily a bad thing for the Community. They sided, to be sure, with the US most of the time; but they were fundamentally more pragmatic and probably more honest. (The Americans were ready to promise heedlessly the reduction of all agricultural subsidies, without acknowledging that it would take them several years to reverse what the US had already set its hand to). If the Cairns group stick together in the forthcoming negotiations in Geneva, they will apply healthy pressure to the US; they can hardly succeed in increasing the pressure under which the Community already finds itself; and they will diversify what could otherwise be an awkwardly confrontational bi-polar super-power set-to between America and Europe.

We put the Japanese under heavy psychological pressure to open up their markets, through our proposal for a "balance of benefits" clause in the Ministerial Declaration, based pretty much on the wording of the GATT preamble (our text spoke of reducing growing disequilibria in the patterns of world trade—something put in at USTR Clayton Yeutter's suggestion—and of achieving a greater mutuality of advantages for the benefit of all Contracting Parties). The Japanese were vehemently opposed to this at Punta and spent most of their time and all their goodwill in ensuring that there was no consensus for it. The Community had in practice few who were prepared to speak out publicly in favour (several Asian countries made it plain that they were scared to do so—claiming that the Japanese had a way with their neighbours). In the end, we reached an acceptable compromise with Japan, in the form of an agreed statement about the need to tackle disequilibria and ensure advantages/benefits to all participants in the New Round, to be read out solemnly by Chairman Iglesias immediately after the adoption of the Ministerial Declaration.

But even this required a little touch of drama and showmanship. At 0530 on the morning of the Saturday, when the last details of the agreed Ministerial Declaration were just being completed, Paul Trân (on the specific instructions of Willy De Clercq and myself, and with the agreement of Paul Channon as the UK President of the Council of Ministers) called for the floor, to declare a Community reserve on the entire package negotiated, in view of the absence of a "balance of payments clause". Consternation! Hundreds of Japanese officials were mobilised, running in all directions in search of a last-minute solution; and the two venerable Japanese Ministerial participants were rousted out of their beds for a crisis meeting with Chairman Iglesias and Arthur Dunkel. Iglesias (briefed by Dunkel, briefed by Trân) then suggested to the Japanese the procedural device referred to above. A text was drafted by the Japanese Delegation. This I then re-cast at 0800 in the morning (fresh from 2 hours' sleep, and comforted by a leisurely prior coffee and croissant at my hotel) and sold back to a grateful Japanese opposite number, in the presence of a gratified Paul Trân and a beaming and complicitous Arthur Dunkel.

Continuing in the vein of *la petite histoire*, I should recall that the Member States were impressively well represented at Punta del Este at both Ministerial and senior official level (almost all the familiar faces from the 113 Titulaires Committee were on parade). The British Presidency chaired the coordinating meetings efficiently and most of the time in very close collaboration with the Commission. The De Clercq/Channon relationship was particularly confident and mutually complementary. The only snag was a certain *excès de zèle* on the part of senior UK officials, which took the form of the doctrine that, in all the Punta del Este negotiations, side talk and informal goings-on, the Presidency should automatically accompany the Commission. This we firmly declined: we had the 'Community Competitiveness' and they did not. The negotiations on agriculture and services with the key Punta del Este players were conducted exclusively by the Commission in various smoke-filled green rooms and late night lobbying sessions. The Presidency did accompany the Commission (at my suggestion) for initial courtesy calls on Chairman Iglesias and Director-General Dunkel; for one confused and never repeated shambles-meeting between Iglesias and 30 or so Ministers representing different regional groups and policy interests; and for one trilateral crisis meeting with Iglesias and Yeutter to do with the way the Conference was being run. But that was the outer limit. We held to our line particularly strictly, because—both at the 1973 Tokyo Ministerial meeting and at the GATT Ministerial in Geneva in 1982—the Commission had done the crucial negotiating unaided; because it is always important in such matters (even with my amiable and usually very efficient compatriots) to establish a certain minimum freedom of manoeuvre; and because we did not wish to set a precedent for future encroachment on our prerogative and Community competence.

As for the Commission Delegation, including the two grossly over-loaded but always cheerful DGI secretaries, plus an equally heroic lady from the Santiago Delegation, their performance was truly remarkable. This is not a routine compliment. Everyone slipped naturally into place and got on with their job without the need for detailed supervision. For a final cutting edge and for much needed Latin American expertise, we had the benefit of Luigi Boselli and Franco Teucci from Caracas; without them, we should have found ourselves out at sea. It was an example of team work in action which impressed even the Member States.

A word finally about Punta del Este as such. It was cold and rainy; the infrastructure was logistically slightly sub-standard and geographically over-dispersed. The town being the sea-side playground of wealthy Argentines, we saw everywhere large and sumptuous villas and blocks of luxury flats, standing well-tended but empty awaiting two months summer occupation by their absentee landlords. Construction of new Hollywood-style residences was in full swing. For me, this manifestation of flight capital put Argentina's debt burden in a distasteful perspective.

Leslie Fielding

Confidential

AUSTRALIA; JAPAN et al.

As I dictate this letter, the XXIV: 6 alarm bells are ringing. Last Saturday, Willy De Clercq and Frans Andriessen failed to find common ground with Clayton Yeutter and Dick Lyng; and the latter returned to Washington on Sunday indicating the likelihood that the US would proceed to take measures against $400 million of EC exports at the end of December, if the EC made no further concessions to the US on Maize and Sorghum access. (We offered an erga omnes, extra EC, reduced-levy quota for the Spanish market of 1.6 million tonnes per annum for the four years 1987-1990, to be shared effectively between the US and Argentina, but with the deduction from this quota of EC imports of maize substitutes such as Corn Gluten Feed. The US side said this was politically unsaleable back home, and demanded 4.4 million tonnes. This we in our turn had to reject, as we calculate Spain's import needs from all sources—intra—and —extra-EC—to be 3.2 million tonnes per annum.) The Commission have proposed a further delay of one month, until the end of January, to permit further reflection by both sides. Reagan will decide one way or another at the EPC meeting he is to preside on 17 December. I shall come back to this matter at the end of the letter. Meanwhile, elsewhere the news is as follows ....

Australia

Willy De Clercq and I, with a large supporting cast, including Peter Pooley from DGVI, visited Australia for High Level Consultations early last month. It was a successful visit, which permitted the necessary fence-mending and hatchet-burying following the bad patch through which EC/Australia relations went earlier in the year.

(PS Readers will remember that Australian Ministers had worked themselves up into a paroxysm of rage with the CAP, which manifested itself in a variety of diplomatic indelicacies, such as a refusal to accredit our new Head of Delegation at Prime Minister level, as already in New Zealand; as the nomination of a Special Trade Representative, based on London, with the declared objective of dealing direct with individual Member States on trade and agricultural matters; as public statements promising a "crescendo of hostility" against the Community. All this quite rightly led the Commission to postpone the High Level Consultations scheduled for Canberra last spring; this, to the disquiet of certain Member State diplomatic representatives in Canberra, but to the wholehearted endorsement of the COREPER. It took the peace-seeking gesture of Prime Minister Hawke's visit to the Commission in April *en catastrophe* to get relations pointed in a more constructive direction, combined with a nice mixture of firmness and flexibility by our Delegation in Canberra. Even then, it was thought better not to pick up High Level threads in Canberra much before the year's end.)

In Canberra last month the atmosphere was much more rational and forward-looking. Prime Minister Hawke informed Willy De Clercq of the Australian Government's decision to re-accredit Ove-Juul Jørgensen at Prime Minister level, as a token of the improved relationship to which they now aspired with the Commission and the Community. Foreign Minister Bill Hayden (basically one of the Community's more bitter critics) was on his best behaviour. John Dawkins, the Trade Minister (responsible for the phrase "crescendo of hostility") was constructive. With a certain reserve (agricultural resentments go very deep) so also was John Kerin, the Minister for Primary Industry. With the ebullient and friendly John Button, Minister for Industry, Technology and Commerce, Willy De

Clercq signed an exchange of letters governing future science and technology cooperation with the Community. Australian officials, always less excitable than their Ministers, and currently a first-class team, were also a pleasure to deal with, from Mike Codd, the Cabinet Secretary, to Vince Fitzgerald and Geoff Miller, the Permanent Secretaries for Trade and Agriculture, and Peter Field from Trade.

Curiously, it was only the people from External Affairs (currently going through a rough patch at the hands of Bill Hayden—too many political appointments and too many creepy-crawlies promoted—and anyway a Ministry in eclipse on economic matters) who tried to cause trouble. Thus, in the Preparatory meeting at senior official level, we had to put the boot in when they came at us with accusations of opening up South East Asia to Soviet influence by our economic and commercial misdemeanours. (There are of course some grounds for thinking that our past sugar policies have hurt the Philippines. But with $10 billion-worth of imports coming into the Community from ASEAN each year, nearly half of which comprising manufactured goods; with our leading role as an investor in the region; and with our entirely respectable ODA performance there and in the South Pacific, it was not too difficult to put the record straight. And to suggest that, with industrial tariffs of 150% mostly directed against Asian neighbours, Australians in glass houses should not start throwing stones.)

Ove's cordial reception when he subsequently presented his new credentials to Prime Minister Hawke last week, was in marked contrast to the curt ungraciousness manifested by Foreign Minister Hayden when Ove had presented his original credentials in March.

The reasons for the Australian change of course are several. Name-calling got them nowhere Australian public opinion blamed their own Government as much as the EC for the Commission's consequent rebuff. Economic difficulties of all kinds have tended to mount, enjoining caution. Prime Minister Hawke's own flexible personal diplomacy and common-sense instincts deserve mention. But perhaps the most important single factor was the Punta del Este experience—educational for Australia and EC alike.

In fact, the Commission had ended up spending quite a lot of time at Punta with John Dawkins' and the Cairns Group. The latter played a responsible hand there (and were markedly less confrontational on agriculture than Dick Lyng and the Americans); and Dawkins and De Clercq happened to develop a mutually respectful and business-like personal relationship. Australian Ministers were also able to measure at first-hand at Punta the sheer weight and power of the European Community in international trade negotiations. (I myself at Punta del Este, watching the Community at work, kept recalling to mind in that respect the description in John Masters' Gurkha autobiography "Bugles and a Tiger", of the dramatic gallop into action in a North West frontier skirmish of a mule Battery[10] with light field artillery.) The Australians certainly found us more unified at Punta than they had expected. They had also seen for themselves that the Commission was firmly in the driving seat as negotiator; and that (what they should have realised all along) the Commission was a power for reason and reform within the Community, not least on agricultural restructuring, and therefore up to a point a friend at Court, as well as an indispensable Australian interlocutor.

And so it was that, in Canberra in November, notwithstanding the for the present unbridgeable chasm between Australia and the Community over agricultural trade policy, we found enough in common to make the visit worthwhile. We agreed that senior officials from Canberra and Brussels would exchange views from time to time on GATT matters and the pursuit of the Uruguay Round. Willy

---

[10] For military history buffs, I hazard the guess, based on dates, that what Masters saw deployed was Bhurtpore Battery, in the subsequent mechanised version of which I had the honour to command B Troop briefly in the 1950s.

De Clercq even felt able to make supporting background noises to John Dawkins' initiative to secure a "ceasefire" in the form of a possible halt in the escalating subsidy war between the US and the EC for the capture of third markets. (I personally doubt whether Dawkins will get anywhere with it; but De Clercq politely said that, if the Americans stopped shooting at us, we would cease to defend ourselves). Incidentally, we found the Australians very disabused with the Japanese; and (discreetly and in private) worried about the down-side of Gorbachov's Vladivostok speech and the reaffirmation of the Soviet Union as an active Pacific power. Current New Zealand policy in this context clearly worried the Australians.

Since we rarely go to Australia, we covered the Continent to the best of our ability, Willy De Clercq delivering speeches and meeting businessmen and bankers in Sydney, Melbourne and Perth. We managed to fit in (at 40°C in the shade) a brief visit to Ayers Rock and Alice Springs, by way of light relief.

All in all, Australia is a fine country; and its countrymen almost invariably decent, straight-forward and companionable folk. But a land not without difficulties. Its agricultural and raw material exports (with notable exceptions such as coal) are not likely to do well in the present international *conjoncture*. Investment (of which the Community is the largest supplier to Australia) is not coming in in the quantities required. People have been gravely shaken by the massive collapse of the Australian dollar over the past 12-18 months—imported necessities have of course become dearer, but exports have not benefited correspondingly. Centralist nation-wide wage bargaining and indexation are certainly now no longer luxuries which the Labour Government thinks that Australia can afford; and there has been a fall in days lost to strike action. But social and industrial rigidities are making it very difficult for Prime Minister Hawke's Government to carry through its re-structuring programme and the cautious progressive reduction of

Australia's outrageous and self-defeating industrial protectionism. Meanwhile, Ministers and officials are talking about facing years of austerity; and are naturally worried about how Australia will survive if there is now a marked and sustained down-turn in the world economy. Oz may therefore, sadly, no longer be quite so much "God's Own Country". But it is well placed to be a survivor country in the XXlst Century—and not only in the scenario of nuclear war in the Northern Hemisphere. Thus still well worth emigrating to, if you are in your twenties, healthy and vigorous, and equipped with some tradeable skill. (Sally and I are too old and ill-qualified; our children too young, and as yet unaddicted to Coonawara Clarets).

Australian Ministers will be paying a return visit to Brussels next July. We look forward to receiving them with affection, as cousins should.

Singapore
On my way back from Australia, I spent a couple of days in Singapore, which I have not seen since I was *en poste* in 1964. Thanks to Lee Kuan-yew, the island was unrecognisable. The swamps, jungle and islands where I used to go picnicing and sailing are now a science park or covered with rising commercial buildings.

Singapore is also one of those rare and happy exceptions—a country where there are no significant bilateral problems with the Community. I had a civilised and profitable exchange of views with senior officials about the multilateral scene, with particular reference to the Uruguay Round.

Like Australia, but for different reasons, Singapore is now also feeling the pinch. Gone for good are the years of 8% per annum growth i they are hoping for 2% this year, and do not expect to rise much above 4%-5% per annum in the 1990s. The Stock Exchange is still shaky and there was less wishful thinking in Singapore than there was in Canberra about the Pacific Rim area being the one white hope for world economic development between now and the end of the century. But, being mostly Chinese rather than hedonistic and complacent, live-now-pay-later, urban Australians, the Singaporeans are vigorously and rigorously carrying through the necessary economic adjustments. For them, everything clearly depends on maintaining the best relations they can with their Asian neighbours (with whom they do not always find it easy to relate, given their own superior efficiency), and on whether or not international economic recovery continues to move slowly forward. With a little wind in their sails, they can still get where they want; but if becalmed, there's not much else for them to do but take in each other's laundry.

Latin America

True to the confident prediction I made in my last letter, we have managed, in our communication to the Council on Latin America, to produce out of our conjuror's hat something which has all the appearances of being a white rabbit, albeit at this stage a rather young and under-nourished one.

The main thrust of what we say is that, with the more developed Third World countries—not only in Latin America, but also in Asia, the Mediterranean and the Gulf—the way ahead cannot lie with trade preferences (two-thirds of Latin American exports already enter the Community at zero or preferential rates) or public development assistance (even a l00-fold increase would barely make a dent on the problems of this sub-continent). Instead we should encourage a higher level of industrial cooperation between private firms, particularly in the form of joint venture investments. Lack of information and the existence of a host of technical and administrative barriers are currently a major disincentive, particularly for small and medium-sized enterprises. The hope is that by setting up data banks and joint investment committees, encouraging the harmonisation of industrial standards, fostering cooperation between chambers of commerce and helping to establish training programmes, the public authorities on both sides will be able jointly to create a more propitious climate for such industrial cooperation.

The effective implementation of this new approach to development cooperation, to which Claude Cheysson personally attaches such importance and which has been the subject of a separate recent communication to the Council, will inevitably require a good deal of time, effort and imagination, as well as some fairly solid support from the public authorities of the Member States and from European industry. We will be keeping our fingers crossed, and advising our rabbit how to avoid the snares that lie ahead.

Japan and The Commission

Our Ministerial Round Table with the Japanese last week in Brussels did not go off too badly. It is now likely to become a regular annual fixture, alternately here and in Tokyo. Despite a charged agenda in the National Diet, we were visited by three Japanese Cabinet Ministers and two Vice Ministers.

As the Japanese Foreign Minister, Mr. Kuranari, confided to me at Zaventem as he wended his way home, the Japanese side had expected worse treatment than they in the event received. Certainly the European Council in London the week before had thundered fresh admonitions. And pressure generally had been building up in EC-Japan relations, as Japanese exports (even denominated in Yen) continued to rise at a faster rate than their imports from the EC; as the famous Maekawa Report on the opening up of the Japanese economy continued to sink into the bureaucratic and party-political quick-sands; and as the authorities in Tokyo continued to debate what they should do on the wines and spirits dossier (a "test case" of Japanese ability to accept fair competition on their home market, on which we are now taking Japan to the GATT for nullification of benefits, under Article XXIII:2).

Once in the Berlaymont, the Japanese team were greeted with exquisite courtesy but considerable firmness on matters of trade friction, while nevertheless assured of our desire to build a more broadly-based and constructive economic relationship for the future. Prudently, Mr. Kuranari and his colleagues had come armed with the minimum necessary offers of appeasement—difficulties about imports into Japan of skis and over standards for domestic appliances magically disappeared; fresh negotiations with Japan on norms and certification procedures for motorcars and medical equipment were hastily assented to; commitments of principle were offered by the Japanese to set up, with the EC, an Industrial Cooperation Centre in Europe, and to negotiate an R and D agreement on nuclear fusion; small but useful new concessions to foreign banks were placed on the table. Only on wines and spirits were the Japanese unclear—but they promised clarity for early January. They also made no bones about continuing export moderation in 1987 in the sectors sensitive to us. Finally, and with a flourish, they pointed to the decision by All Nippon Airways to purchase 10 Airbuses and take an option on 10 more. (Naturally this was presented as a purely commercial decision—but Japanese Ministers clearly expect to bask in our appreciation).

The two lead-players on the Japanese side performed with charm and skill. Kuranari, an adept at after-dinner conjuring tricks, knows the Community extremely well; and his MITI colleague, Tamura, while less at home with Euro-foreigners than Kuranari, had clearly knocked his officials' heads together in advance of the meeting. At dinner, Tamura privately professed himself (in the light of Nagasaki and Hiroshima) as more inclined to do business with the EC than .... (wait for it) .... with the US.

So while, in Macro terms, Japan continues to move further out of kilter with the rest of the world, defying the usual economic laws, nevertheless in Micro terms and in the Japan-EC context, it was the season for small gifts and large smirks. The New Year will see whether the smirk fades—or gets wiped off by events beyond everyone's adequate control. The boiler gauge has risen close to red again, I am afraid.

EC-US Round Table

George Schultz imposed his personal style and priorities as usual on his Ministerial team at the annual Round Table in Brussels last Friday. But there was an air of unreality as marked, in its way, as it had been at the Japan Round Table the previous day. Me, I felt as if monsters slumbering beneath the earth were beginning to stir; and that, sensing this, everyone was trying to make polite and cheerful conversation in loud voices.

In his press conference, Schultz readily pronounced the meeting the best of the six in which he had ever participated—a verdict which he had clearly already reached before setting out from Washington. Following "Iranagua", and Schultz's evident success in establishing his own integrity and continued grasp upon his office in the associated Congressional hearings, the Secretary is now setting about the systematic demonstration of continuity and success in US foreign policy, wherever that can be credibly established. While in Brussels, he reassured NATO Ministers at Zaventem that the fundamentals of US strategy and support for the Alliance remained unchanged; while the Schultz message, in the Berlaymont, was that the economic side of the US-Europe equation also remained reliably in hand.

At the Round Table therefore, all was mostly sweetness and light. Schultz gave an economic history lecture starting from the 1930s, supported by graphs distributed en séance, to the effect that the West was now emerging from inflationary excesses and economic mismanagement into a period of potential widespread prosperity, provided always that the LDC debt crisis could be managed, that Europe carried through its full share of structural reform, that—as hitherto—the genie of protectionism could be kept firmly in the bottle, and that the lessons of the past could be applied to the future. The secret of success lay in the unleashing of market forces and the consequent gains in efficiency. Europe and Japan were now happily poised to assume a bigger share of the burden for the expansion of world economic growth. The US and the EC should join forces to solve the problem of agricultural over-production, so as to bring supply into line with demand. And both parties should keep fresh capital flowing to the debtor countries. Notwithstanding Congressional changes, the US Administration intended to move next year "from the defence to the offence on trade liberalisation" and the fight against protectionism. The EC should draw the right conclusions. Finally and ultimately, the key to everyone's welfare lay in acceptance of the impact of technology. The days of "sailing ships and customs forms" had now gone by.

This little number was followed on by Secretary Baker (graciously passing through Brussels on a trip to Bonn, London and other more important venues, to talk about the dollar) claiming that, while the present US trade deficit was neither economically nor politically sustainable, and notwithstanding the risks of protectionist trade legislation from Congress, nevertheless the US economy was on an even keel, the inflationary cycle broken, unemployment falling, and tax reform and new budgetary rigour each promising good things for the future. Against that background, and provided that the EC Member States fully understood the "gravity of the situation" in regard to protectionism, (since the US business and farming communities were now moving away from their past enchantment with free trade, and sweeping Congressmen along with them), the Reagan Administration expected to be able to "sit down and work things out" with the new Congress.

Both USTR Yeutter and USDA Lyng subsequently dwelt on certain unresolved bilateral issues, such as XXIV:6 and the prospect of show-downs on hormones and the Community meat directive in 1987. Yeutter struck a further slightly awkward note in his announced policy intention, in the Uruguay Round, to try and bring four or five areas of negotiation to a successful conclusion before leaving office in 1988. But this did not prevent George Schultz from picking up a suggestion of Frans Andriessen that the two sides should work together on agriculture and, from Willy De Clercq, to collaborate closely in advancing the Uruguay Round. Schultz quoted figures to show how the Community and the US accounted for over half GATT trade and why therefore common strategies were not only desirable but natural in the commercial and agricultural fields.

It was only in a side meeting with Yeutter that the bilateral issues assumed a sharper edge—and where we pointed out that the latest US protectionist moves on the Super Fund, customs-user fees etc., threatened as much damage to Community trade with the US (up to $500 million) as Yeutter was claiming for US exports to Spain and Portugal following Community enlargement. The XXIV: 6 negotiation, mentioned at the Plenary Round Table only as an issue requiring urgent political solution, came to a head in a much more menacing way with Yeutter and Lyng on the Saturday morning, after Schultz and Baker had left town breathing optimism and goodwill.

While Jacques Delors found his private *tête-a-tête* with George Schultz cordial and constructive enough, the President commented to EC Foreign Ministers privately on 15 December about the Round Table that US "unilateralism" had never been more evident. Certainly, I myself saw little sign that the US were ready to listen seriously and put themselves in other's shoes. They were too much preoccupied by domestic worries.

Sussex

Most, but perhaps not all, of you, will have heard about my own personal plans for next year. I have accepted the offer of the post of Vice-Chancellor of the University of Sussex, with effect from October 1987. Certainly, I shall look back on my time as a Eurocrat with vivid remembrance, and much nostalgia. More than that, having joined the Commission in my forty-first year with UK entry in 1973, and by the time I leave having served 5 years as Director-General, I will always be glad to have been able to devote my peak years of professional energy and inventiveness to the Community cause, as my father and grandfather would have wished if they had lived to see it. I shall be retaining my links with the Commission, and expect to continue to serve the European cause in other ways, from my new power base. My successor will not be chosen until the spring or early summer of next year, and there will be the opportunity for a careful hand-over, in which I shall be bearing your various individual interests very much In mind.

Christmas

I wish you all a Very Merry Christmas. I shall spend some of it by a log fire at home in the Welsh Marches, swotting up back-numbers of the Times Higher Educational Supplement, and arguing for more money from the Chairman of the University Grants' Committee, who happens to be a Shropshire neighbour. (I will see to it that the vintage port is of the best.)

Leslie Fielding

Confidential

Brussels
30 January, 1987

WAR OR PEACE WITH THE USA? EASTERN EUROPE

After a sniffly Christmas and New Year holiday in which all members of my family, including Nanny, had 'flu simultaneously, the Fieldings got back to Brussels by car in arctic conditions (-17°C and British motorways almost impassable in the snow and ice) only for me to encounter the toughest working January that I can remember.

La guerre de Troie n'aura finalement pas lieu. (Ouff!)

Today the US had intended to introduce measures to interdict $400 million of EC exports, on account of US dissatisfaction with the XXIV:6 negotiations. But this particular balloon will not, in the end, go up. An hour or two ago, the last EC Member State agreed, by written procedure, to endorse the Agreement for the Conclusion of the XXIV:6 Negotiations, which the Commission *reached ad referendum* with USTR yesterday morning.

The Agreement is pragmatic and constitutes essentially a political compromise, in which both sides have had to give ground. Apart from a long conceded EC move to fix the tariff of the Twelve at the level of the Ten for products of significant interest to the US, the deal consists of a 4-year arrangement under which the US will be able to benefit from special *erga omnes* import quotas for maize and sorghum into Spain; from untrammelled access to the Portuguese market for cereals; and from autonomous unbound *erga omnes* tariff cuts on two dozen particular products.

As regards the grain, both sides finally settled on a 2 million tons per annum MFN quota for maize for the Spanish market for 1987-1990 (up from the 1.6 million tonnes we offered last time, but down from the original US request for over 4 million tons); plus a 300.000 tonnes per annum similar such quota for sorghum. From these figures, will be deducted *pro rata*, ton for ton, the Community's imports over the 4 years in question of cereal substitutes such as Corn Gluten Feed. In addition, the Community will waive the reservation to the Ten of the 15% of the Portuguese cereals market from 1987 to 1990 for which the Accession Treaty makes provision. (Note that this does not require amendment of the Treaty, which allows for the provision to be waived on Portuguese initiative—and in effect with the tacit consent of the Ten.) As regards the temporary tariff cuts, these will cover $400 million worth of imports from the US, spread over 24 products (9 agricultural and 15 industrial). The tariff changes vary between 0.5% less for certain kinds of aluminium to 9% less on cigars. This compares with the much deeper cuts, on over 40 products, initially demanded by the US.

The EC-US Agreement also contains a review clause in which the position will be re-assessed in mid-1990; and the Agreement specifies that each side sticks to its own interpretation of the GATT and reserves its own GATT rights. The review clause contains, however, no obligation for the Community to continue these various temporary arrangements beyond 1990. Our hope is that, come mid-1990 (US exports having in the interim picked up, if only as a result of the devaluation of the dollar), we shall be able to demonstrate from the trade figures that the US, far from suffering from, will actually have benefited from, the overall liberalisation in Spain and Portugal resulting from their accession. Meanwhile, the final clause of the Agreement specifies that the EC-US XXIV:6 negotiation is concluded. We understand that the Americans will be re-binding the tariffs which they unbound last May in preparation for sanctions against the EC.

So ends the toughest and most dangerous bilateral confrontation with the US which the Community has known since the "Chicken War" of the 1960s. It could easily have triggered off a succession of retaliatory and counter-retaliatory moves which would have been disastrous not only for bilateral trade, but for the future course of US trade policy, and for the successful pursuit of the Uruguay Round (on which see below). The US negotiators were as keenly aware of this as we were, lamenting in private that a tit-for-tat trade war could only result in the loss of their control over US trade policy, to the benefit of a now clearly protectionist US Congress. No doubt for that reason alone, the Americans made a significant move at 10 minutes to midnight, to cut down their demands for maize and sorghum access from 4 million tons to 2.7 million tons per annum. This in turn enabled us to reciprocate and to produce the compromise described above, with the "Portuguese Card" (worth maybe 0.3 to 0.4 million tons of additional US cereals exports) as our Trump.

Pour la petite histoire, the Americans had agreed at the last moment in December (after my letter of 18 December was signed off) to extend the deadline until the end of January, so as to permit both sides a final margin of manoeuvre. After an eyeball-to-eyeball session in Geneva ten days back between Woods, Amstutz, Legras and myself, Willy De Clercq and Frans Andriessen flew over to Washington last week to meet MM Yeutter and Lyng for a Ministerial show-down, with senior officials to hold their jackets. Because of unusually severe blizzards, this Ministerial meeting nearly never took place, Andriessen being stuck in London and De Clercq being diverted to Montreal. Rod Abbott and I succeeded in arriving first, just making it to New York before La Guardia closed, thanks to having been transferred at no extra cost from Jumbo to faster-flying Concorde. This was followed for both of us by an epic 11-hour journey by coach, Amtrack, Metro, taxi and on foot from New York to Washington in conditions of unimaginable disruption, across an ice-bound landscape and through outraged hordes of stranded US citizenry on the verge of civil riot. Only a half-bottle of whisky and the DGI tradition kept us going. Nevertheless the Commission team (in the end fully staffed, with Roy Denman also on board and all the stragglers gathered in) broke the back of the negotiation in Washington. We returned to Brussels to receive the broad support of the Council of Ministers on 26 January for one last effort to settle. This final phase was conducted by telephone round the clock over three days from the austere comfort of our Brussels offices; but at the price of 2 nights largely without sleep, followed by a nine-hour marathon session of the COREPER, extending until 0200 this morning (effectively, our third night of negotiations).

It would be tempting to add that "All's Well that End's Well". However, fresh troubles with the US (admittedly of lesser magnitude) are already flagged on the horizon, in the shape of rows over Airbus subsidies and over the EC's insistence on hormone-free beef. In the words of the famous Old Norse ballad, "Let no man call the day good, until it be eventide".

Uruguay Round

Against the background of an imminent EC/US agreement on XXIV:6, the Contracting Parties were able, in Geneva in the small hours of yesterday morning, to reach final agreement on the structure and organisation of the new MTNs. Those of you who have followed this question will recall that these matters were supposed to have been settled by the end of December. This proved impossible, and the deadline was postponed until end-January. It looked at one time as if the Community might become dangerously exposed on the question of agriculture, where we were determined to fend off demands by the US and others to have a "fast track" negotiation on agriculture, regardless of the rate of progress in other sectors. In the event, compromise wording was adopted which avoided any firm commitment to start actual negotiations on agriculture at the beginning of 1988. For this, much credit is due to Paul Trân and his team in Geneva, as well as to Paul Luyten and my other GATT experts here in Brussels.

Now that the "talks about talks" have been concluded, we have to get down to the serious business of identifying problems, preparing documentation and establishing in more detail our negotiating directives. The Commission recently approved a modification of the DGI organigramme to prepare for this, involving the creation of a new A/2 (Principal Advisor) post under Paul Luyten, as well as modest additional supporting staff. These extra staff are essential if we are to defend properly the Community's interests, and to continue to play the leadership role which the Community has already earned for itself at Punta del Este and in Geneva.

Getting the *minimum minimorum* of such assets in the Berlaymont (as opposed to Whitehall, which is more flexible and vastly better resourced than the Brussels Commission ever will be) is like getting blood out of a stone, as we all know. So, *Gott sei Dank*!

Relations With Eastern Europe

This month saw, here in Brussels, the first round of bilateral contacts between Commission and USSR experts, following Willy De Clercq's exchange of correspondence with the USSR Foreign Minister Mr. Shevardnadze. The meeting, chaired on our side by Pablo Benavides, was devoted mainly to discussing the modalities of the establishment of formal diplomatic relations between the USSR and the Community, and in particular the question of their accrediting an Ambassador to us. True to the Gorbachov *operation de charme*, the USSR delegation showed quite exceptional cordiality. They were at pains to point out that, however unreasonable they thought the US position on disarmament to be, there could be no question of the USSR's trying to split the Community from its US allies. We, for our part, intend to proceed with great care. While we welcome, in principle—and indeed want to encourage—the official recognition of the Community by the USSR, we remain uncertain about their real motives, and fully conscious of the practical difficulties, particularly of a security nature, which inevitably surround the establishment of a Soviet mission to the Communities in Brussels.

As regards the other member countries of COMECON, we now have our negotiating directives for Czechslovakia and Rumania, although we have yet to begin official negotiations. With Hungary, however, as previous discussions have shown, there is an unwillingness on the part of certain Member States to give economic expression to their political rhetoric. At present, our proposal for negotiating directives is bogged down at technical level in a Council Working Group. A further initiative at the level of Ministers or COREPER will probably be needed if progress is to be made.

Meanwhile, in line with our policy of strict parallelism, we are for the moment hastening slowly as regards fixing a date for our second expert meeting with the CMEA Secretariat.

Looking Ahead

With the XXIV:6 dossier behind us, we can now breathe again and start to give some thought to the many other dossiers which will have to be tackled in 1987.

Only a week away now is the San José III Ministerial conference in Guatemala, which Claude Cheysson and DDG Jean Durieux will be attending, along with Ministers of the Member States and the countries of Central America. Next week in the GATT, we shall be pressing for a GATT Panel to be set up to examine Japan's import *régime* for wines and spirits. By the end of February the Commission will probably have to bite the bullet and decide what sort of agreement with the Gulf countries we wish to propose to the Council. On the multilateral side, the usual hardy annuals of the OECD Ministerial and the Western Economic Summit (I am off to the ECSS in Paris next Tuesday, then to the Sherpa meeting on Thursday in Florence) will be complemented this year by UNCTAD VII, which will be taking place in Geneva throughout most of July.

But for details of these, and other, burning issues you will have, I fear, to wait a little longer.

Lecture Material

I enclose, *à toutes fins utiles*, a copy of the lecture I gave over the holiday period to a Conference of UK University Professors specialising in European studies. Some of you might find it useful for your speaking tours up-country.

New Faces In The Officers' Mess

Two new Heads of Delegation are to join us, coming from other Regiments. Thus, the Commission has designated Mr. Arnandio De Azevedo, a former Portuguese Minister with a distinguished record in that country's return to Parliamentary democracy, as Head of the Delegation in Brasilia; and have similarly designated Mr. Andries van Agt, the former Netherlands Prime Minister, as Head of the Delegation in Tokyo. Neither of these appointments is official, as we are still awaiting agrément from the Brazilian and Japanese Governments. But we trust that everything will go smoothly and that both gentlemen will shortly be donning their DGI uniforms. I invite you all to make them welcome in the Mess; I am sure they will rapidly, and with pride, respect the shibolleths and follow the traditions of the "Big Red One".

Yours sincerely

Leslie Fielding

Brussels
Confidential   12 June, 1987

G7 SUMMIT IN VENICE

If you are busy, read the last two paragraphs of this letter (Venice in a nutshell). If you have more leisure and greater curiosity, read on. (It was not so awful after all!)

A Certain Sinking Feeling?

Reclining in soapy warm water, contemplating the grey marble bathroom walls in my luxury hotel suite on the Grand Canal, and sipping an ill-earned gin and tonic, I had my misgivings, on that first evening, about the Venice Summit. The President himself had had doubts—and expressed them openly to the General Affairs Council before he set out—as to whether he should even actually attend the Summit. And on arrival in Venice, in flaming June, the Community team found the city covered with grey clouds, the waters of the lagoon lashed by a downpour of chilly rain.

E Pur Si Muove!

But let me quickly now recant. As the debate moved forward among the Palladian splendours of the island of San Giorgio Maggiori, that slight sinking feeling (however appropriate to Venice) gradually dissipated. In bright sunlight on the third day, 10 June, Prime Minister Fanfani was able to read out, in the Sala degli Arazzi, what turned out to be quite a workmanlike and constructive, if still in some ways modest, final Declaration. I enclose:

- the main text;
- the separate Declarations on East-West Relations, on terrorism and on the Persian Gulf;
- the Chairman's statements on AIDS; and
- the Chairman's statement on drugs.

<u>Technical Exegesis and Political Overview</u>

Quickly dictated while my memory of the debates is still fresh, my own personal impression of the texts and their implications, are more or less as follows:

(a) wise and realistic consensus on trade and agriculture (paragraphs 13 to 20). The foundations had been laid at the OECD Ministerial meeting last month. All went well at Venice, thanks to firm persuasiveness from Vice President Willy De Clercq in the Finance Ministers Group (it was they who handled trade and agriculture, not the Foreign Ministers) and President Jacques Delors in Plenary; and to skilful pre-dawn draftsmanship by the President's *Chef de Cabinet*, the admirable Pascal Lamy. As all this is of great importance to DGI, I go into more detail below;

(b) a small but significant shift on debt. Chancellor Kohl set the tone ("A major point for the Summit. Press and public opinion are watching. Need for a clear political message and a framework for concerted action".) We are still wedded to "case-by-case" and the Baker tryptich, at least for the major middle-income debtor countries. But their problems are "a cause of economic and political concern" (paragraph 21). And there was real recognition, thanks to the Community (Commission, France, UK and Italy together with Germany), of the need for special treatment of the 'basket cases' of sub-Saharan Africa (paragraph 27). There are also some not unhelpful noises about a general capital increase of the World Bank (paragraph 22);

(c) a distinctly useful step forward on macro-economic and monetary coordination (called "international group therapy" by Sir G Howe) in the Group of Seven. The latter will now move on to more structured surveillance and the use of special indicators of performance (paragraph 11). As Finance Minister Giovanni Goria said in presenting his G7 report to the Summit, in some respects the present situation is not sustainable and action has to be taken in the positive spirit of the Louvre;

(d) grimmish realism behind closed doors. Beneath the minimum necessary surface optimism of the Declaration (see e.g. paragraph 2), there was genuine recognition of the dangers of the *conjoncture* (paragraph 4); and of the consequent need for action (paragraphs 5 to 7), and maybe more action still (paragraph 10) to avert a major recession. While Jim Baker had said (rightly) to the press on his way to Venice that he did not agree with the apocalyptic view that everything was going to blow up, no one gainsaid Margaret Thatcher when, *en séance restreinte,* she asserted that, behind all the "fancy vocabulary" of the draft communiqué, the Summit in reality was facing the prospect of serious international economic difficulties. And even Nakasone spoke of "light and shadow". In particular, no one wanted the US dollar to decline further;

(e) some exercise of cool and even-handed judgement (see the different tasks set for surplus and deficit countries in paragraphs 5 and 7);

(f) no roses for Japan. Despite Prime Minister Nakasone's skilfully contrived pre-Summit package of measures to stimulate growth, and to channel aid and investment to the Third World, there was little eulogy and strictly no adulation.

It was the best package to date; but the atmosphere of scepticism and déjà vu was so thick that you could cut it with a blunt knife. Mrs Thatcher questioned whether the package would achieve its declared purposes, and archly enquired whether, in an environment of "shrinking trade", Japan could be counted on to take in the imports which the US was no longer able to ingest. And there was sharp criticism of Japan's relative ODA performance (see further below) on the last day;

(g) good work on political and strategic issues. The three political cooperation texts, which George Schultz described as "basically what we want", were put together without too much hassle (thanks to neat work by DSG Horst Krenzler and the Political Directors until 4.30 a.m. on the Tuesday). Because Kohl and his Government had already moved beforehand on the "double zero" option, the expected wrangle over missiles did not take place. On the Gulf, the feared commitment to risky military specifics was never in the event sought by the US; Reagan was cautious. Both the EC and Japan made clear the limits to which they were prepared to go (they agreed to "consult" but declined more constraining US formulae, such as "cooperating" or "working together"). Similarly, it was agreed to call for "effective", but not "enforceable", measures by the UN—Mitterrand said that the Summit was not a substitute for the Security Council. On East/West, a slightly hawkish US text circulated on the eve of the Summit was set aside in favour of more balanced (if still a little bit "NATO-like"—e.g. "each of us must remain vigilantly alert") language mostly prepared by the Europeans. And such was the speed with which all these issues were dispatched, that they did not squeeze out or even in any way compress the debate on central economic issues;

(h) a minimum acceptable acknowledgement of the problems and concerns of the developing countries. The justified jab at the MCs (paragraph 6) and the grudging acknowledgement of the imminence, but not the vital importance, of UNCTAD VII (paragraph 28) did not mean that the now traditional hard-nosed US attitudes had it all to themselves at Venice (witness paragraphs 4, 24 and 26, as well as the sub-Saharan Africa development mentioned at (b) above, and the reference to the 0.7% ODA target in paragraph 22);

(i) the right noises about the environment and AIDS. (Both issues are still generally the subject of jokes in bad taste. But each of them is the cause of what is now scientifically well-founded, long-term concern—and even of some degree of hidden governmental panic.)

Trade and Agriculture: Flashback to OECD Ministerial

To explain the Community's grip on these issues at Venice, it is necessary to go back to the Commission's little success story at the OECD Ministerial meeting of 11-13 May in Paris.

At Paris, on the New Round, we had headed off Canadian and American smart-ass procedural gimmicks, such as "Fast Track for Agriculture" or "Early Harvest" or "Let's have another GATT Ministerial meeting". We did this by putting the focus on the substance. Thus we wrote into the Communiqué that "OECD countries will prove their determination by tabling in the coming months comprehensive proposals covering the various fields of the negotiations". We secured a reaffirmation of earlier anti-protectionist 'Stand Still and Roll Back' commitments. And we slotted in the Punta del Este language of last September about the Round being a "single undertaking". As Willy De Clercq put it at one of his press conferences, the Community are not fast track or slow track, but one track.

Thus, at Venice this week, a last ditch pig-headed effort by Canadian officials in favour of "early progress" and a Ministerial jamboree in mid-1988 was easily swept aside. All the Venice Summit does is to toe the OECD line referred to above, but with a ritual genuflection towards the usefulness, "as appropriate", of a Ministerial meeting in Geneva "in the course of the negotiations".

At Paris, on agriculture, the Community had pulled off something much more remarkable. The Commission had the advantage of tide and time. We were able to turn to good effect both the gathering momentum of agricultural restructuring in the Community, and the excellent and intellectually un-challenged recent work of Secretary General Jean-Claude Paye, identifying the causes of, and suggesting the remedies to, the current situation of chronic world over-production. So, instead of playing games, we decided to steal a march on our critics and go for a full-bloodied if balanced OECD commitment to change. So—with the prior blessing of my great buddy, our splendid Director-General for Agriculture, Guy Legras—Rolf Möhler, Hugo Paemen and I duly worked round the clock, in 113 coordination and in the OECD communiqué drafting group. The outcome was paragraphs 19-25 of the Paris Communiqué, which Ministers adopted without fuss, and which constitute a major pointer to the future.

The key OECD concepts were:
- supply greatly exceeds demand for various reasons (including excessive support policies, but also technological change);

- responsibility is shared. No finger-pointing or name-calling;
- therefore concerted reform is called for;
- in the long term, there must be freer play for market forces and a progressive reduction of support;
- at the same time, consideration has to be given to social and other non-economic concerns to do with agriculture and rural areas generally; and there must also be flexibility in the choice of means;
- meanwhile, comprehensive proposals on agriculture, as in other fields, should be tabled by everyone in the Uruguay Round, and credits given to those who have already (like the EC) started the reform process;
- and, short-term, a truce must be called in agricultural tensions. Everyone should "refrain from confrontational and destabilising trade practices".

Even the Americans described this as a "remarkable" OECD outcome. And so it came to pass that this kind of approach prevailed without too much trouble at Venice. We were, I suppose, helped by the fact that the UK Prime Minister made only a brief appearance before returning to the general election campaign. She was blistering about uneconomic farm surpluses; and might have been tempted to try to go a bridge further than the OECD, if the US and Canada had insisted. But when it came to draft the Declaration, she had long since left; and the Commission, France, Germany and Italy took a firm line. President Reagan did not seem to be too worried and Secretary Schultz went so far as to say that the OECD consensus could be sufficient to the day. We then brushed aside half-hearted efforts by Prime Minister Mulroney to get more, in the name of the Cairns Group and the Canadian peasantry. We were helped, too, by the proposed EC oils and fats tax, which came in, on Tuesday, for attacks not only from

Ronald Reagan and Jim Baker, but also even from Mrs Thatcher. It became a splendid whipping boy/red herring/universal scapegoat; and it harmlessly distracted everyone's attention on the final morning's Plenary Session, when the section of the draft Declaration on agriculture went through smoothly. Finally, the Venice Declaration assigned no special monitoring role on agriculture or trade to the Summit countries as such. Low-key US suggestions that Summit Ministers of Agriculture and/or Trade might meet informally between now and the next Summit were ignored. François Mitterrand said he would have "no G7 for agriculture" That quashed the opposition.

Wall Flowers and Warriors: The Commission, the G7 and the EC 12

There was a curious paradox at Venice. The 'bicephalous' (Commission plus Council Presidency) Community worked impressively behind the scenes, but was not very evident up stage. The media hardly noticed us. Even the Italian press banged on and on about the "Summit Seven", despite the visual and aural evidence of the presence of President Jacques Delors and Prime Minister Wilfred Martens, and the excellence of Commission/Presidency cooperation.

This superficial impression of our own marginality was not improved by the quite considerable strengthening of the G7 which was consecrated at Venice (see paragraphs 9 to 12). And, make no mistake about it, the Finance Ministers and Central Bank Governors of the Seven, impelled by inner anxieties, have indeed been busy behind the scenes. They intend (see that all-important paragraph 11) to be busier yet, with surveillance, performance indicators and the rest of the paraphernalia necessary to economic and monetary coordination and possible remedial action. The Louvre and Washington meetings in February and April 1987 will be followed up. All this is balm to the soul of two late-comers to the circle, Canada and Italy; but a closed door to the Commission. There was at Venice once again no consensus to let the Commission into the G7. Gaston Thorn, if he had been there as President, might have been apoplectic. But the present EC team took all this in its stride.

On matters of direct Community competence, Willy De Clercq and Jacques Delors spoke authoritatively for the Twelve at Venice. On sub-Saharan Africa, supported by France and the UK, the Commission took the lead, having prepared the ground with COREPER and Council beforehand in Brussels.

On economic coordination in the face of a worrying conjoncture, Jacques Delors, made a decisive contribution, in my view, to the pre-Venice intra-Community debate, and added his voice effectively to those of Member State Heads of Government. On the *conjoncture* (as on sub-Sahara) the Commission had written, for and at the request of the General Affairs Council, a prior orientation paper which, while judged a little too pessimistic by some Member States, nevertheless helped clear the air and identify common ground in advance of Venice. I enclose a copy, as also (because it goes into more detail on the reasons for the Commission's disabused outlook in this matter) of the economic steering brief which the President brought with him to Venice.

As to the G7, I personally am not too upset for the time being about the Commission's continued absence from it. Time is on our side. We need, in my view, to wait until:

(a) the UK will (following the Thatcher election victory) have joined the EMS—if not in 1987, then in 1988;

(b) Italy and Canada will have concluded that the cement is no longer still wet on their membership, and that talk of bringing in the

Commission will not drive the original members of the G5 back into their inner laager.

That could well do the trick for us in 1988 or 1989.

Pour la petite histoire

Some miscellaneous observations and anecdotes are, I suppose, expected.

- The Canadian Prime Minister (host to a Commonwealth and a Francophone Summit in Vancouver and Montreal later this year; and unencumbered by any direct stake in, or helpful influence over, South Africa) wanted Venice to issue a lengthy admonitory Declaration on South Africa. No one else had strong feelings; and some felt unhappy, mainly because the timing and content of such a Declaration was thought likely to harden racism and nationalism among white nationalists in the Republic, following the recent electoral swing to the right. Instead, at UK suggestion, Fanfani made an oral public statement from the Chair at the end of the Summit, deploring apartheid.

- On this, and indeed on all other major points where the Canadians were tiresome and importunate, there was little or no disposition to take them very seriously. But this will not prevent them from continuing to try and organise everyone for the Ottawa Summit, thereby institutionalising their self-importance. We will have to watch this aspect. Already their Sherpa has been to Geneva and attempted to organise the GATT!

- The French President (supported by the Belgian Prime Minister and the Federal Chancellor) gave short shrift to attempts by Nakasone to pass off the increase in Japanese ODA ("Japan the world's second largest donor") as the best thing for the planet since Scotch whisky and sliced bread. Implacably, François Mitterrand pointed out that Japan was still only diverting 0.29% of GDP in 1986 to ODA—cf EC average 0.52%, UN target 0.7%, and France 0.78%. (I did the calculation in my head that, to reach even 0.5%, Japan would have to spend an additional \$4 billion per annum; at present she devotes \$5-6 billion to ODA.)

- This was, in more than a geographical sense, a European Summit. Nakasone looked stoical but shorn of glamour and short on credibility. Reagan was affable, conciliatory, but sometimes tentative, and always unenergetic. Mulroney (domestic opinion polls plummeting) cut very little ice. Thatcher, however, was on peak House of Commons form; Mitterrand turned in an economical, saturnine but highly telling performance. Kohl was more active and outspoken than usual. Fanfani was a witty, brisk and effective Chairman. And Delors and Martens rode shotgun together, in a confident bicephalous partnership, like Yul Brynner and Burt Lancaster in a Western movie.

Venice, in a Nutshell

President Delors got across his message on the need to develop world trade, to stabilise the international monetary system (he recalled his first aspiring for this at the Versailles Summit in 1981), and to get something as concrete as possible done for the LLDCs. There has been some progress since Tokyo, especially within the G7 (of which Delors says that he was not sure, 12 months' ago, that it would live). Of the three Summits he has attended as President of the Commission, Jacques Delors rates Venice the most positive from the EC view point; although he continues to believe that the tree can be judged only by its fruits.

I would sum up by saying pas mal, at any rate by the circus-like and over-institutionalised and bureaucratic standards of what Western Economic Summits have now become. Or so I felt, as I had my second, better deserved, gin and tonic on the Presidency plane back to dear old Brussels. Later by 48 hours, I still drink to that judgement. So, unexpectedly, it was not a case of "Death in Venice".

Yours sincerely

Leslie Fielding

THE DIRECTOR-GENERAL'S VALEDICTORY

Directorate-General for External Relations
The Director-General
Brussels
17 July, 1987

Dear Colleagues,

This is my final private letter as your Director-General, before I leave in 10 days' time for a different world, and for my third career, at the University of Sussex. Apart from what I have to report on my successor (see below), I have given the letter a more general and reflective character, as befits a "Valedictory".

My Successor: Wait And See
He will be chosen by the College on 29 July, at the final meeting before the summer recess. Rumours abound: I will not add to them. It is still an open question who he will be. Whoever is selected, I know you will all join me in wishing him every success as Director-General in the years which lie ahead.

Apologia Pro DGI Saeculi Sui
In recent months, I have been writing a pamphlet on the evolution of the Community's external relations over the past 15 years. [Europe as a Global Partner—see Background Reading]. I thought it useful, for a wider audience outside the Commission, to set out something of what has happened since Edmond Wellenstein's rather shorter but similar work of the early 1970s; and to attempt to place all the nitty-gritty and ephemera, with which we are so intimately engaged, into wider historical perspective.

When I arrived in the Commission at the beginning of 1973 on UK entry, I brought with me 17 years of

355

professional experience in the UK Diplomatic Service. I had done various political jobs in the Foreign Office in London; and had served in British Embassies in Europe, the Middle East, South East Asia and Indo-China, including 3 years as Head of Mission. But, on arrival in the Berlaymont, I knew by definition almost nothing about in-house EC matters; and not a great deal about economics. (My student days had been spent, in the then not un-typical English way, studying medieval and ancient history; and scrutinising the Persian mystic poets in the original tongue[11]) . Thus, I was initially the victim of what I believe is called "culture shock". So my early apprenticeship years here under the friendly tutelage of Edmond Wellenstein and Theo Hijzen and Jos Loeff were a vivid learning experience; just as my more operational subsequent years, both under Roy Denman and later as his successor were never to know a dull moment.

It feels good therefore to have at least made the attempt to distil the professional experience of 1973-1987 into its quintessence. Whether or not you will agree with all I say, it may be that the booklet will prove of assistance to some of you in the field. Behind the technical and the day-today, it is the etching of what I consider to be a substantive and stabilising Community achievement in a transitory and turbulent world.

Personal Retrospect On 5 Years As Director-General

Looking back over the past 5 years, one tends to think first of the frequent tough times.

There has been the steady run of "close shaves" and "macho" confrontations in EC/US relations, beginning with steel and the gas pipeline problem in the autumn of 1982

---

[11] To be truthful, I later studied economics as a hobby when I was in the British Embassy in Paris; and was put through a gruelling four-month course by the Treasury just before coming to Brussels. But all that gave me was the ability to conduct a conversation with a _real_ economist!

and extending through citrus and enlargement (XXIV:6) to the as yet finally unresolved pasta dispute. I still marvel (as I am sure Gi Giola does, too) at the time and energy that EC/US relations have consumed, at the expense of other things. Perpetual crisis-management can be a drag, even if one is as personally committed as I am to good Transatlantic relations. Then too, there has been the endless struggle with Japan over burden-sharing and reciprocal market access (another time-consumer for both Jos Loeff and myself). I recall the UNCTAD VI nightmare in Belgrade in June 1983—chaotic, confusing and shot through with North-South mistrust. I will not forget, either, the great GATT battles, from that of the bitter and uncreative Ministerial of 1982 (thoroughly messed up by the Americans and by certain Third World rhetoricians and ideologists; but enlivened by the Quixoticism of M. Jobert; and dignified by a remarkable farewell feat of arms by Roy Denman in the thick of the Geneva fray) to the final victory of commonsense, and Community diplomacy, at the Punta del Este Ministerial last autumn. Let me not fail also to mention the endless struggle to get from the Council and the Parliament additional human and financial resources, more political initiative and creativity, with which to develop the Community's relations with others than the super powers—for instance with Turkey, Yugoslavia and India, and with neglected partners in Latin America and the Gulf; or to do something concrete for the refugees in their camps in Palestine and on the Thai/Cambodian frontier, or for the victims of natural catastrophes whenever the need arose. Jean Durieux could confirm, with feeling, how uphill the struggle has been this past 18 months.

But there have been easier times also. To cite a few examples among the many, our relations with ASEAN continue to run quite smoothly. (I recall with pleasure my four visits to the area while Director-General—to Bangkok and Jakarta with Willi Haferkamp, to Jakarta with Gaston

Thorn, and subsequently on DGI business to Manila and Singapore). So, too, have our relations with the EFTAs—collectively our biggest trade partners, and on the whole a very agreeable and like-minded set of people. Our ties with China have developed successfully, to the point that a Delegation will be opening in Beijing in December. Closer home, the Community role in the OECD and at Western Economic Summits (at both of which, in the CESS and among the Sherpas, I myself have been regular in my attendance) is now, in its different and more modest way, as fully accepted as our monolithic presence and active negotiating role in the GATT.

In both good times and bad, while ranging the world scene far and wide, the Director-General has always had to have an eye to his base camp and an ear for noises off. Confident and cordial relations with Member States are naturally essential. Their officials and diplomats are our colleagues—and often also our personal friends. While I have sometimes had to goad and to argue, it has never been my practice to treat with them as if they were representatives of some foreign power. Then, developments on the home front, within the Community, were and remain of vital indirect importance for the conduct of the Community's external relations. The failure of Summit after EC Summit to get to grips with budget burden sharing and with agricultural reform were to cast a pall over external relations fully as palpable as e.g. such obvious spasms and contortions as Poitiers and the French import levies in the autumn of 1982; or as the dither and indecision about commercial defence and the "New Instrument"; or as the row over the Greek balance of payments crisis in 1983. The doldrums and drawn-out agonies of the negotiations for Spanish and Portuguese entry cast their own shadow over the 1980s. On the other hand, the renewed EC economic vigour and intra-Community dynamism of present times—the settlement of old quarrels and the move to *la Grande Europe* of 1992—are reinvigorating our approach to external issues. Euro-diplomacy grows best where Europessimism lies buried. (Don't worry too much about passing clashes of personality and conviction between the leviathans of the European Council.)

For sheer purgatory, I would cite the burden of laborious and frequently pettifogging personnel and administration work which falls to every head of a large department in the Berlaymont, (and even more to his long-suffering Assistants—I would wish this latter job on no one). This is still in my view the weak spot of the Commission. Any attempt at significant innovation can take years rather than months (remember the Fortescue Report?); a major set of staff moves will usually occupy weeks rather than days of to-and-fro negotiation; promotion procedures leave me at times apoplectic. Happily, a dedicated attempt is being made by Henning Christophersen and Richard Hay to bring reform to a system which is in many ways ill-suited to a public service of the size and complexity which the European Commission has now attained.

But "begone dull care"! For sheer fun, I look back upon the glamour of President Thorn's official visit to Delhi, in company with Manfred Macioti and a supporting cast of Bengal Lancers; upon colonial Williamsburg, with Roy Denman and assorted Heads of State and Government; upon a carefree open air Mechoui at Paul Tran's hill-side Geneva residence, with a cheerful Arthur Dunkel and a very cheerful Robin Gray; upon the Tien Anmen, during the 35th Anniversary celebration of the People's Republic, occupied by two million Chinese servicemen, dancers, firework artificers and simple citizens; upon Ayers Rock in the sweltering central Australian desert, with Ove-Juul Jørgensen and the local aborigines; and upon celebrating the 30th anniversary of the Treaties, with champagne galore, Luigi Boselli and half Caracas, on my first visit to Venezuela.

A Source Of Satisfaction: The New Round Initiative

One source of personal satisfaction for me has been, quite unexpectedly, the GATT (of which I had had little experience before becoming Director-General). I am thinking in particular of the protracted process of leading the Community from agnosticism to active commitment, in the matter of a New Round of trade liberalisation. The GATT team and I had to establish credibility and create momentum by committing the Community, in successive meetings of the CG18, to some form of roll-back (we succeeded with QR packages and tariff accelerations). We had to lay with the 113 Committee in Brussels the analytical basis for a New Round in the famous five "Alpha-Epsilon Non-Papers". These last were an intellectual pleasure to write; but we had to stick our necks out, in writing them. (It was a delicate initiative, given the *ambiance* in the Community at that time; our professional reputations had to be put on the line.) And we had to fight off continued efforts by the US and others to force the Community to run before it could walk (including having to frustrate Ronald Reagan and his sympathisers at the London Western Economic Summit). It fell to Willy De Clercq and to me to steer respectively the Council and the 113 Titulaires, in a marathon session on 12 March 1985, through at times heated discussion to a carefully qualified but meaningful commitment of principle. That was then only the beginning. Next came, on the one side, our infinite labours to rally doubtful or hostile developing countries (with Paul Luyten, Rod Abbott and I quartering the Third World between us); and, on the other side, in one damned Quadrilateral after another, our constant effort to dissuade the US from too extreme and dictatorial a GATT crusade for the New Round which would have destroyed the international consensus we were painstakingly building up. A decisive majority of GATT Contracting Parties need to be convinced, not just corralled. (I think especially of the Sintra Quadrilateral last September, where the US became quite *intraitable,* denouncing us for laying the foundation of a workman-like bargain on services with the Third World very close to that which Clayton Yeutter was himself to grasp thankfully a few days later at Punta del Este). All that, and the persuasive diplomacy of the EC Delegation and its Head in Geneva, finally paid off, in the triumph of constructive compromise at Punta del Este, with the Community playing the pivotal North/South role upon which success or failure depended. I look back on the whole process with pride; because what we did served not only our enlightened self-interest as Europeans, but also the wider interests of an expanding world economy, and with it the deeper needs of the developing countries. It still seems to me probable that, if the Community had never come into being, and Europe's wisdom and weight in Geneva were still divided among twelve purely national Delegations, the GATT would have collapsed for lack of centripetence and cement, and protectionism would be running amok through the World.

Towards A European Foreign Service

I will mention one other personal satisfaction, the origin of which goes back, however, some dozen years. I refer to the steady growth of professionalism in our external Delegations. I am well aware that there is more to be done: the MMI Delegations, for example, urgently require additional infrastructural support; the DGI "desk" service to some of you people in the field could be further improved; I am still dissatisfied with the financial conditions of service at certain posts; the quality of man-management, while usually good, and sometimes quite outstanding, still tends to vary from Delegation to Delegation.

It does, indeed, take time to acquire expertise and to create a tradition. When I first started work in the

Berlaymont, one of the responsibilities of my Directorate, especially given me by Christopher Soames and Edmond Wellenstein, was policy governing external offices. There were then in fact very few offices, and there was almost no policy. I discovered that only Washington possessed a cypher machine—no one there knew how to operate it and it was kept locked away in a cupboard somewhere and never used. There was no diplomatic bag service. Allowances were haphazard. Apart from the Geneva Delegation, ably and forcefully led by Paul Luyten, most offices in the Spring of 1973 were poorly organised and directed. (I remember receiving two separate telexes from the Washington Delegation reporting the same trade policy development, one from the Commercial Section and one from the Press Section; things improved when Jean-Pierre Leng arrived and got a grip on the Delegation.) Traditional diplomatic ranks and titles were not in use and traditional diplomatic procedures rarely observed (for example, formal *agrément* was not sought for Heads of Mission and the latter presented no formal Letters of credence on arrival). Coordination at overseas posts between DGI and DGX was lacking—the former usually claiming to be a 'Delegation' and the latter an independent 'Press Office', yet all within a single set up.

There were exotic episodes. Let me recount a Uruguayan anecdote. I remember in the mid-70s having to fly out to Montevideo, where there used to be located an antenna of our then regional Delegation in Santiago, to prevent the rather brutal Colonels then in power in Uruguay from arresting, on mysterious charges, and probably torturing, the Head of that antenna. The Head, a local agent, was Czech by birth, claimed German nationality, but had Argentinean and Uruguayan passports. It turned out that he was under suspicion of having abused the diplomatic privileges of the sub-office to import motor cars duty-free in order to raise funds for a local political party. He finally confessed, to Wolfgang Renner and myself; we secured his on-the-spot resignation; and the man left the country within hours. In the absence of more secure means, and since the Colonels had blithely told me that they were able to listen to my transatlantic phone calls, I had to make the key report to Soames, and get his approval for my proposed course of action, by sending a telex from the Montevideo Post Office in Persian (a language I hold in common with David Hannay, then the Chef de Cabinet, but not one which the Colonels were likely to be able to decypher in the twelve hours within which I needed confidentiality).

Looking back, it is clear that the external representation of the Community has come a long way since the first enlargement, not only quantitatively but also qualitatively. We now unquestionably have the makings of a professional foreign service for Community matters, and one in which our two Commissioners can justly take growing satisfaction.

The Future

Over the next 5 years, much can be expected to stay the same: continued crisis-management requirements with the US; continued pressure and persuasion to get Japan to open up and behave responsibly; continued hard-grinding negotiations in the GATT (including the on-going saga of textiles, as well as New Round stuff); continued economic and commercial consolidation with EFTA and the Mediterranean partners; continued efforts to secure closer relations with the Gulf; continued endeavours to expand and improve our DGI development activities in the countries for which we have responsibility (already a budget of well over half a billion ECU a year); continued expansion and professionalisation of our external diplomatic network; continued battles with the Council over budgets, in alliance with the Parliament; and so forth and so on.

But there will be some new and potentially exciting external developments too: among them, the slow unfolding of a more substantive relationship with Latin America (itself a process initiated, before Spanish and Portuguese adhesion, by Willi Haferkamp's paper to the General Affairs Council in August 1984); the steadily strengthening position of the Community in the UN; the cautious opening up of our relations with the Comecon countries; the start of an EC policy on debt; the development of new EC competences outside the straight commercial policy context (monetary, environmental, financial etc) and their incorporation within, or harnessing to, a coherent EC external policy; the late, but not for that the less sweet, fruits of political cooperation in the form of some kind of genuine European foreign policy.

We shall have to take care for the further viability and development of the EC/US/Japan triangle. (Will the US blow their top? Will Japan pull the roof down? Will Europe continue to shoulder its own responsibilities?) We will want to keep an eagle eye fixed on certain up and coming bilateral partners (China and Russia, of course; but also, for example, Korea, a country where we will need to be diplomatically represented before the decade is over). We will need to give special succour to the key multilateral institutions—especially the GATT, which is shifting like sand under our feet. (Will the US stop the bus and get off? What effect will China's re-entry have? Could the GATT survive Soviet membership, even of the Gorbachev type?)

And there will be two major factors which will affect decisively the framework within which we operate, over which DGI has no control at all. The first will be the continued growth (or the progressive collapse) of the world economy; the second, the degree of success (or failure) of the internal drive to the Great Market—with all that both imply for future Community strength and cohesion.

It adds up to quite a challenge for all of you, for our two Commissioners and for my still unannounced successor.

The Coldstream Of The Commission
DGI works. Indeed, a very senior official of the Council Secretariat, speaking last month at a dinner at Val Duchesse in honour of Paul Luyten, described ours as *la Direction Générale la plus prestigeuse de la Commission européenne.* I am glad to have served with DGI for over 14 years in both Brussels and (after an eight-month sabbatical at Oxford) in Tokyo; and to have had the pleasure of heading the Directorate General for the past 5 years. It is a professional body, not only here at home, but increasingly now overseas also; and presided over by two first-class political professionals in Willy De Clercq and Claude Cheysson. Our best, these days, is fully as good as what we usually meet among the Member States, who I think generally give us peer approval. So DGI has some claim to be *Nulli Secundus* in the Commission.

Last Words On Riding Off Into The Sunset
There is always liable to be something slightly ludicrous about last words or final gestures. Like the terminal utterances of Socrates or Rabelais or Goethe. Or like when, at the end of some Western movie, the lone cowboy swings into the saddle and rides off into the sunset—only to fall off, necessitating an expensive retake (it is said to have happened once to Ronald Reagan). Nevertheless, I feel moved to write the following last words. When I vault lightly into the saddle of my battered family Volvo, and zoom up the rue de la Loi and out onto the Zeebrugge road at the end of this month, I shall wave a cheerful farewell to the formal minuets of the COREPER; and the rustic charms of the 113 Titulaires Committee; and the challenge of non-stop jet-setting round the world; and the adrenalin of rough and tumble, all-night negotiating sessions; and the gastronomic delights of the Villa Lorraine; and the tinsel crown of petty privilege and empty acclaim. And I admit I

can do without working steadily round the clock, year in year out, without seeing very much of my wife and children, or opening a book, or saying my prayers properly. But I shall miss and remember the men and women of the Directorate-General whom I have been lucky enough to know and serve with, past and present, the living and the departed. My best wishes for your future careers. My blessing on you and your families. Goodbye—and thank you.

Yours sincerely

Leslie Fielding

8. STAFF IN CONFIDENCE

"In these pages, the history is not of the Arab movement, but of me in it. It is a matter of daily life, mean happenings, little people. Here are no lessons for the world, no disclosure to shock people".

T.E. Lawrence: 'The Seven Pillars of Wisdom'

REFEREES AND THE CIVIL SERVICE COMMISSION

SCHOOL:

He was a Prefect, and a good one, Editor of the Magazine, a Colour in the First XV, a leading actor in School plays, prominent in debates—in short, an able and public-spirited all-rounder.

It is, of course, over four years since he left, but I have been in quite reasonable contact with him (three or four meetings or private chats a year) since he left, and have no reason to change the very good opinion I had of him when he left.

His character is sound, he has personality and polish, and he has an active mind in which seriousness and humour are combined. In short, he is, in my opinion, a really good candidate.

E.H. Jenkins, Headmaster
Queen Elizabeth's School
Barnet, Herts

February 1956

UNIVERSITY:

He began his connection with us by rejecting a place at University College, Oxford, awarded to him on the result of a Scholarship Examination there, he thinking that the History Tripos here would supply his wants more effectively than would Modern Greats. This ability to look and think ahead is one of his outstanding characteristics. It is the rarest thing for an undergraduate to come and tell me the answer to the question which I am going to ask him in six months' time, but this is what Fielding has done throughout his time here. With this forward-looking way he combines habits of extreme tidiness, both in mind and in external appearance. He has his own ideas of protocol in the relations between Tutor and pupil but his rather sly, but rich, sense of humour makes it quite plain that he is well aware of the difference between the real and the formal. Behind the formal, there is a most attractive and extremely able undergraduate. He is near the first class all the time and I hope that he will find himself classed as such in his last examination. He works hard, he can assimilate fresh material very quickly and his judgment, at least in terms of the Historical Tripos, is good. He is highly regarded by his contemporaries and has earned a great reputation in the Debating Society, first as its Secretary and later as its Vice-President. Unless I am greatly at fault in my judgement, Fielding is one of the strongest candidates for the Civil Service that we have had in this College for several years.

P. Hunter-Blair, M.A.
Senior Tutor
Emmanuel College
Cambridge

February 1956

CIVIL SERVICE COMMISSION

Fielding has an active mind in which seriousness and humour are combined. He works hard, he can assimilate fresh material quickly, and his judgment is good. On every kind of problem he is thoroughly competent, systematic and reliable. In written work he has a good solid style, handles an argument well and uses a wide range of factual illustration to advantage. Moderation and a sense of proportion are high among his virtues; he is careful to balance issues but not afraid to come down decisively. Perhaps his greatest assets are reliability and integrity. He has a keen conscience, a strong sense of responsibility, and his professional approach to whatever he does makes him incapable of producing anything shoddy. Although his imagination does not always sparkle, he thinks well ahead and is a born planner. Calm and courteous, he speaks with a quiet assurance and a sense of real authority, though a trifle unbending until he feels himself firmly established; if serious minded, he is in no way dull or humourless, and colleagues will like as well as respect him. Behind the slightly formal manner there is a most attractive and extremely able man, with great scope for development, and a genuine desire to use his ability in the public service.

May 1956
F.S.B. Mark 270 F.S.

JUNIOR DIPLOMAT, TEHRAN

Initial Report

Pen Picture of the Officer

Leslie Fielding has some very solid qualities behind a slightly precious appearance. Although his tastes are more intellectual than sporting, he is quite tough[12]. Fond of amateur dramatics, he is gay and imaginative. Friendly, courteous and well turned out he is excellent in social life. His integrity and consideration for others make him liked by everyone. He has settled down well in Chancery and his Persian is now extremely fluent. He also plays a considerable part in extra curriculum activities ranging from the Embassy library to the sports club. He has a good brain; is extremely thorough and hard working. He is quick in action[13] and ready to take responsibility and use his initiative. His modesty probably conceals considerable strength of character. His good temper, judgment and gift of sympathy make him excellent in helping with the welfare side of Chancery work.

It is difficult to tell yet just how able he is or whether he has a gift for any particular side of Foreign Service work, but his qualities of character alone should make him an excellent member of Branch A.

George Hiller
Head of Chancery
December 1958

During the short time I have been here, I have formed a high opinion of Fielding's capabilities and potentialities.

Sir Geoffrey Harrison
Ambassador
January 1959

---

[12] Probably an allusion to the author's participation in a mid-winter earthquake relief expedition in the snows of Kordestan.

[13] Possibly an allusion to the author's handling of a hostile mob (see 'Kindly Call Me God', p.21

Mr. Fielding has clearly come on, since he went to Tehran. My first impression was of a slightly gloomy young man who might develop chips on his shoulder. Sir G. Harrison thinks him eminently steady and conscientious, but not in the first flight. I think he will be a useful member of the Service.

John Henniker-Major
Head of Personnel Dept FO
October 1959

Final Confidential Report, Tehran Embassy

Pen Picture of the Officer

He is a pleasant-mannered young man of good appearance and considerable charm. His tendency here towards excessive pomposity and formality of behaviour will no doubt wear off with the years.

In the Chancery at this post, Mr. Fielding was an able and efficient Junior Secretary. After completing his period as a language student he quickly picked up the requirements and procedures of Chancery work, and was able adequately to take charge in the Head of Chancery's absence. He was a hard and willing worker, and very keen to improve his knowledge. Occasionally this keenness led him to pursue subjects beyond what was necessary, and he was over-fond of writing lengthy and rather pompous minutes. But when given a particular job of research or compilation to do, he did it quickly and effectively. His political judgment at this post was, not surprisingly so early in his career, slightly immature; but he showed keen interest in political work and may prove very suitable for this type of work in the future. He was good at picking up information and developed contacts in a variety of circles. He acquitted himself very well when he accompanied me on a week's tour of the oilfields in Southern Iran. He took the initiative in introducing himself at social gatherings, attended competently to such matters as arose during the tour, and proved an entertaining companion with a wide range of interests.

He is a sensitive young man, and has probably not yet fully found his emotional and temperamental feet. But generally feeling, he has the makings of an excellent Branch A officer.

Sir Geoffrey Harrison
Ambassador
August 1960

Mr. Fielding has evidently learnt Persian extremely well. In Khorramshahr, I met a senior Iranian official of the Oil Consortium who had been very highly impressed by Mr. Fielding's Persian at the time of the Ambassador's official visit. He said that, but for his appearance, Mr. Fielding could even be taken for a Persian, as his vocabulary and accent were so perfect.

Personnel Dept., FO
September 1960

DESK OFFICER, WESTERN ORGANISATIONS DEPARTMENT, LONDON

Initial Report

Pen Picture of the Officer

He is very keen and, I think, ambitious. During my time as Head of the Dept. he has worked extremely hard and is now an expert in the intricacies of NATO and WEU. He likes detail and is thoroughly reliable. I never have to check his facts. He enjoys especially the quasi-legal aspects of Treaty interpretation: he would have been a good lawyer. His drafts are always clear and well-written—sometimes too long-winded. He takes immense pains to ensure that all the action is complete before he presents papers.

His keenness sometimes leads him to overstate his case and to propose a hammer when a smaller instrument would do.

He has a forceful character, and accepts responsibility easily. His manner, however, can be brusque and he can be irritable if he does not get his way. Sometimes a bit brash, he needs to be gently sat upon periodically. To get the best out of him he needs to be given constant and active work. But he has the makings of an extremely competent officer.

I find it hard to assess his personality—he is probably not very sure of himself yet, nor of his relations with other people. I think he probably irritates a few. In some ways, he seems rather young, for 30. It is time he got married and had children.

I like him, but never managed to get to know him very well.

Peter Ramsbotham
Head of Department
October 1962

Final Report

Pen Picture of the Officer

He is full of energy and his output is high. His enthusiasm sometimes runs away with his drafts. But he has a very thorough grasp of his job and can always be relied upon to find the relevant precedent on Treaty provision in NATO and WEU affairs with the minimum of delay.

He is also an able organiser and operator with a cheerful extravagant manner and plenty of self-confidence. This has stood him in good stead both in the Department and as Resident Clerk. On the same basis, he is a bit inclined to show pained surprise when his drafts are not accepted just as they flow from his pen. But he readily resumes his equanimity and comes back for more punishment.

He seems to make friends quickly and to keep them. On social occasions with foreigners, his manners are pleasant and forthcoming and he speaks to the point when business is being discussed.

Despite his rather *fin de siècle* appearance, I think he would be an adaptable member of any team and I think he is certainly fit for promotion to First Secretary.

He should be used in a large post where there is plenty of work and where his public spirit will also help. But I could also see him being very valuable in a tight corner, where his practical common sense and power of making things happen could be exploited. He still needs the supervision of a cautious supervisor for a bit.

John Barnes
Head of Department
February 1964

CHARGE D'AFFAIRES, PHNOM PENH

Regular confidential personal reports were not written, during the author's spell as Chargé d'Affaires in Phnom Penh, because he had no one in the Embassy above him to undertake them. The only reports, therefore, are episodic, in the form of what follows.

H.M. Inspector's Report INDIV, July 1964

Mr. Fielding was transferred from Singapore to May in exchange for Mr. Shakespeare. Before my arrival in Phnom Penh, the Ambassador had already left and Mr. Fielding had become Chargé d'Affaires. Although at the post for only a short time and in charge for only a few days he was very much in command and dealing quickly and capably with a fair range of problems. He also seemed to me to be getting on well with his staff (despite some feeling of mild resentment at being led by such a young newcomer to the post), and with others with whom I saw him dealing. It must have been something of a gamble to send a bachelor A.8 to a tricky post of this kind; but I shall be surprised if the gamble does not pay off. Incidentally, Mr. Fielding has a pop painting on his wall and a Beatles record on his gramophone: how "with it" can the younger generation get?

Harold Brown

Letter from Edward Peck, Assistant Under Secretary of State, FCO, 28 September, 1964

I was delighted to hear such good news of you from William Hayter when I met him at a conference in Oxford last week. I had not realised he had been travelling in South-East Asia until he gave me a glowing account of the *langouste flambeé* you gave him for dinner. After this recommendation I need hardly add that we in the Department are very pleased with your excellent reporting and your handling of a tiresome, but not yet troublesome, situation.

Extract from Report by Rt Hon Malcolm MacDonald of his private meeting with Prince Norodom Sihanouk, Cambodian Head of State, in the latter's villa in Grasse, 15 September 1965

Prince Sihanouk said that the present Chargé d'Affaires [Leslie Fielding] is "helpful and sensible (*très sage*)".

INDIV: Confirmation As First Secretary
L. Fielding

Mr. Fielding was promoted to Grade 5A in July 1964, shortly after his posting to Phnom Penh, where he is still serving. He has been Chargé d'Affaires at the post throughout the period since his promotion, and has thus been his own master. The Head of South East Asia Department has told us orally that he considers Mr. Fielding has carried out his duties in admirable fashion and we have received tributes to his effectiveness from a number of other sources. There is no doubt that his performance fully merits confirmation of his promotion.

Personnel Dept. FO
June 1966

Letter To H.M. Ambassador, Paris, from Chief Clerk, July 1966

You will recall that when you were over here earlier this month, you suggested that it would be as well to stagger the coming changes in your Chancery ....

We have a good replacement available at the end of this year in Leslie Fielding, whose curriculum vitae I attach. Fielding is a bachelor, aged 34. He has done well in the Service. As a Persian language student and in his time in the Chancery at Tehran both Roger Stevens and Geoffrey Harrison spoke well of him. He worked for a time in Western Department and Western Organisations and Planning Department under Peter Ramsbotham who described him then as keen, ambitious, and a good drafter, and added: "To get the best out of him he needs to be given constant and active work, but he has the makings of an extremely competent officer". His latest appointment, that of Chargé d'Affaires at Phnom Penh, has been unusual for so young an officer, but he has carried out his duties in admirable fashion and we have had tributes to his effectiveness from a number of sources.

Fielding has in the past shown some tendency to overvalue his own capacity, considerable though this is, and it should therefore be a useful corrective at this point for him to serve in a large Chancery where there is strong competition. He is personally agreeable, and his French must be pretty competent by now. He took a five week course at the Sorbonne while serving in the Foreign Office, and has been using that language daily for the past two years. I hope that you can accept him. I am sure that he will measure up very well.

July 1966

[For Ministerial comment on Despatches from Phnom Penh, see pages 58, 80 and 150 above]

POLITICAL FIRST SECRETARY, PARIS

Initial Report:

1. He has specialised on the external political subjects, other than European/Atlantic questions—and has been especially active over Viet-Nam, Rhodesia and the Middle East. From his previous service with me in Western Organisations Dept, five years ago, I knew him to be a good performer, competent and quick, with an orderly mind and great deal of determination—with a tendency to want to press on too fast and to show his exasperation when

restrained. In the four intervening years, he has noticeably matured. Undoubtedly his experience as Chargé d'Affaires in Cambodia for so long has been turned to good account. His zest is undiminished, but better controlled. His judgement has improved, and he is quicker to sense and identify the finer points in an argument.

2. His conscientious attention to duty is almost exaggerated. True, he has had to tackle two 'crisis' subjects—Rhodesia and the Middle East, with neither of which he was familiar—but I sometimes thought he was overzealous in the amount of time he would spend at his desk in the evenings and often at weekends. Nevertheless, he so obviously enjoyed it all (and he has no domestic ties), and I do not think he will lose his sense of proportion.

3. His is a character which is very hard to assess. Six months in Paris was too short a period in which to build up a circle of friends and develop any outside interests. He is already inclined to corpulence, and his somewhat effeminate traits[14] probably lead him in the direction of the arts. Certainly his dress is often startlingly flamboyant. I doubt whether he has a fondness for sports, though he seems to be keen on dancing (at which he is surprisingly nimble). He has already shown himself to be kind and considerate towards junior staff, ready to join in the Embassy's "welfare" activities and to co-operate in any way he can be useful. In fact I was struck by this cheerful keenness to play an active part in the Embassy.

4. He is full of self-confidence, and enjoys being given responsible tasks; nor does he seem to feel the need to seek guidance in his work, though in fact he does so

---

[14] Not the view of George Hiller DSO, wartime hero in the French Resistance, (see pp 293 and 294).

very readily. There is a certain artificiality about his relations with his seniors. He is not fully at his ease; but this may largely be due to the transition from three years as acting Head of Mission in Cambodia and the junior First Secretary in the Paris Chancery. I think this is an important period in his development.

Peter Ramsbotham
Head of Chancery
August 1967

I agree with Mr. Ramsbotham's excellent report on Mr. Fielding, who has made a very good start in Paris. He has done some excellent major drafts. Indeed I would be in inclined to rate his work all round a little higher than Mr. Ramsbotham does. I have been particularly struck by the sensible and pleasant way in which he has fitted into a relatively junior job in this top Embassy after having run his own show so young for so long. I think it does him great credit.

If he does not rate outstanding/exceptional under Part 6 (and personally I am inclined to think that he does), he comes very close to it.

Sir Patrick Reilly
Ambassador
August 1967

Further Report:

His job in the Chancery has been to deal with the Third World diplomatic business at the "desk" level. He has been eighteen months here and has made a considerable success of this job. In fact I have no criticism of the way he has done it. [In the *Powers of Leadership* box. 'He could be first class in a crisis'.]

Leslie Fielding is a clever man, very well read and with a considerable variety of cultural and intellectual interests. He is widely respected by diplomatic colleagues and French officials for knowledge and judgment of the questions he deals with. [In the *Languages* box: 'His French is exceptionally good, both spoken and written. He can even tell stories in provincial accents etc!' In the *Contacts* box: 'French officials seem to dote on him']. He is very conscientious and "serious". Yet his appearance is far from solemn. On the contrary, his aspect and clothing are on the flamboyant side and his manner is open and easy. He finds himself at home in most circles, ranging from the Embassy club bar to the drawing rooms of the Faubourg. He is widely liked, being good company and a talented mimic.

In short, Fielding is a delightful fellow as well as an able one—he may go a very long way in the Service (although this may depend a bit on whether, and if so whom, he marries).

Alan Campbell
Head of Chancery
August 1968

This is a very good report with which I entirely agree. Mr. Fielding's work here has been consistently first class. As I have previously reported, I have greatly admired the way in which, in spite of having been his own master so long, he immediately fitted in here in the most sensible and non-fussing way possible. He should go a very long way. I hope he can get married soon. His neckties continue to startle me: but this is no doubt one further proof that it is time to get out.

I told him today that I had given him a first class report and that I saw no reason why he should not go to the top of the Service. If he could find himself the right wife, he would get there all the quicker. He promised to try.

Sir Patrick Reilly
Ambassador
August 1968

Further Report:

His job in the Paris Chancery has been to deal with diplomatic work relating to the Third World for his first years, and (since November 1968) to Europe and NATO. He has been quite first class in every aspect of the job and I have therefore given him an excellent report.

His more obvious qualities are already well known to the Dept. He is a gay, presentable, extrovert, amusing attractive fellow. But he is also fundamentally serious and surprisingly thorough and conscientious in his work. I have formed a great liking for him and a high opinion of his ability. As an example of his seriousness, he followed a correspondence course and subsequently took an A level in Economics in order to broaden his general knowledge of affairs while at the same time fully carrying out all his duties at a very busy time in the Chancery. He is widely read and intellectually active, so that he has successfully made himself master of several complicated but important questions of current interests, such as *La Francophonie* and the intellectual and philosophical background of the 1968 student revolt.

His next job should be on the economic side. He wants this and I gather it is agreed. He would be a great asset in any job concerned with the negotiations to get into the EEC.

As to the more distant future, all depends on whether he marries and if so when. If he remains a bachelor, I doubt if he will stay in the Service more than another five years or so. But I may be quite wrong about this!

Alan Campbell
Head of Chancery
August 1969

This good report is well-deserved. Leslie Fielding is bright, sensitive, hard-working, gay, and, I think, ambitious. An adaptable person who I'm sure will do well wherever he goes. I would certainly be glad to have him in any team I was connected with.

Sir Christopher Soames
Ambassador
November 1969

Final Report

Mr. Fielding is a round, comfortable, red-headed man of exceptional social gifts and intellectual stature. He did a first-class job in Paris both in the office and outside it as a First Secretary in Chancery, concerned (while I was Head of Chancery) with European questions and the expanding framework of Anglo-French relations. The ratings in Part 2 show how highly his performance appears when subject to individual points of analysis. The general effect was outstanding.

Mr. Fielding had a wide circle of interesting friends in Paris and a busy social and cultural life, yet found time for intellectual endeavours outside his work—the study of mathematics and economics, research on Cambodia (where he was en poste) and writing.

He is of unimpeachable integrity and universal popularity.

Peter Marshall

Head of Chancery
April 1971

I would have thought that Leslie Fielding was an example of the very best which, thank goodness, the Foreign Service attracts. He is an excellent, attractive and well-rounded character. Though by no means objectionably ambitious, he is keen and optimistic. I would expect him always to put his best into his job, and to get the most out of it. He is a bright, lively and enjoyable companion, with an excellent intellect. I hope and expect that he will go far and fast.

Sir Christopher Soames
Ambassador
June 1971

DEPUTY HEAD, PLANNING STAFF, LONDON

Initial Report

Mr. Fielding has been with the Planning Staff since September 1970 as Assistant Head of the Department. He is in charge in my absence. Otherwise he takes part in normal planning work. We are too small and too busy a unit to have any hierarchical structure. Mr. Fielding has shaped Planning papers, takes part in the discussion of others and the continuing debate on general issues within the Planning Staff and the Office in general. He participates in seminars and has undertaken some speaking engagements.

Mr. Fielding is an agreeable and intelligent young man. His bonhomie, sense of humour and considerable social talents conceal a thoughtful disposition. He reads and reflects. He is well informed, but anxious to extend his knowledge, particularly on the side of economics. He has great tact and gets on well with all conditions of men. He has imagination and he writes well, with a genuine literary flair. These are all plus points for a Planner.

There are, however, some anxieties, or rather questions. He has been rather slow at finding his feet, as many are, in what is an unusual department. He has also been detached on other work [attached to Sir F Warner for work on the Rhodesia crisis]. He has not been particularly productive and has been rather over-shadowed by his two colleagues. Occasionally I have had the feeling that he is coasting, and regarding the Planning Staff as a kind of superior interlude between real jobs. His mind is good, but I would not really call it first class. He lacks edge and incisiveness. There is tendency to produce a graceful rephrasing of accepted positions, rather than take up a subject by the roots and really analyse it.

This is hypercriticism from a hypercritical department. Mr. Fielding is well up to and above normal standards for first class officers and I have no doubt about his fitness for top jobs. But my present feeling is that he is primarily a practical diplomat—an operator or fixer. I should like this to be regarded as a temporary judgment as I come to know him better, or as he gains confidence in his present job. I may wish to modify it.

I suggest he should be allowed to deepen his knowledge of economics (possibly a sabbatical) and then be given a post in the politico-economic field. As regards area, I think Europe would be right. His tact and diplomacy would no doubt soothe the savage breast of the Afro/Asian, but would also be useful in more important fields e.g. dealing with a prickly Frenchman.

Percy Cradock
Head of the Planning Staff
May 1971

Further Report

Mr. Fielding is an agreeable and highly talented man. In an earlier input on him, I set out his considerable merits; I suggested that he was a first class diplomat; I wondered whether he was a really first class planner. On the whole I adhere to that position. He has knowledge, judgment and flexibility; good manners, good humour and good drafting. He also thinks more than his manner suggest. He has been particularly helpful in negotiating difficult and contentious drafts; he has a good sense of reality; and he has run the department well in my absence. But his papers tend to be the 18th Century ideal "what oft was thought but ne'er so well expressed"; there is some lack of intellectual power and incisiveness; and I would tend to look to elsewhere for ideas.

I would therefore give him a very good mark as a practical diplomat and hope that he can be promoted rapidly. His qualities are those the Service requires in most of its manifestations; the fact that he is not the planners' dream should not detract from that.

Percy Cradock
November 1971

FCO Personnel Department Comments: Grade 5 Flyers List

Mr. Fielding is an outstanding officer on the brink of promotion to Grade 4, ... having for the past 18 months been No 2 in the Planning Department of the FCO. He is one of the best French speakers in the Service.

Personnel Dept, FCO
February 1972

Final Report

[In boxes: *Judgement*: occasionally almost too good for the heretics of the Planning Staff. Ability to produce *constructive ideas*: his ideas are not always very profound, but are sometimes more practical for that very reason.

Drive and determination: his enthusiasm is occasionally intermittent. *Interest in welfare of staff:* always remembers little attentions to typists.]

Paradoxically Mr. Fielding's greatest value to the Planning Staff—and he is the colleague I shall be most reluctant to lose—is that he is in some ways not a natural choice for the job. He is by temperament an operator and a tactician, rather than a thinker. As a result he is constantly able to remind us of what is practical and expedient, to diagnose the general climate of opinion and to predict the likely responses of senior officials. He is also a master of office drafting. If I tell him what I want, he will very quickly produce an admirable draft which, in nine cases out of ten, I have only to initial. He shows the same ability in administrative matters.

When it comes to the production of Planning Papers, he is perhaps better as a critic and collaborator than as an initiator.

I find the natural *bravura* of his personality stimulating and amusing. He altogether lacks the subdued drabness of so many of our colleagues and is a lively and agreeable companion. But the austere Mandarins might regard him as somewhat self-indulgent. To them his pleasure in picking up gossip, in his own cleverness, in his command of tactics and in the perfection of his French may sometimes be too apparent. He has nevertheless, in the ten years I have know him, conquered his earlier impetuosity and improved his ability to restrain his exuberance in the interests of the immediate objective. He has the talents to support his considerable ambitions: it will be interesting to see whether he also has the self-discipline.

He has many interests outside his work, leads a lively social life and is always eager to broaden his experience.

James Cable
Head of the Planning Staff
November 1972

THE BRUSSELS EUROCRACY

Initial FCO Impressions

UKREP say that, while he is finding it tough going, and needs some reassurance from time to time, he is settling down well and performs ably in COREPER.

Personnel Dept, FCO
July 1973

First FCO Report

Since this report covers a period of four years it must necessarily be somewhat telescoped and historical. Leslie Fielding was parachuted into a senior post in the EEC Commission when we joined, without having had any previous experience directly of Community work or international organisations. In the early months, he certainly found the surface slippery and the problems complex and not always easy to handle. But within a period of eighteen months he had really mastered the situation, gained the respect of those who worked with him and since then he has never looked back. He was almost single-handed responsible for the negotiation of the EEC/Canada agreement which was itself a substantial innovation in Community practice. He played a major part in the establishment and smooth running of the annual or bi-annual consultations which the US, Canada, Australia and New Zealand. He has improved out of all recognition the quality of the day-today contacts with the missions of the countries for which he is responsible. He has shaken up and re-organised the Commission's protocol service. He has brought some order into the administration of the Commission's overseas delegations. And he has handled with skill, tact and determination that hottest of potatoes, the external aspects of the Community's agricultural policy. Perhaps the best tribute was that of his (Dutch) Director-General who, when recently discussing a switch of posts at Director level (it did not in the end happen), said "Leslie Fielding is the only one of my six Directors whom I would happily transfer into any of the other jobs and know that in six weeks he would be doing it terrifically".

Mr. Fielding has now achieved and shown great aptitude for a wide range of political and economic work. He has also demonstrated his ability to run, and run well, a substantial administrative unit. It is clear that he lacks any commercial experience and this could be a gap to fill. But even without that he is exceptionally well suited to take a senior post in any of the industrialised countries (in or out of the EEC) or in any other part of the world.

David Hannay
Head of Cabinet, Vice-President Christopher Soames
November 1976
Further FCO Report

Leslie Fielding has proved an extremely effective official in the European Commission: hard working and dedicated, wholly reliable, sensible and cool under strain, imaginative, and rarely lacking humour. For as long as I have known him here, he has more than held down a job which gave him more responsibility and scope than most others in his grade. In this curious organization, where people of quality are able to do their own thing, he has done his with distinction, and will be sorely missed.

In spite of his charm and bonhomie, he is a very solitary person. Some people, while admiring his talents, have found him hard to work with, and I doubt he gets the best out of subordinates or has easy negotiations with his equals. His new job as Head of the Commission office in Tokyo will be the test in this respect. He is an actor who likes to play a lot of roles, whether the diplomat, the man-about-town, the buffoon, the dedicated worker, or the country gentleman. In a way he is all of them, and in another, he is none of them.

I have known him for 15 years, yet the central ambiguity about him remains. There is, as someone remarked to me the other day, a hole in his character, or at least a thick screen around it. I suspect he is more vulnerable than he looks. At one time he wanted to get married, but he did not succeed; and now seems resigned to his own company. But I do not know whether he really is. Nor, I think, does anyone else.

So lively, endearing and intelligent a person and so effective an operator deserves the trial of high office.

Crispin Tickell
Head of Cabinet, President Roy Jenkins
December 1977

[No further FCO Personnel Reports were written, after the author transferred permanently to the European Civil Service in 1979. Nor were reports subsequently written on me by the European Commission. Whether as Head of the Delegation in Tokyo, or later as Director-General in Brussels, I had no immediate civil service superior, and was in any case by then sufficiently well known to appropriate Commissioners and senior officials.]

Is Diplomacy Dead?

9. THE ASSESSORS ASSESSED

The following, in alphabetical order, is a list of the Assessors who signed off the FCO personnel reports in Chapter 8 above, with notes on who they were and what they were like. All great men in their different ways. I was glad to have served with them: I owed them a great deal.

John Barnes

Head of Western Organisations Department in the FO, 1962-66. (In succession to Peter Ramsbotham). A fire-eater and controversialist, very quick and decisive. Later, Ambassador to Israel and KCMG; but never quite made it to the top, because of his temperament. Tough to one's face, but generous and appreciative behind one's back.

James Cable

Head of South East Asia Department in the FO, 1963-66 (while the author was serving in Phnom Penh). Head of the Policy Planning Staff in the FCO 1972-75 (in succession to Percy Cradock). A bearded and slightly eccentric intellectual, much respected in and outside the FO. Author of books on naval power. Later, Ambassador to Finland and KCVO.

Alan Campbell

Head of Chancery in Paris, 1967-69 (in succession to Peter Ramsbotham). Urbane, sympathetic and astute high-flyer; later Deputy Under Secretary of State in London, Ambassador in Rome, and GCMG.

Percy Cradock

Head of Planning Staff in the FCO, 1969-71. Brilliant late entrant to the Service, having started life as a Law don at Cambridge; one of the outstanding intellectuals of the post-war Diplomatic Service. Later, Ambassador to China, Hong

Kong negotiator and Foreign Policy Adviser to Prime Minister Thatcher. GCMG and Privy Counsellor.

David Hannay

The outstanding Diplomatic Service officer of his generation. Chief of Staff to Vice-President Sir Christopher Soames in the European Commission 1973-77, while the author was serving in Soames' Directorate General. Later, Ambassador to the EU in Brussels and to the UN in New York. Later, Special Representative for Cyprus. GCMG, CH and active Life Peer. (Was to have become Permanent Under-Secretary of State and Head of the Diplomatic Service, but Mrs Thatcher objected).

Geoffrey Harrison

Ambassador in Tehran in 1958-63. Cold, austere, shrewd and highly competent Wykehamist. Later Deputy Under-Secretary of State in London and Ambassador in Moscow (from which post he punctiliously asked to be withdrawn, after an affair with a Russian domestic of which the KGB might have taken advantage). GCMG.

John Henniker-Major

War hero (MC) and aristocratic Head of Personnel Department in the FO 1953-60, credited with broadening the base of recruitment to the Diplomatic Service, to bring in bright people from non-privileged backgrounds. Later, Ambassador to Jordan and to Denmark and Director-General of the British Council. KCMG. Became the eighth Baron Henniker, 1980.

George Hiller

War hero (won the DSO with SOE, in occupied France— he was bilingual, his mother having been French). Head of Chancery, Tehran 1956-59. Later also, very briefly, the author's superior in Singapore in 1964, in the Office of the Political Advisor to the C in C Far East. Introverted, but kindly. Never spoke of his war experiences, but was, we all guessed, much marked by the loss of friends in the Resistance. Retired from ill health before reaching the upper ranks of the Service. CMG.

Peter Marshall

Head of Chancery Paris 1969-71 (in succession to Peter Ramsbotham and Alan Campbell). Later, Assistant Under-Secretary of State in London, Ambassador in Geneva and Commonwealth Deputy Secretary General. KCMG. Friendly, hard-working all-rounder of great charm, with wide contacts in Whitehall.

Peter Ramsbotham

Head of Western Organisations Department FO 1961-62 and Head of Chancery Paris 1962-67. Son of a Tory Viscount. FO grandee of the Old School, later High Commissioner in Cyprus, and Ambassador in Tehran and finally Washington (from which post he was prematurely—and undeservedly—withdrawn by Prime Minister Callaghan, to make way for a political appointment; but consoled with the Governorship of Bermuda). GCMG. Despite being slightly crippled by polio when a lad, did well in the Intelligence Corps in Europe during the war (Mentioned in despatches and *Croix de Guerre*.) Beneath the charm, there was both resolution and ambition.

Patrick Reilly

Ambassador in Paris 1965-68. Before that, Deputy Under-Secretary of State in the FO and Ambassador to Moscow. Fellow of All Souls College and intellectual of the highest quality. Kindly but sensitive—he found it difficult to cope with the aggression and the sheer rudeness of George Brown as Foreign Secretary. GCMG.

Christopher Soames

Ambassador in Paris 1969-73 and Vice-President of the European Commission, 1973-77. Well-connected Europhile Tory politician and former Cabinet Minister of vision and charisma, married to Sir Winston Churchill's youngest daughter, Mary. GCMG and Life Peer. Got on famously with the mandarins, whom he handled astutely and who respected his political judgment.

Crispin Tickell

Chief of Staff to Roy Jenkins, President of the European Commission 1977-81. Before that, served with the author both in the Western Organisations Department in London and in the Paris Chancery. Formidable diplomatic operator, and also an intellectual of wide (including scientific) interests, credited with convincing Prime Minister Thatcher to take action on the depletion of the ozone layer. Ambassador to Mexico and to the United Nations and Permanent Secretary of the Overseas Development Agency. President of Green College Oxford. GCMG, KCVO.

10. ENVOY

Readers of this book will have learnt that Harold Wilson, when Prime Minister, and R.A. Butler and Patrick Gordon Walker, when Foreign Secretary, took the trouble to read the key despatches of a junior Chargé d'Affaires in the middle of an international crisis, and took some account of his youthful judgement (pages 58, 80 and 150). Likewise, Prime Minister Edward Heath, with my work, along with that of others in the team, on Anglo-French relations. Successive Presidents and Vice-Presidents of the European Commission came to rely on the author, similarly.

In the post WWII era, time was, indeed, when the considered view of a professional diplomat counted for something with Cabinet ministers, with whom relations were close and confident. When Truth was spoken to Power, albeit with total loyalty and discretion. When the entourage of Prime Minister Harold Macmillan, on his official trips abroad, was normally confined to one man: Philip de Zulueta, the Foreign Office official then serving as Private Secretary at No 10. When Harold Wilson, coming from the opposition benches to become Prime Minister, took over his Tory predecessor's official staff without hesitation. When the sofas at 10 Downing Street were unencumbered by spin doctors and 'special political advisers'. When, without question, the British Ambassador on the spot took place and precedence at his leader's right hand. When diplomats were not bean-counting "managers" beholden to the Treasury, focussed on artificial "targets" and "delivery"; but could concentrate on their real job: knowing the foreigner well; speaking his language fluently; getting to grips with overseas ruling elites—all in the promotion of the British national interest.

Of course, methods of communication have changed radically; the digital revolution has opened up a new frontier; 'social media' cannot be neglected. But, as Britain's youngest and most 'with it' emissary acknowledges[15], "there is still a need for direct private conversations between leaders, for intelligence and confidential analysis, for robust discussion of national interests .... Much has to be handled backstage, however many of us become what *The Economist* calls 'Tweeting Tallyrands'."

The fundamental point was hammered home, in a public lecture in 2011, by a distinguished former Head of the Diplomatic Service, Lord Wright of Richmond, (on the theme, *Do We Still Need Diplomats?*), as follows:

> "I maintain that the main duty of a diplomat abroad is to develop as wide a circle of contacts as possible, and to understand the culture, the history, the politics and the language of the country or Institution where he or she is serving. The best advice I ever received myself was from a predecessor, when I was about to take up my post as Ambassador to Saudi Arabia. "If it moves", he said, "call on it".

William Hague as Foreign Secretary exercises greater clout in Whitehall than any of his predecessors since Douglas Hurd. Particular interest therefore attaches to his speech in the historic Locarno Room on 8 September 2011 (*"The best diplomatic service in the world: strengthening the Foreign and Commonwealth Office"*). Hague began by acknowledging that "the FCO's stature in government has diminished in recent years .... devalued and sidelined .... too often ignored by the Prime Minister and weakened as an institution". He said that "the pendulum had swung too far in recent years away from policy-making expertise and towards cumbersome bureaucracy often imposed by the

---

[15] Tom Fletcher, Ambassador in Beirut: *The World Today*, December 2012

centre of government—a perception I know was shared by many within the FCO itself". Language teaching, also, had declined—the Foreign Office Language School was axed in 2007. Yet "our country needs the skills of the Foreign Office more than ever". To correct this, he assured his audience that embassies were in fact now being reopened. He announced the launch of a new "Diplomatic Excellence Initiative", to cover every aspect of the work of the FCO, including linguistic skills—the language school being re-opened. (Not before time. Stephen Barclay MP, of the Public Accounts Committee of the House of Commons, is reported, last year, to have discovered that only one in forty British diplomats spoke the language of their host country—something inconceivable in my day.)

The bottom line has to be this. Diplomats are necessary, but not sufficient, to keep the world turning. They must not get too uppity or élitist. Individual Ambassadors can occasionally—if the Foreign Office Establishment as a whole, only rarely—be mistaken in their judgements. Like all Civil Servants, they should be on tap, not on top. The final shots have to be called by democratically elected and accountable politicians. But "abroad" can be a funny place, where UK instincts and purely British domestic assumptions have little or no validity. If skilled and informed professional advice is not part of the foreign policy making input, the output is likely to be garbage— and damaging to the nation's interest. If they did not exist, our diplomats would have to be invented. This country will always stand in need of their craft—in a highly uncertain and possibly perilous future world, perhaps more than ever before.

Despite the difficulties, our Diplomatic Service has moved with the times, or rolled with the punch, as it always has. Whether or not we succeed in 'punching above our weight', as Douglas Hurd hoped we could, we most certainly now need to 'box clever'. The Office still enjoys world-wide 'Street Cred'. The Government of the day, present and to come, will do well to keep it that way. And to listen to what it has to say. For what is the point of keeping a pedigree guard dog, if it is not permitted to bark?

The author accordingly welcomes the determination of the Coalition Cabinet, with the clear cross-party consent of the Foreign Affairs Committee of the House of Commons, to strengthen the Foreign and Commonwealth Office as an institution and restore it to its rightful place in government.

BACKGROUND READING

On diplomatic 'despatches':

Matthew Parris and Andrew Bryson:
> *Parting Shots,* 2010;
> *The Spanish Ambassador's Suitcase and Other Stories,*
> 2012

How British Cabinet Ministers have viewed diplomacy:

Geoffrey Howe (Lord Howe of Aberavon):
> *Conflict of Loyalty,* 1998
David Owen (Lord Owen of Plymouth) and others (Peter Carrington, Geoffrey Howe, Douglas Hurd and Malcolm Rifkind) in:
> *British Diplomacy: A Foreign Secretary Reflects,* 2007
Chris Patten (Lord Patten of Barnes):
> *East and West,* 1998;
> *Cousins and Strangers,* 2005;
> *Not Quite the Diplomat: Home Truths about World Affairs,* 2005;
> *What Next? Surviving the 21ˢᵗ Century,* 2008
Douglas Hurd (Lord Hurd of Westwell):
> *Memoirs,* 2003;
> *Choose Your Weapons,* 2010
William Hague:
> *The best diplomatic service in the world: strengthening the Foreign and Commonwealth Office as an institution* (speech in London), 2011

How the 'professionals' have viewed diplomacy:

Henry Kissinger:
> *Diplomacy*, 1994

Sir Percy Cradock:
> *Experiences of China*, 1994;
> *In Pursuit of British Interests*, 1997;
> *Know Your Enemy*, 2002

Sir Peter Marshall:
> *Positive Diplomacy*, 1997

Sir Marrack Goulding:
> *Peacemonger*, 2002

Dame Margaret Anstee:
> *Never Learn to Type: A Woman at the United Nations,*
> 2004

Sir Christopher Meyer:
> *DC Confidential*, 2005;
> *Getting Our Way*, 2009

David Hannay (Lord Hannay of Chiswick):
> *Cyprus: the Search for a Solution*, 2005;
> *The New World Disorder*, 2008
> *Britain's Quest for a Role: A Diplomatic Memoir from*
> *Europe to the UN*, 2012

Sir Leslie Fielding:
> *Before the Killing Fields: Witness to Cambodia and the*
> *Viet-Nam War*, 2008

Adam Holloway MP:
> *In Blood Stepp'd In Too Far? Towards a Realistic Policy*
> *for Afghanistan*, 2009

Sir Nicholas Bayne:
> *Economic Diplomat*, 2010

Jonathan Powell: *The New Machiavelli – How to Wield Power*
> *in the Modern World*, 2010

Frank Ledwidge:
> *Losing Small Wars: British military failure in Iraq and*
> *Afghanistan*, 2011

Sir Sherard Cowper-Coles:

Cables from Kabul: *The Inside Story of the West's Afghanistan Campaign,* 2011
Rory Stewart (with Gerald Knaus):
 Can Intervention Work?, 2011
Robert Merrillees:
 Diplomatic Digs, 2012
Prof. Iver B.Neumann:
 At Home with the Diplomats, 2012
 Diplomatic Sites, A Critical Enquiry, 2013

About diplomatic life:

Sir Alan Campbell:
 Colleagues and Friends, 1988
Sir John Barnes:
 Footsteps on the Backstairs, 1992
Lord Greenhill:
 More by Accident, 1992
Sir Nicholas Henderson:
 Mandarin, 1994
Sir Donald Maitland:
 Diverse Times, Sundry Places, 1996;
 The Running Tide, 2000
Richard Faber:
 A Chain of Cities, 2000
Hugh Cortazzi: (ed.)
 Japan Experiences, 2001
Lord Henniker:
 Painful Extractions, 2002
Sir Rodric Braithwaite:
 Across the Moscow River, 2002
Sir Christopher Audland:
 Right Place – Right Time, 2004
Andrew Palmer:
 A Diplomat and his Birds, 2005

Brigid Keenan:
>*Diplomatic Baggage*, 2005

Sir John Leahy:
>*A Life of Spice*, 2006

Sir Alan Munro:
>*Arab Storm: Politics and Diplomacy Behind the Gulf War*, 2006
>*Keep The Flag Flying, a Diplomatic Memoir*, 2012

Rory Stewart:
>*Occupational Hazards*, 2006

Sir Hilary Synnott:
>*Bad Days in Basra*, 2008

Sir Leslie Fielding:
>*Kindly Call Me God: the Misadventures of 'Fielding of the FO', Eurocrat Extraordinaire and Vice-Chancellor Semipotentiary*, 2009;
>*Twilight Over the Temples: The Close of Cambodia's Belle Époque*, (screen play) 2011

Sir John Whitehead:
>*Counterpoint*, 2011

Sir Roger Carrick:
>*Diplomatic Anecdotage, Around the World In 40 Years*, 2012

A 'European' perspective on diplomacy:

Lord Jenkins of Hillhead:
>*European Diary 1972-81*, 1989

Sir Leslie Fielding:
>*Europe as a Global Partner*, 1991
>*Changing Horizons: Memories of Britain's European Pioneers, 1973*, (contrib.) 2013

Sir Roy Denman:
>*Missed Chances*, 1996;
>*The Mandarin's Tale*, 2002

Derk-Jan Eppink:
>*Life of a European Mandarin*, 2007

Sir Stephen Wall:

A Stranger in Europe, 2008

David Rennie:

> *The Continent or the Open Sea: Does Britain Have a European Future?*, 2012

The Home Base: British Self-Scrutiny

John Dickey:

> *Special No More*, 1994

Andrew Marr:

> *Ruling Britannia – The Failure and Future of British Democracy*, 1995

Peter Hitchens:

> *The Abolition of Britain*, 1999

Roger Scruton:

> *England, an Elegy*, 2001

Nicholas Faith:

> *A Very Different Country*, 2002

Clifford Longley:

> *Chosen People*, 2002

David Marquard:

> *Decline of The Public*, 2004

Christopher Foster:

> *British Government In Crisis*, 2005

George Walden:

> *Time to Emigrate?*, 2006

Peter Oborne:

> *The Triumph of the Political Class*, 2007

A.N. Wilson:

> *Our Times*, 2008

Larry Elliott and Dan Atkinson

> *Going South: Why Britain will have a Third World Economy by 2014*, 2012

David Goodhart:
: *The British Dream, Successes and Failures of Post War Immigration*, 2013

FOOTNOTE: THE GOD KING OF CAMBODIA

In the 1960s, the Cambodian Head of State, the former King Norodom Sihanouk (he had stepped down from the throne in 1955, to enter active political life), was by far the dominant national figure. A figure, too, in the affairs of South-East Asia as a whole. Controversial, egotistical and by most standards highly eccentric, he often got under the skins of the Americans and occasionally of the phlegmatic British.

I saw a great deal of him, face to face or in small groups, during the three years of my time, as a youthful Chargé d'Affaires in Cambodia. I taught his favourite daughter to dance The Twist. He apparently thought well of me and described me to others as helpful and *"très sage"*. I for my part had a sneaking admiration and affection for 'Samdech Sahachivin'. But I had to stand back, also, and place him in an objective, professional, perspective. The difficulty lay in explaining this quixotic *enfant terrible* to British Governments in a light which was broadly sympathetic, but which did not conceal his powerful idiosyncrasies.

Once I was sure of my man (from close personal observation, careful analysis, and consultation of other trustworthy observers), I wrote a long despatch to key people in London, of a kind never before or since attempted. It was hailed enthusiastically as a kind of Michelin's Guide, by the small coterie of Ministers and senior officials in London who had dealings with the Prince and were required to make the policy decisions. It was also judged 'definitive' by the scholarly FO Research Department. By my desk officer, however, it was deemed— no doubt correctly—too detailed and pedantic for wide circulation. Released to the public only since Sihanouk's death in October 2012, the text is reproduced in Chapter 4 above ("The Personality of Prince Sihanouk: Some First Impressions" 2 March, 1965).

In the mid-1960s, I knew personally, and flagged up in several reports, the two men (General Lon Nol and Prince Sirik Matak) who eventually, in 1970, launched the bloodless *coup d'état* which ousted Sihanouk. And I was aware how much, even in the space of my brief service in Phnom Penh, the Prince's position was suffering erosion. But, in my own time, a domestic coup was not immediately on the cards; Sihanouk was better than any likely alternative; and we could, within narrow limits, do business with him. The fact that, after the eventual coup, things went from bad to worse for the Cambodians themselves (open guerrilla war; foreign military intervention; the Pol Pot takeover in 1975; genocide; misery, even after the 1991 Paris Peace Agreement and extending into the present time), has served only to reinforce in me my conviction about the positive side of Norodom Sihanouk, warts and all.

The obituary published by The Times on October 16, 2012 concludes with the following judgement:

> "Norodom Sihanouk is inseparable from the history of 20th Century Cambodia, and a balanced view of his 70-year career is difficult to assemble. He was a hard-working patriot whose unpredictable actions often had deleterious effects. An ardent Francophile, he also befriended the Chinese Prime Minister Zhou Enlai, and after 1970 he never challenged Chinese policy. This alliance led him to support the Khmer Rouge for much longer than most Cambodians would have liked. His opponents also criticised his autocratic, ego-driven style, his fondness of flattery and his intolerance of dissent.

His supporters, while admitting his flaws, pointed to his unswerving devotion to Cambodian independence and praised his affection for Cambodia's rural poor. Moreover, unlike many southeast Asian rulers, Sihanouk made no effort to enrich himself during his years in power."

The Australian scholar and former diplomat in Cambodia, Professor Milton Osborne (possibly the shrewdest and best informed of all western observers and author of a remarkable biography: 'Sihanouk, Prince of Light, Prince of Darkness') acknowledges, in the obituary he wrote for the 'Phnom Penh Post' that:

"By any standards, Norodom Sihanouk was one of the most remarkable political figures of the twentieth century. During the course of a lifetime that lasted eighty nine years, he filled the roles of king, prime minister and chief of state of his country and in doing so took actions for good and bad that had profound effects on the course of Cambodia's modern history".

Pithily, Osborne concludes that:

"For all of the good things which he did, or tried to do, his greatest weakness was his inability to recognise that he was not the only person in Cambodia possessed of wisdom. In speaking of his people as children who had no right to their own ideas he crippled political development in the years before 1970 and contributed to the tragedies that followed his deposition in that year. As I have written previously, he was a 'prince of light and a prince of darkness'. In personalising politics while he held power, he deserved praise for his achievements, but insured that he would also be judged for the main failures of his long time as Cambodia's leader".

In retrospect, I dissent from neither of the foregoing judgements. But I will always retain in my memory a certain soft spot for 'Monseigneur'. On my departure from Phnom Penh, in October 1966, I wrote him a personal letter of farewell, to which he replied immediately, as follows:

> "*A cette occasion je suis heureux de vous assurer de mon estime et de rendre un vif hommage à vos efforts pour améliorer et développer les relations entre nos deux pays. Il m'apparaît d'ailleurs certain que votre compréhension de nos problèmes ainsi que vos relations personnelles avec nos compatriotes ont contribué à dissiper de nombreux malentendus.*
>
> *Je vous félicite de votre nomination à Paris où je vous reverrai avec plaisir et vous adresse tous mes voeux de bonheur et de succès dans votre carrière.*"

In the event, neither the FCO nor the newly appointed British Ambassador in Phnom Penh wanted me to open a 'back channel'. Accordingly, I did not take up the Prince's invitation to call on him when in Paris—experiencing in the process a strange mixture of both relief and regret. I was never to see him face to face again.

Index

Also by Leslie Fielding

BEFORE THE KILLING FIELDS: WITNESS TO CAMBODIA
AND THE VIETNAM WAR
(2008)

Hugely germane to many of our present preoccupations in international relations.
Lord Patten of Barnes

A vivid picture of the life of a diplomat abroad; usually arduous, sometimes uncomfortable and dangerous; pompous routine varied by passages of the comical and wildly unexpected.
Philip Zeigler

Matches that other outstanding account of duty done on a far frontier—John Master's 'Bugles and Tiger'.
Professor Milton Osborne

Leslie Fielding was one of Britain's more unorthodox and original diplomats.... For all students of diplomacy and of Cambodia, this book provides a vivid and colourful picture of life at the sharp end.
International Affairs

Written with panache and verve.... a joy to read.... reminds us of a seemingly lost world of good fun but also serious thought and action.
Asian Affairs

Fielding gives a gripping account of Cambodia under the mercurial Sihanouk, as the shadows closed in.
Literary Review

Fielding.... cuts a dash in the drawing rooms and opium dens of Phnom Penh.... As 'Number One Twister', he developed a better relationship with Sihanouk than his US counterpart.... He is proud of a time when Britain stood up to America and did not go to war.

Daily Telegraph

KINDLY CALL ME GOD: THE MISADVENTURES OF 'FIELDING OF THE FO', EUROCRAT EXTRAORDINAIRE AND VICE-CHANCELLOR SEMIPOTENTIARY
(2009)

This is an entertaining and instructive book, which will give particular pleasure to those of us who have watched with sadness the decline of the Foreign Office as a force in our political life. There are signs now that a Conservative Government would correct the balance and return the FCO to its proper place in forming and directing British foreign policy. Leslie Fielding's book is based on hard reality flowing from practical experience and I strongly recommend it.

Lord Hurd of Westwell

As the reader is taken on a fast canter round the distinguished career course, there are many laughs and no yawns.... We hear the voice of a serious scholar and public servant and cease to be surprised at his success in the world he so engagingly mocks.

Country Life, July 15, 2009

Fantastic! Great reading. Hugely entertaining.

Sir Christopher Ondaatje

I read it with great enjoyment and much admire the wry, irreverent tone.

Tony Howard

How much I enjoyed 'KCMG', both as a roller coaster of adventures/experiences and as a record of diplomatic skills. The final chapters on the role and future of the Foreign Service should be compulsory reading for our political masters, and many others.

John Harding

The brilliantly titled 'KCMG' brings together the wide range of cultures encountered by the author and chronicled with consummate panache. Each chapter is crafted like a classic short story and the prose is bursting with energy and sharp observation.

Professor Howard B. Clarke

TWILIGHT OVER THE TEMPLES: THE CLOSE OF CAMBODIA'S BELLE EPOQUE
(2011)

A young diplomat pursues honour and glory in an exotic and distant land. He takes on the world, charms a king and falls in love. But the fairytale fades. His duties draw him deep into the turbulent world of plot and counterplot in pre-revolutionary Cambodia. Betrayal comes from an unexpected quarter and paves the way to personal tragedy and national disaster.

A highly entertaining read, which is all too relevant to some of the difficult issues we face in international relations today. This is a book to enjoy and to learn from.
Lord Patten of Barnes

A tragic, exotic love story, powerful and well told.
James Lee

Captures the bitter-sweet essence of Cambodia's modern history, where laughter so often was stilled by tragedy: the actors in the country's drama a fateful mix of heroes, fools and truly evil.
Professor Milton Osborne

Love in an exotic setting, laced with authentic Indo-Chinese politics and old school British diplomacy. Written in dialogue that informs with pith and wit.
Peter Burden